NAKED SPIRITS

NAKED SPIRITS

A Journey into Occupied Tibet

ADRIAN ABBOTTS

CANONGATE BOOKS

First published in Great Britain in 1997 by
Canongate Books Ltd,
14 High Street, Edinburgh EH1 1TE

Copyright © Adrian Abbotts 1997

The moral right of the author
has been asserted.

All photographs, unless otherwise credited
are copyright © Maria Salak, 1997

British Library Cataloguing in Publication Data

A catalogue record for this book is available on
request from the British Library

ISBN 0 86241 617 5

Typeset by Palimpsest Book Production Limited,
Polmont, Stirlingshire
Printed and bound in Finland by WSOY

For Jovian

in all his happiness,
that he may know a free Tibet in his lifetime

And for the people of Tibet

in all their suffering,
that they may also

Contents

Acknowledgements

PARAMOUNT AMONG ALL DEBTS OF gratitude accrued in the production of this book is that which I owe my agent, Marilyn Malin, whose belief in the manuscript while still far from finished has now been rewarded. Through Marilyn I have learnt so much about the publishing world, and in her I hope I have acquired not only a highly regarded agent but also a much valued friend. To Stephanie Wolfe-Murray I am indebted for her initial interest in the manuscript and recognition of human rights everywhere as the highest cause; without her, this work may not have come to fruition. To Jamie Byng and Hugh Andrew at Canongate I am grateful for their faith and enthusiasm in picking up the ball and running with it, to Hugh especially for the wisdom of his structural advice which so transformed the finished product.

Many people were helpful in the early stages, when this book was little more than an idea, and as idea became reality the value of friendship became clear. My squash and drinking partner, Phil Dudman, has my gratitude for sustaining me with his repertoire of awful jokes – oh yes, and also for his extensive advice and assistance, particularly with the troublesome earlier drafts of the manuscript. The generous time, comments and resourceful efforts on my behalf of Carol Tibbs and Terry Richards were also invaluable. The early comments of Roger Butler, like the brave – and, I hope, *largely* successful – attempts of Ruth Turner to render my language and prose non-sexist, fully deserve recognition. The thoughts and suggestions of Kate Saunders, of Free Tibet Campaign, corrected some important omissions and were much appreciated. Also generous with his time and advice was Asaf

Hussain, while to Freda Hussain and Su Walls I owe thanks for providing me with employment when funds had run out.

I am especially grateful to Pam and Wasyl for regular Sunday babysitting while the manuscript was revised. The cheerful commitment of everyone involved in the Leicester Free Tibet Campaign has similarly been much appreciated, and encouraging. Further thanks go to Ollie Thomas for the mugshot on the jacket, and to the Tibet Image Bank for supplementing Maria's more humble selection of photos. The karmic debt owed to Maria herself, first of all for so readily casting off house, job and security, and then on return for the innumerable sacrifices and (almost) uncomplaining perseverance which made the task of writing possible, can surely only be repayable over many more lifetimes together. Without her this journey would not have been made, nor would my own inner journey have been so rich. And lastly, Vinod and Suresh Pandya and their wonderful staff at Leicester's Sayonara restaurant cannot go without mention, for supplying us with the best Indian vegetarian food in Britain while this book was being written.

Prefatory Notes

NATURALLY, IN A BOOK SUCH as this, it has been necessary on occasion to confuse identities and places in order to protect people in vulnerable positions.

The attention of the reader is also drawn to the use of the religiously neutral CE and BCE (Common Era and Before Common Era), rather than the parallel Christian dating of AD and BC (In the Year of the Lord and Before the Messiah), which would have been particularly out of place in a book on Tibet.

Also, transliterating Chinese is never easy, especially when there are several accepted systems. Generally, I have retained the older Wade-Giles system for older names which are more familiar in that form (e.g. Han Fei Tzu), but opted for the modern pinyin system when transcribing more contemporary names (e.g. Mao Zedong). With Tibetan, which in its classical form involves numerous redundant letters, I have approximated pronunciation rather than faithfully reproducing the true spelling (e.g. Tenzin Gyatso, rather than Bstan.'dzin.rgya.mtsho).

Author's Foreword

TIBET, ROMANTIC AND MYSTICAL, A smile in the Eastern mind's eye, a land of levitating lamas, mysterious monasteries and yak-butter tea, a natural home on the roof of the world to the mythical Shangri-la, is also a real place with a two thousand-year-old history. It is about to end the 20th century as an independent state under illegal, wrathful occupation.

This occupation began on October 7th 1950, a year and a week after Mao's establishment of the Peoples' Republic of China, when 40,000 Chinese troops invaded Tibet on a wave of genocidal, nationalistic hysteria. Tenzin Gyatso, His Holiness the fourteenth Dalai Lama, on the advice of the State Oracle, fled to seek exile in India.

In May 1951, using seals of state forged for the purpose in Beijing, the collaborator Ngawang Jigme Ngapo, who remains the most powerful man in Tibet today, signed Tibet over to China in exchange for high office. Returning to the capital, Lhasa, in August 1951, the Dalai Lama refused to accept the validity of this agreement and strove for eight years to establish non-violent co-existence with the Chinese.

On March 10th 1959, continued repression and systematic attempts at ethnic genocide in the province of Kham culminated in an uprising against Chinese forces in Lhasa. In the next three days alone, by Chinese not Tibetan statistics, 87,000 Tibetans were killed. Tenzin Gyatso, foiling an attempt on his life, fled in disguise to India.

Subsequently, almost half of geographical Tibet and two thirds of its population were annexed and absorbed into the Chinese provinces of Yunnan, Sichuan, Gansu and Qinghai. Before the Cultural Revolution began in 1967, all but a small handful of Tibet's six thousand monasteries had already been reduced to rubble, their monks and nuns forced to copulate in public and defecate on holy scriptures before being used for forced labour.

In 1960 the International Committee of Jurists accused China of committing 'acts of genocide – in an attempt to destroy the Tibetans as a religious group'. Like other statements by an otherwise idle and complacent outside world, it made no difference. By 1977, more than one in six of Tibet's population of 6 million had died from torture, murder or starvation – a population loss comparable with that of Poland during World War Two.

China's justification for its treatment of Tibet and her people is that Tibet has been an 'inalienable part of China' since the 13th century, when China came under direct Mongolian rule and Tibet – under Mongolian military protection but not direct rule – provided a religious teacher as supreme pontiff. The absurdity of this argument, which is the heart of the Chinese legal claim to Tibet, has been likened to suggesting that France should be governed from London since both experienced Roman domination.

Today, over 120,000 Tibetans live in exile, mostly in India. Large numbers, especially children whose parents wish them to be educated in their own language, continue to flood over the borders into India, Bhutan and Nepal.

A population transfer of Chinese into Tibet however, fuelled by financial incentives and in violation of the 4th Geneva Convention of 1949 which prohibits population transfer into occupied territory, has continued unabated since 1983. At present Chinese outnumber Tibetans in Lhasa by three to one, entire districts of traditional Tibetan houses are being pulled down and the Tibetan presence in Lhasa is being forced into a 'quarter' of their own city; a 1993 survey on a street close to the central shrine found that 46 out of 50 shops were Chinese owned or operated.

As further evidence that China remains committed to the eradication of Tibetans in race as well as in culture, first-hand accounts of enforced abortion and sterilisation of Tibetan women, as well as of Chinese medical infanticide of Tibetan children, are frequently cited by refugees arriving in India.

Inside Lhasa, Tibetans have to put up with continuous anti-clockwise circumambulation of the holy Jokhang temple by forty-strong platoons of stormtroopers with machine guns, sentries on rooftops with guns aimed into the streets, and video surveillance of most of the city centre. Imprisonment, and routine torture, of Tibetan men and women is so frequent that every family is believed to have had at least one person in jail for 'political offences', let alone relatives who have 'died' or 'disappeared' since 1950.

Yet in spite of the rule by fear which ranks Tibet as a police state alongside the likes of Iraq under Saddam Hussein, dissent and organised protests continue with remarkable regularity. In 1987, 1988 and 1989, what began as peaceful street protests in Lhasa exploded in a violence that sacrificed hundreds of lives. Tibetans as people possess a fighting spirit that ranks alongside the Vietnamese, and for all their vulnerability they are not likely to give up.

The question is whether the outside world will continue to kowtow to an evil and repressive regime for essentially economic reasons. While it does so, inside Tibet other plans are made, and it is not the inextinguishable flames of romantic butter lamps, but of real spirits which burn.

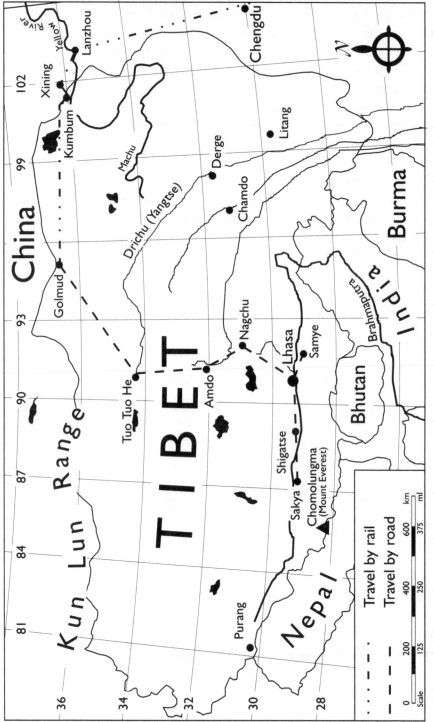

MAP SHOWING TIBET BEFORE ANNEXATION, INCLUDING THE AUTHOR'S JOURNEY.

Prologue

Once in the past the Marquis Chao of Han got drunk and fell asleep. The Keeper of the Royal Hat, seeing that the Marquis was cold, laid a robe over him. When the Marquis awoke, he was pleased and asked his attendants, 'Who covered me with a robe?' 'The Keeper of the Hat,' they replied.

The Marquis thereupon punished both the Keeper of the Royal Hat and the Keeper of the Royal Robe. He punished the Keeper of the Robe for failing to do his duty, and the Keeper of the Hat for over-stepping his office. It was not that he did not dislike the cold, but he considered the trespass of one official upon the duties of another to be a greater danger than cold.

THE SENSE OF HISTORY repeating itself is much stronger in Han China than in the West. Perhaps, as some claim, this impression was influenced by the old Chinese calendar of sixty-year cycles. Then again, perhaps ancient patterns of human behaviour really were somehow sealed into the souls of those who, through history, have been fated to rule the Middle Kingdom. The gentleman who penned this little anecdote as an advice on good government, Han Fei Tzu (c.280–233 BCE), a prince in the royal family of the Kingdom of Han, would certainly be inclined to believe it were his ghost unfortunate enough to haunt the creaking, possibly already collapsing, corridors of power today, for he – who should have been no more than an accidental bit-player on the stage of Chinese history – was responsible for the script which Mao picked up and dusted down, over two millennia later.

Han Fei Tzu was a founder of the Legalist school, the last of many doctrines arising from the 'Hundred Schools of Thought Era' that had begun, three centuries before him, with Confucius. Han Fei Tzu had been a student of a Confucian scholar, Hsun Tzu, whose defining characteristic was a belief that human nature was intrinsically evil and required external discipline to control it. Although he was to turn on Confucianism with a vengeance, Han Fei Tzu seems to have absorbed this aspect of his mentor's teaching. Freedom of behaviour, he said, is what throws society into confusion, and what brings order to society is enforced, rigid adherence to the Law. The quip about the Keeper of the Hat and the Keeper of the Robe was intended to show that application of the Law should take no account of individual circumstances. The business of achieving social order left no room for such deviations as pity or compassion.

To a large extent Han Fei Tzu was a disaster waiting to happen, a grimly smiling embodiment of death hovering to collect when the tracks ran out under the locomotive of China's early philosophical direction. That locomotive of course had been set in motion by Confucius (more properly Kung Fu Tzu, c.551–479 BCE). Unlike his subsequent followers, Confucius himself had made no definite statement regarding the virtues or otherwise of human nature. His concerns were wholly social and in no way 'religious'. He was after all a politician, an itinerant civil servant whose middle-life was spent pestering various rulers to adopt his moral codes, but to no avail. He retired in despair to his home province of Lu, where he instructed a small coterie of disciples in the notion that the hidden pearl of social order could be found in the oyster of his Rules of Proper Conduct.

When I think of Confucius I imagine a tall, imposing, wispy-bearded figure, somewhat haughty and self-righteous, rigidly upright in posture as well as in views, standing perhaps on the verandah of a large wooden town-house while awaiting his middle-aged, aristocratic students. His arms would be folded in baggy silk sleeves, his wife neither seen nor heard within. When his students arrived he would encourage them to develop the virtues of benevolence and righteousness, of brotherliness and filial piety. It sounds noble, and yet the minutiae of his lectures, as they have come down to us in the *Analects*, consisted of such memorable advice as:

> In one's household it is the women and small men that are difficult to deal with. If you let them get too close they become insolent. If you keep them at a distance they complain.

Confucius preached an ideal world wherein each person knew their place and behaved accordingly, and where place was determined as much by age, gender and class as by merit. The bedrock of society was the family, which was held together by filial piety:

> Give your father and mother no other cause for anxiety than illness.

In return for such devotions however, Confucius counselled:

A gentleman always keeps aloof from his son.

Indeed, his world was certainly a cold one:

He did not converse at meals; nor did he talk in bed.
He did not sit, unless his mat was straight.

and thoroughly hierarchical, with women at the bottom and animals outside the scheme completely:

The stables caught fire. The Master, on returning from court, asked,
'Was anyone hurt?' He did not ask about the horses.

At the top of the hierarchy, Confucius taught that there were four stages of moral perfection – the Gentleman (*chun tzu*), the Complete Man (*ch'eng jen*), the Good Man (*shan jen*) and the Sage (*sheng jen*). He indicated that Sages were so rare he was never likely to meet one (and was not one himself), and that he had never met a 'Good Man' either:

I suppose I should give up hope. I have yet to meet the man who is as
fond of virtue as he is of beauty in women.

The man who ought to represent perfection was, of course, the ruler. Confucius venerated the ancient 'Yellow Emperor' Huang Ti, a semi-mythical figure who ruled in a previous Golden Age. Confucius desired to re-establish this Golden Age, to bring earthly affairs once more in line with the 'Will of Heaven', but despaired of finding a ruler capable. He despaired even more of ordinary people, whom he considered as possessing neither moral nor intellectual capacity. It was this attitude which became a foundation stone in Chinese thought, firmly in place ever since, whereby the masses had to be 'moulded' from above:

The common people can be made to follow a path,
but not to understand it.

After Confucius, the next stop on the Philosophy Line was Mo Tzu (c.470–391 BCE), who clearly had no time for his predecessor at all:

The Confucians corrupt men with their elaborate and showy rites and music, and deceive parents with lengthy mournings and hypocritical grief. They propound fatalism, ignore poverty and behave with the greatest arrogance . . . They are greedy for food and drink and too lazy to work . . . They behave like beggars, stuff away food like hamsters, stare like he-goats, and walk around like castrated pigs . . .

From a modern perspective however we could hardly consider Mo Tzu preferable. In spite of a doctrine he called 'Universal Love', he preached a strong line on capital punishment to be inflicted on those who disagreed with him. Mo Tzu's analysis of society led him to the profound conclusion that discord was due to people having different views about things:

The more people there are, the more there are different concepts. Each man approves of his own view and disapproves of that of others, so there arises mutual disapproval among men. As a result father and son, and elder and younger brothers become estranged from each other . . .

Mo Tzu's cure for such worldly discord was not to preach tolerance for alternative opinions, but to establish one supreme opinion, in the body of the ruler, and make everyone else adopt it. He called this the doctrine of Absolute Obedience:

What the Superior thinks to be right, all shall think to be right.
What the Superior thinks to be wrong, all shall think to be wrong.

In a further, chilling foreshadowing of modern Han China, Mo Tzu even advocated that people should be ready to inform on each other for the good of the group:

Whoever fails to report a malefactor of the clan upon seeing one will be equivalent to being a malefactor to the clan himself. Knowing him, the Superior will punish him; hearing of him, the group will condemn him . . .

Following the same train of thought was Hsun Tzu (c.312–230 BCE) who, although a Confucian, shared Mo Tzu's hatred of music and other leisure activities:

Man is born with the desires of the eyes and ears, with a fondness for beautiful sights and sounds. If he indulges these, they will lead him into license and wantonness, and all ritual principles and correct forms will be lost. Hence, any man who follows his nature and indulges his emotions will inevitably become involved in wrangling and strife, will violate the forms and rules of society, and will end as a criminal.

Thankfully for the common people, none of these stations was halted at long enough for their systems to be ruthlessly applied. That was until the line came to an end with Hsun Tzu's student, the Legalist Han Fei Tzu. Han Fei Tzu's own fate, as recorded for us by the historian Ssu Ma Ch'ien, is a study in irony. He stuttered, and because he stuttered he could not present his views personally at court. Therefore he wrote treatises, and he wrote them primarily for the ruler of his own state of Han, King An, who would not listen. When faced with invasion by the powerful neighbouring state of Ch'in however, King An selected Han Fei Tzu as an envoy to appeal to the king of Ch'in to desist from attack. Now it so happened that the ruler of Ch'in, King Ch'eng, was a fan of Han Fei Tzu's works, and was pleased to receive him. In King Ch'eng's ears, Han Fei Tzu's beliefs that morality was a redundant weakness, that the common people should be kept mercilessly in their place, that whole families should be exterminated for every criminal deed, that the only value the common people had for the state was in increasing production and providing military service, were eagerly received. More eagerly, unfortunately for Han Fei Tzu, than his plea to save the state of Han, which was attacked anyway.

The man who gave Han Fei Tzu recognition, King Ch'eng, was himself a complex character, a man of tremendous authority yet who seems to have been easily swayed by others, who applied a ruthless and irreligious creed to the process of government but was privately obsessed with the pursuit of immortality. Assisted by the application of Han Fei Tzu's advice however, he succeeded in unifying China for the first time in recorded history. His first step upon doing so was to abandon the lesser, more regional title of 'King' (*Wang*), and to grandly (*very* grandly, for he consciously applied to himself the title of the original, deified ruler of the Golden Age) declare himself *Ch'in Shih Huang Ti*, First Ch'in Yellow Emperor. It is from the title of his dynasty that 'China' got its name, but the re-establishment of the 'Golden Age', if it was ever one of his intentions, was *not* one of his achievements.

The immediate effects of Ch'in Shih Huang Ti's rule were so far-reaching that, to its roots, China would never be the same again. He abolished feudalism – replacing it with governmental bureaucracy – redistributed land to the peasants, divided the country into easily administrated sectors, reformed the written script and standardised weights, measures and currency across the realm. But he also uprooted thousands of people from their homes in a massive population redistribution scheme, conscripted thousands of young men to fight at the fronts of new and aggressive wars and to form construction gangs to work on roads and other projects, all of which were financed by unbelievably punitive taxation. He is mostly remembered today as the man who had thousands of terracotta warriors buried with him in the capital he established at Ch'ang An (now Xian), who built the Great Wall (largely with slave labour), and who decreed a great 'Burning of the Books' in 213 BCE whereby, to stop people using philosophical and classical literature as a basis for criticising him, he ordered every book in China that was not to do with divination, medicine or agriculture to be destroyed. People caught hiding books were either executed, or branded on the face and sent to prison camps to build the Great Wall.

While immersing himself at court in the perverse pursuit of the elixir of eternal life, patronising at great expense strings of alchemists (*fang shih*) and obeying credulously their every whim (on their say-so he had every walkway in his palace covered so that his whereabouts could not be known by bad spirits, and despatched boatloads of young male and female virgins to find the mythical island of P'eng Lai where the Immortals dwelt – inadvertently, it has been suggested, thereby colonising Japan), Ch'in Shih Huang Ti presided over terror in the land. The sad news for Han Fei Tzu is that he never lived to witness the unification of China that resulted from his ideas. The keenness with which the state of Ch'in had received him proved similar to that with which a praying mantis receives her mate – his purpose served, he could comfortably be disposed of. Ch'in Shih Huang Ti's Prime Minister, Li Ssu, a jealous rival of Han Fei Tzu, persuaded his ruler that his adviser could not be trusted as he came from the Kingdom of Han. With Han Fei Tzu in prison, Li Ssu sent him poison. Interpreting it perhaps as the painless option, Han Fei Tzu drank it.

In 210 BCE, Ch'in Shih Huang Ti died. In keeping with his obsession, he died on the eastern coast, hoping for a glimpse of P'eng Lai. The good news for his subjects was that he had kept all able successors out of reach, and three years later his dynastic reign of terror was ended at the hands of a peasant rebellion. The leader of the rebels, a farmer named Liu Chi, made a speech before entering the capital to take power. To the gathered crowds, who would have taken happily to living in trees after their recent experiences, he promised the extinction of the entire edifice of Han Fei Tzu's Legalism:

> *Gentlemen, for a long time you have suffered beneath the harsh laws of Ch'in. Those who criticised the government were wiped out along with their families; those who gathered to talk in private were executed in the market place ... I hereby promise you a code of laws consisting of three articles only: 1) he who kills anyone shall suffer death; 2) he who wounds another or steals shall be punished according to the gravity of the offence; 3) all other laws of Ch'in are abolished. Let the officials and people remain undisturbed as before. I have come only to save you from injury, not to exploit or oppress you ...*

The dragon slain, Liu Chi went on to become the first emperor of the Han Dynasty. In time it would become as corrupt as any other, but for a while at least there was a period of benign rule by a true 'man of the people'. There have not been many such windows in Chinese history, where totalitarianism has been the only real understanding of power, and that, really, is the present problem. Thankfully, Ch'in Shih Huang Ti was not directly emulated for over two thousand years, but when the terror came again, the sense of history repeating itself was not lost. The man at the helm of the new terror, on record as admiring Ch'in Shi Huang Ti beyond all other emperors and with Han Fei Tzu (along with a few pornographers) as his favourite bed-time reading, was Chairman Mao. Having already effectively unified China when he proclaimed the People's Republic in 1949, Mao first had to look outside his country to flex his military might, and the terror his reign unleashed was not only on his own citizens, but on the people of Tibet.

If what is can only be contextualised by what was, and the function of the past is to illuminate the present, then the causes, effects and nature of the consequent occupation of that country can only be properly understood through a Han psychology which, set in tablets of Confucian and Legalist stone, has remained literally petrified, afraid and unwilling to change, since Chinese history began.

Part 1

'SICHUAN'

Sichuan is not all it is made out to be.
Approximately fifty per cent of it was,
until 1950, the Tibetan provinces of Kham
and Amdo.

The town of Lijiang, a hundred miles
south-west of Chengdu, alternated between
Tibetan, Mongolian and Chinese control
for most of its history.

Its people, both pure Tibetan and the
Tibetan-descended Nakhi, were only finally
brought within the Chinese empire by force
of arms in 1723.

The nearby town of Chung-tien was
held by Tibetans as late as 1942, until
beaten off by Japanese, not Chinese planes.

The Giant Panda, symbol of China,
is native to regions of Kham now
annexed into western Sichuan, and not
Chinese at all.

*If heaven is the Lord's, the earth is the
inheritance of man, and ... consequently any
traveller has the right to walk as he chooses,
all over that globe which is his.*

MME ALEXANDRA DAVID-NEEL

Tienanmen

THE EVENTS OF AND SURROUNDING June 4th 1989 were so momentous, they have defined everything said or written about China ever since. Though unrest and slaughter occurred in many Chinese cities that day, the name of a Beijing square – Tienanmen – has become a symbol for the worst that a government can do to its people, the entirety of the drama which unfolded there being beamed live by satellite into Western living rooms, complete with journalistic analysis and bullet-by-bullet commentary.

For the Chinese however, Tienanmen has long been pregnant with meaning, a stage on which several episodes of recent history have been played. The May 4th Nationalist movement began there in 1919 with a rally of 3,000 people – small by today's standards but considered powerful at the time. On October 1st 1949, Mao proclaimed the People's Republic from the Gate of Heavenly Peace overlooking the square. He then quadrupled its size by levelling the surrounding historic buildings, to organise parades of a million people in iconic adulation of himself.

On April 5th 1976, in the original Tienanmen Incident a few months before Mao's death and the disgrace of Deng Xiaoping, several hundred thousand people poured onto the square at the Ching Ming festival, to mourn the death of Zhou Enlai. It turned into an anti-government demonstration, the PLA (People's Revolutionary Army) were sent in, and it finished in the same way as the 1989 protest, if on a smaller scale. Later, the Tienanmen Incident was reinterpreted as revolutionary rather than counter-revolutionary, so that Deng could portray himself as ruling with the will of the people.

Two years later, in November 1978, the square again found itself a focus of popular expression when the Democracy Wall movement began. Wall posters openly critical of Mao and (with a curious frequency) praising of Deng began to be pasted up; one giant *dazibao* stuck to the wall of the History Museum, which would have got its authors executed a year or two previously, labelled Mao as '70 per cent good and 30 per cent bad', which has since become the official line on the monster. Alas, when the poster campaign no longer suited Deng's interests he moved to end it, originally by the imaginative method of sending gangs of plain-clothes police to beat up anyone who stopped off for a read on the way home. Eventually, at the end of 1979, he just decreed the whole thing counter-revolutionary. 'Human Rights is a bourgeois, European concept', said the *Peking Daily* at the time, and Wei Jingsheng, one of the leading poster writers (and previously a leading Red Guard), has had only six months of freedom since (which, out of pure coincidence, happened to be the six months prior to the 1994 Olympics bid). In 1996, Wei was nominated for the Nobel Peace Prize and awarded the Sakharov Prize for Human Rights.

The more recent protest began with the death by heart attack of Hu Yaobang. There had been some pro-democracy student demonstrations in 1986–7, tiny by comparison, but Hu had been criticised for letting them get out of hand, and dismissed from the Party. Two days after his death, students from Beijing's People's University held a mourning rally in Tienanmen. There were obvious parallels with the 1976 Tienanmen Incident, and students hoped that Deng, as he had in 1978 rehabilitated Zhou Enlai, would now do the same for Hu. Wall posters in praise of Hu appeared, student associations multiplied, and an atmosphere of challenge conflagrated across China.

On April 18th there were student sit-ins in the Great Hall of the People (the Chinese Parliament), at Party Headquarters and at Zhongnanhai, the governmental residences. On April 22nd, funeral ceremonies for Hu went off peacefully, but unofficially. Then, demonstrations were forbidden, and steps were taken to cordon off the square. A number of students entered it first, pre-empting the police action. The government continued its hardline stand, the refusal to compromise inflaming student anger. Demonstrations proliferated and grew larger across the city and the country, and then it became impossible accurately to describe it all as a 'student movement'. Workers and citizens joined in, and on May 4th the demonstrations were infinitely larger than the historically ground-breaking one seventy years previously. Still the government did nothing, and although dialogue at this stage could have led to compromise, it refused.

In the middle of May, Gorbachev arrived on a state visit. His was the first visit by a Soviet leader since Mao famously received Kruschev in his swimming trunks. His arrival, as a symbol of the possibility of democratisation within a totalitarian country, intensified people's hopes. The students camped in Tienanmen upped the stakes by going on hunger strike. On May 17th and 18th a million people were in the square, the largest numbers since Mao's parades, but now with very different motives.

The next day Martial Law was declared, and the PLA was ordered in. Citizens around Beijing erected barricades, talked to the soldiers, chanted 'the army loves the people', and for a fortnight the army allowed itself to be held off. Debate spread about the streets as to which units could or could not be trusted. Troops were brought in from Tibet and Heilongjiang, guaranteed to be unfamiliar with the build-up to the situation. The Western media analysed the possibility of civil war, and for a while this seemed a viable scenario. Meanwhile, a thirty-foot plaster-and-foam statue, named the 'Goddess of Democracy' and modelled after the Statue of Liberty by students from Beijing's Art College, was erected in the square under the gaze of Mao. The tension could scarcely have been increased. Something had to give. The students themselves were divided. Some mooted returning to campus, to show goodwill and consolidate the allowance of this much expression. Others disagreed. In one incident, ink was thrown across Mao's face. Sensitive to the degree of provocation this could constitute, all the student organisations condemned it.

On June 3rd the inevitable happened, and the PLA opened fire. Troops from the hardline 27th opened up first. Tanks rolled over barricades, and over any people who got in the way. Approaching the square, they fired at anything that moved, and into apartment windows to keep witnesses away. In Western countries, people sat glued to every bulletin, to live pictures of familiar journalists ducking and diving with the frantic crowd. Realising the decision and the odds, demonstrators remaining in the square in the early hours of June 4th attempted to go home, but were mown down in surrounding streets while tanks rolled up and down the square itself, flattening everything and everyone left behind. On the morning of June 5th, only a few, isolated people were about. A poignant image of a young man bringing a column of tanks to a halt with his jacket in one hand and a white carrier bag in the other epitomised the heroism, the nakedness of the human spirit, and it was one of the last images to be transmitted before satellite links were belatedly cut off, though in China executions associated with Tienanmen were publicised for weeks afterwards. It also took weeks to scrub the blood away, before Tienanmen would be opened again. A decree was issued ordering future Beijing University students to serve a year in the PLA before commencing their studies. On June 4th 1990, Tienanmen was used for cycling proficiency displays; one man attempting to lay a wreath in honour of Hu Yaobang was arrested, and declared mad.

And then there was, and is still, the dissembling, the perversion of truth into the highest obscenity, that no citizens died at all. What is Truth? It always seemed to me quite a good question really. The subjectivity required for its construction makes it very easy to manipulate, when you control the information. Thus there were not really millions of protestors, but 'a handful of misguided persons'. The army had to restore order because it was attacked, but still the noble PLA refused to open fire. The only people who died were soldiers. It can be proved. A book in the Beijing Friendship Store was full of grisly photographs of charred bodies, frozen by the flames into horrifying positions of agony, white teeth shining through burnt flesh, yet still wearing their green army caps with plastic visors that mysteriously refused to burn with the rest of the body. The situation, at first tolerated by a lenient government, had finally got out of hand. What choice did it have? The wonder is that the PLA were so restrained, refusing to shoot back under fire like that. So once again the PLA are the People's heroes, and the people of Beijing love them.

But who, I wanted to know, had the job of carrying a green hat around Beijing for the photographer?

1

I HAVE BEEN TRAVELLING AS long as I can remember – even if, before
the addiction began for real when I acquired a passport at sixteen and ran
away to Paris, it was largely in the mind, my imagination fired by the
pictures in *National Geographic*. At an age when my wife, Maria (who
became a teacher), was arranging her obedient teddy bears in front of a
blackboard and her sister (who became a nurse) was smothering her sick
ones in bandages, I was leading mine over the Himalayas. 'Yeti ahoy!' I
would inform my portentously malnourished Teds on reaching the top of
the stairs, though they may have thought themselves more subject to enforced
moulting than triumphantly entering Tibet.

I have yet to find out whether divination by teddy bear is an infallible
method of determining the future of one's offspring. Equally intriguing
however is the hard-to-explain affinity which some people have with
certain countries, frequently from an early age. For many it is India; for
others, South America; for others still the obsession of life is Africa, as if
some invisible umbilical cord were connecting them to a place they had
never visited, and could be known only through the collision of imagination
with literary text or photograph, or the apparent memory – for those who
believe in such things – of reincarnation.

With me, it was always Tibet, the country whose map on the wall in
front of me as I write so closely resembles the human brain, and which has
come to be known (due to the altitude, Bede Griffiths believed) for its rarefied
religious perceptions, for its sublime and gentle subtleties of human thought
and spirituality. Yet I had not been born when China invaded in 1950,

and when the Dalai Lama escaped nine years later I was three. When the Sixties came along however, when my own cognitive processes were riper and images of Tibet more commonly seen on TV, I remember being angered by a propaganda film of Chinese actors dressed up as happy Tibetan road-diggers, the fraud given away even to my young eyes by the richness and unsuitability to the task of their clothes. And there was a mystical element, too. I remember on one occasion entering the living room mid-programme, to see a line of shaven-headed, meditating monks sitting silently in a cave, candlelight playing catch-and-kiss on their loosely closed eyes. Never having seen such a sight before I stood transfixed, with the feeling of someone who, selecting a channel at random, is presented with an image of themselves.

When an obsession with a place is so deep-rooted, it seems inadequate to describe the desire to go there as 'ambition'. It is not ambition that attracts metal to a magnet, but a fate determined by its composition. The only difficulty for me was that my particular object of attraction had been defended by force of arms for the best part of a century. Only in the early 1980s had the door to foreigners become slightly ajar, and even now it nudges open and shut with political whim and tide. When we arrived, close to the anniversary of the first modern uprising of 1987 (now a reliably regular hot-spot in the Sino-Tibetan calendar), the tide seemed most definitely out, the door most literally closed.

'Individual travellers aren't allowed in Tibet. You have to take a tour.' The woman behind the desk of Chengdu's China International Travel Service was sour-faced and unconcerned. Used to a daily stream of such enquiries, she turned away and pretended to busy herself with something at the back of the little office.

'But we've met people coming out who weren't on tours,' Maria insisted. This was true, although we knew they had not entered recently. We were conscious of going through the motions with CITS (more commonly known to independent travellers as the Criminals Incorporated Travel Service) in case, as is often the way in China, the ruling had changed with the wind. It had not, and the woman, annoyed at having to complete the conversation, did not bother to hide the fact that she regarded us as a nuisance.

'You're lying.' Turning to face us again, she replied with the crisp bluntness characteristic of Chinese officialdom. 'I told you, tours only. If you want go Tibet, you pay one thousand dollar. Five days Lhasa, good hotel. OK?'

'Not OK,' I answered.

'So bye-bye.' She began to usher us out. 'Now time for lunch,' came the functional excuse, with something extra in Chinese as the door to Tibet closed behind us.

Talk of Tibet was on everyone's lips at Chengdu's unworthily famous Traffic Hotel, the grubbily dysfunctional tower of greyness which was the only place allowed to take the budget travellers China accepted out of sufferance. A desire for foreign currencies and a need to be seen as playing by the rules of an 'open door' had resulted since 1980 in an unprecedented granting of access – even if other international standards, such as human rights and a basic politeness to one's foreign guests, went blatantly unheeded.

For their part, the Western independent travellers, or 'backpackers', tolerated the rudeness with only the occasional exasperated fit in front of a ticket counter, and generally went about their business of getting from A to B with a modicum of good humour. This was to their credit not only for the restraint shown in the face of unreasonable stubbornness when attempting what would have been fairly routine procedures in the West, such as obtaining a sheet for one's bed, but also because Western tourists included their share of those who seemed insensitive to any cultural nuance, in spite of having travelled several thousand miles expressly to expose themselves to a culture whose flowers, branches and trunk came from seeds and soil completely unrelated to their own. In tribal regions especially we had seen the integrity of indigenous people transformed into trophies like exotic butterflies, pinned into albums by cameras poked into faces, and wondered whether it was actually to *their* credit that they were not moved to anger. This was no false puritanism on our part, for such Western behaviour was playing into the hands of a government which, having failed to eradicate indigenous culture by power politics, was now trying power tourism instead; the policy of reducing people in their own land to insects in a vase would come to the fore when any travellers coalesced into a group, and gave us our own dictum that one is a better ambassador for one's culture when one is alone. It was another reason, out of many, why China preferred people to visit Tibet in groups, and the main reason why we wanted no part of it.

Western travellers divided, we deduced, into two clearly discernible types, those who travelled with humility, and those who travelled with egotistical pride. There was a third group whom we called 'the adventurers', which drew its numbers from both of those types and became more evident the further one got from conventional tourist trails. The difference was that whereas the humble adventurers would venture into a void with a curiosity for the unknown and an empathy with what they might find, the proud type travelled purely to prove themselves in what they construed as a hostile environment. If there were a difficult journey going, such as Kashgar to Beijing on one leg in a crowded bus, they would do it and then live for a week on the kudos this gave them in the dormitories where they spent time recovering. To us, it seemed a matter of maturity. Endurance of hardship was actively sought as a way of measuring their strength in the world; like the taking of drugs, it was a substitute perhaps for the rites of passage into adulthood their own cultures had forgotten.

But did the journey to Tibet require that we, too, became adventurers? Alongside those who wanted to go there precisely because it was forbidden, we wanted to see for ourselves the persistence of Tibetan culture under Chinese oppression. There were those who argued that merely to visit was to bestow respectability on the evils of the regime, an old but understandable argument we had once tussled over regarding Burma, before deciding that while package tours undoubtedly confer acceptance, individual travellers do not, and are ultimately priceless to the people. The citizens of such regimes need to see us to tell their stories, to know they are not forgotten by the outside world, not locked in a madhouse with the key thrown away, and from the point of view of information, without going there is no knowing – and no telling either. We were determined of course to enter Tibet without contributing to the profits China was making from its illegal occupation, and attempts by Chinese officialdom to stop us only fired our desire with a fox-like cunning. We thus found ourselves curiously unable to look down on the adventure motive, and the need to conspire and plot was transforming our journey. The lure of Lhasa, by historical tradition the 'big daddy' of forbidden cities, imbued it in our minds with almost mythological status. We had our own golden fleece to chase, our own labyrinth to penetrate, and if the authorities insisted on making it difficult, we decided we may as well relish the challenge.

News from other travellers however was not favourable. It was impossible in Chengdu to obtain a permit for Tibet without booking a thousand-dollar tour. Rumours that it remained possible to enter Tibet by bus from Golmud, a town in the south of Qinghai about a thousand kilometres north of Lhasa, were countered by those arriving in Chengdu who had tried that option, and failed. A third route, a fortnight's bus and truck journey across the mountains of Sichuan into Tibet's eastern province of Kham, seemed ruled out by the dearth of traffic and the ease of being picked up by police while waiting in a three-house town for a stray truck to replace the one that had broken down. We favoured the second option, if only because the Golmud road was the major supply link for Lhasa, so important that it was kept open throughout the depths of winter and at least held the promise of regular, alternative traffic. The journey ahead would be difficult and testing regardless of whether we succeeded, and we decided to spend a few days in Chengdu as much to rest and gather strength as to further investigate our options.

'Have faith in your own karma,' Maria reminded me, as ever a rock-like support when my doubts began to seem too real.

Chengdu is one of China's pleasanter cities. It has been compared to Paris, though it is only by the pavement restaurants along the banks of the Nanhe that one has this impression. Elsewhere the city is a seething mass of chaos, of overburdened boulevards and unreconstructed backstreets, of garish neon-lit soda bars and Karaoke joints, recently sprung up like splashes of spring colour in previously bare winter soil.

As the hometown of that capitalist roader Deng Xiaoping, free enterprise took off here before the Special Enterprise Zones were thought of. Consequently there is a definite zest that one does not find in Kunming, say, or Xian, and much of it is, in Chinese terms, rather alternative. One road is lined with stalls selling Western fashions such as blue jeans, another with stalls run by artists exhibiting and selling their own work. At the entrance to its bridges, peasant artisans craft bicycles from single strands of wire, model insects from blades of grass. Hobbies, here, are public. One can scarcely move outside the Post Office for the legions of stamp collectors displaying their albums, and a narrow lane close to our hotel was blocked solid one morning a week by bird fanciers, archetypal old Chinese men with white beards and Mao suits, beamingly exchanging advice on their lovingly caged possessions. From our room at the top of the Traffic Hotel we could see the ballroom dancers on a patch of green the other side of the Nanhe, a ghetto-blaster set up at five o'clock every afternoon to drown the horn and engine noise with strains of waltz and tango, and no shortage of people willing to put down their string bags of fruit and vegetables for a quick but wooden whirl with a stranger, usually of the same sex.

Chengdu is also a university town, and an abundance of English students are ever on the lookout for opportunities to practise their grammar. Before 1980, talking to foreigners would have been even more proscribed than any of the forementioned activities, yet on such occasions the hidden history of the city is given away by the subject matter. In 1989 Tienanmen got the world's attention, but there were disturbances all over China. Chengdu was second in the league of casualties, at the hands of toughened troops brought in from Tibet. Most of the dead were students, and they do not want the fact to be forgotten.

'My friend was killed by a bullet, during the demonstrations,' said one young man who walked a little way with us outside the International Department Store, his words at odds with the bustling normality around us. 'By day they only used batons, but at night they used guns against us. I saw him fall, but the bullets were so many we couldn't help him. Everyone ran. Only later I found out he was dead – a long time later. For one month his own family didn't know where he was.'

The man's name was Wang. Now a computer programmer, his one aim was to get to America. His hair was raven and hung limp, long and unstyled, neglected almost, over his ears. His thick glasses contributed to a great intensity of manner, as if he were focusing with all his might on a task that lay two inches from his nose, and his easy ambling at our side seemed therefore like a cover, a mask of nonchalant pretence.

'Were you part of the Democracy movement?' Maria enquired, leaning in front of me as we walked along.

'I am now,' Wang replied. 'But I wasn't then. Or I was, but only in a little way. I had little interest in politics before 1989, but the events of that time politicised me. It's like this with many people. Since 1989 no-one believes the word "Communism" anymore. Even the Party doesn't. The only system they believe in is protecting their own power.'

We waited to cross a road while a battalion of bicycles went by, overtaken by a green-tarpaulined army truck belching black exhaust, two rows of soldiers inside lurching with its sway. Next to us, pacing up and down in the strong sun was an 'old auntie', a tiny, wrinkled, retired woman in a blue Mao jacket with an armband and red flag, whose job it was to watch for traffic offenders, as well as any pedestrians who might spoil the pavement with sputum or cigarette stubs. From the look of the ground, she had an uphill task.

'But recent changes are bringing greater wealth,' Maria persisted.

'True, but only for people in the private sector,' Wang replied. 'For others, there are no improvements. We're seeing two societies again, just like China was before 1949, just like it's always been.'

The lights changed, and we crossed. 'So will there be disturbances again?' Maria wanted to know, dodging an old man coming towards her with a live turtle dangling helplessly on the end of a piece of string threaded through its body, its feet paddling fruitlessly in the air.

'Not for a long time,' Wang was definite. 'It's no crazy thing to be afraid of bullets. And what happened afterwards was like the Cultural Revolution all over again. A number of student leaders escaped, and we were interrogated about them in the street. I had eight people screaming at me. They said, "If you don't tell us, we'll take you to prison." But I knew they couldn't prove I knew anything, and of course I didn't. For the parents of the hiding students it was worse. They had to denounce their children on TV. You know, we've a great tradition in China of family loyalty, but Communism's destroyed that. For me, that's the worst evil. Family loyalty is like the bonding of molecules in society. Without it, society will fall apart.'

I remembered an article by the journalist Edgar Snow, in which he lamented how even friendship itself had been supplanted during the Cultural Revolution by the cooler, more professional idea of 'comradeship'. I mentioned this, and Wang nodded vigorously.

'We have to be careful who our friends are, even now,' he said. 'There are people to whom we can speak our true feelings, and there are people in front of whom it's a good idea to be heard praising the Party – like the boss at work for example.' His earlier intensity working off, Wang allowed himself a smile at the absurdity of it all, flicking his hair away from his face and blinking behind his glasses. With a few more strides we reached another boulevard. 'My bus stop's this way,' he gestured.

We stood on the corner. Tied to the railings where the road curved was a family planning poster, its words in English as well as Chinese: 'Raise Population Quality, Not Quantity'. I grimaced. It was a sign of how eugenics had passed into Chinese law, providing local authorities with a statutory duty 'to avoid new births of inferior quality and heighten the standards of the whole population'. Several states were already legally forcing sterilisation on anyone with unspecified diseases, and in 1994 a law would be passed precluding the physically and mentally infirm from marriage.

'Will China change, then?' Maria pursued, testing Wang for his optimism. Merely to stand still was creating congestion, but he answered oblivious to the muttered complaints, reverting in immobility to his previous engrossment.

'The question is how, not if. You have to look at Chinese history. We've always had totalitarian rule. For three or four thousand years we haven't known anything else. It's a strong habit to be cured of. I think our situation is similar now to the end of the Ch'in dynasty, when the government lost its strong emperor and the power vacuum was filled by the people. Of course, that's not what we were consciously trying to do in 1989, but it nearly happened. At other times in our history when a dynasty has been weak, the whole empire has split up. I can see this happening too. Tibet will go. Xinjiang will go. The Special Economic Zones will go. Beijing will have no authority beyond the northern provinces. In my opinion, only democracy can stop this. But the Party believes the opposite, because the transition to democracy created the break⁄up of the Soviet Union.' Wang paused, looking along the street and back again. 'Perhaps China will break up anyway, with or without democracy. It's our fate perhaps, as history repeats itself.'

While we stood engaged in conversation, several people in poorer dress had gathered to hear the strangeness of another language, and the resulting blockage was now large enough to force others off the pavement into the road.

'It's alright to speak to us?' Maria wondered, prompted to concern perhaps by the openness of his words.

'Of course. Maybe there are some police, but I can say I'm practising my English. There's no law against that!' He pulled a pen and paper from his pocket and scribbled down his telephone number. 'Come for dinner on Sunday. I'll meet you here at three o'clock. Phone me if you can't make it.'

Wang's bus appeared, a huge concertina affair, and we watched as he fought through the crowds to get on it. Take away the signs of modernity, I thought, and we could have had the same conversation with a young trader perhaps, at any of several moments in China's long, authoritarian history.

On Sunday afternoon, we set off to meet Wang. Unable to judge the journey correctly, we arrived an hour late – a great *impolitesse* in China. We found him waiting dutifully at the bus stop, still wearing the same clothes as two days previously, a red gingham shirt and blue jeans. It was a short ride to the housing estate where he lived with his wife and daughter, whose little bicycle was propped against the door on the fourth-floor landing.

We stepped around it as he let us in. His wife Li, a doctor, came to meet us, and we shook hands. A tall, alert woman, she was smiling broadly; it was always exciting to have foreign guests. We gave her the modest gifts we had been carrying, a tin of biscuits and a box of chocolates from the International Department Store, and she thanked us shyly.

'Would you like to wash your hands?'

It was not the first thing we would say to visitors. It sounded like a purification ritual on returning home from the outside world, and was suggested so strongly we hardly felt inclined to refuse. While we stood around in the hall waiting for each other and they bustled with the gifts and the kettle, we had the opportunity to take the place in. The flat was tiny. The hall was almost the largest area; it had a hat and coat stand, towel rails, shoes. In the main room, tea and crisps were laid out in readiness on a folding table. Their few possessions so compressed their living space that nowhere could two people pass without touching. We could see nothing resembling any form of heating, for which we assumed they had to use space heaters – portable stoves perhaps – which were kept in cupboards until their use could be postponed no longer. It was an austere existence. In the whole flat there was nothing to cover the bare, concrete floor, and nothing to decorate the once white-painted and now flaking walls. They could have done infinitely more to make it attractive for little outlay, Maria mused quietly to herself, while I reflected on what their standard of living would have been as middle-class professionals in Britain.

In their thirties, combining energy with know-how, Wang and Li were typical of the engine room of modern China. Yet they seemed throughout their lives to have been the victims of social experiments. They grew up and went to school – when school was open – during the Cultural Revolution, which did not end until their early twenties. Then, with coloured clothes and modern goods suddenly appearing in the shops as a result of Deng's 'openness' policy, they were to find, on the threshold of marriage and a new life with great expectations, that the greatest possessions of all were denied them, not by low wages but by the one-child policy. Theirs had been a life of many vistas, of serial ironies and the dashing of hopes. Theirs was an unfortunate generation, I said to Wang, pushed by promises, punished by policies.

'All generations in China are unfortunate,' was his answer, as we sat on the bed and he sat on the bamboo sofa at right angles to us, his familiar intensity embodied in his hunched shoulders, his hands that were clasped between his knees. And then I thought it was wrong to call it an intensity of manner, when he was really speaking only with passion. 'But of course we don't feel it all the time,' he continued, releasing a hand to tap his forehead in indication of trickery, 'as the government is clever to always give us hopes. Before, the hope was a Socialist society based on fairness. They gave up that idea. Now the hope is economic prosperity. I don't think they will give up this idea so easily, but it won't lead to universal happiness. People like us, professionals, and private sector managers, will do well, but most people could become more unhappy. The government's promising to make everyone rich, and the promise keeps everyone going, for now. But what'll happen when only a few are rich, and most are poor? Already corruption's everywhere, the government's losing control in the provinces, and people in the countryside are so poor they're coming to town to beg for food.'

This was certainly true, and visible on the streets. It pointed to a growing gulf between the cities and the countryside, where unemployment was rife and the Party already admitted, in an article in *China Daily*, to fifty million people it could neither feed nor clothe. Since the revolution was nurtured in the countryside, there would be many who would think this a betrayal.

'We read in *China Daily*,' said Maria with one eye on the little electric organ, 'that young people have so many possessions now not because they've earned them, but because their parents insist on buying them things. Is this true?'

'Oh yes!' said Li, standing in the doorway and swinging her daughter between her legs. 'It's quite common for old people to buy a colour television for their children, while they only have a black and white one for themselves, or to buy their children a fridge, while they don't have one at all. They say things like: "We've never had anything, so why start now?"'

'Old people are so used to hardship,' added Wang, 'they don't know what comfort is. But they want their children to have everything, so life continues to be hard for them. For my generation it can be easier, because they sacrifice themselves for us.'

'Even so,' said Maria, 'we can't imagine what your lives were like during the Cultural Revolution.'

This was true of course; it was like peering into an abyss, knowing it to be deep but having no idea how deep it really was, or what monsters lay hidden in the darkness.

Wang said: 'The little red books we waved!'

'Those parades in Tienanmen!' enjoined Li. 'How exciting they were!'

Maria and I looked at each other. They may have been speaking of a childhood picnic. But they were the children of unpersecuted officials, and could look back on it fondly, even if they now viewed the period intellectually as a disaster. Li skipped out of the room.

'I show you photos!' she said, and came back with a glossy album, an autumnal country scene on its cover, all blue sky and fallen leaves.

The photos were old. Black and white and brown and faded, they were stuck to brown paper pages by old-fashioned black paper corners. Many were loose, especially the tiny ones of people, just faces or standing, posed by a chair or a set of steps. They had put both families together, the beginnings, perhaps of an heirloom. Maria and I held the album between us on the bed, while Li knelt in front of us and pointed here and there, beaming at the exercise. She put her finger on a photo of a young woman, pretty, her hair tied behind in a bun.

'That was my mother,' she said. 'My real mother. My father remarried after she died.'

'How did she die?' Maria asked.

'In the great famine of 1960, which killed twenty-four million people. I was five years old.'

'But you survived,' I said.

'What food they had, they gave to me.' She said it bluntly, without emotion.

I swallowed. There was the abyss again, the unimaginable with half-formed pictures shifting in its mist. This woman was telling us her mother starved herself to death in order that she may live, and we could only hover on the verge of comprehension. I looked at her. Her eyes flickered. Yes, times were bad her eyes said, but we want to hear worse? Go talk to the next person. Chinese lives seemed such stuff as films were made on, designer tragedies for Westerners to read or watch after Sunday dinner.

We flicked on. Most of the photos were Li's. Many were taken in the same year, 1972, when she was seventeen, and showed her in school and in Tienanmen, in all the photos wearing a blue Mao-suit and holding a copy of Mao's little red book. Several photos were stereotypical of newspaper copy at the time – there was Li, in close-up or with schoolfriends, clasping the book to her chest or raising it aloft with a beaming face. It looked like she meant it.

'We did, of course we did. At that time everyone believed in Mao. Everyone did. I did. With all my heart.'

The last expression amused me. It suggested either a crush or a religious devotion, and I teased her with the choice.

'Oh, it was religious!' she said, laughing. 'He was like a god, every bit a god to us, to everyone. There was no idea of questioning anything!' She paused briefly, and leaned forward conspiratorially. 'You know, every mealtime in my house, before eating, we – the whole family – would stand around the table. My father would choose a verse to read from that book, and then we'd all turn and look at a large picture of Mao that hung on the wall, and my father would say: "Thankyou, Chairman Mao, for all the food and everything you've given us." Isn't that just like a religion?' They were laughing, looking at our expressions, how our mouths had dropped in disbelief.

'Just like a religion,' nodded Maria.

'A *false* religion,' said Wang, smiling, as if some others were true.

We went through to the tiny kitchen to eat, where Li had prepared a veritable banquet, a dozen dishes taking perfect account of our vegetarianism, which in Chinese cuisine meant preparing tofu to resemble meat. The spread must have cost them dear. Wang opened one of the many bottles of beer lined up for the occasion, and offered a toast to our mutual health and prosperity. One glass went straight down for the appetite.

'Do you ever think to yourselves,' asked Maria, staying with the interrupted conversation, '*why* you believed those things?'

'It's to do with information.' Wang replied with such immediacy, that we were sure they had thrashed this one through many times. 'We had no knowledge of the outside world. We didn't know the alternatives – or even that there *were* any alternatives.'

'What about your parents, though?' I wanted to know. 'They were older. They knew.'

'Not really, they didn't. Before the Communists, you see, there was the civil war, the war with Japan, the first revolution . . . By the time the Cultural Revolution happened it had been several decades since China had a free flow of information.'

'In fact, we've never had *that*,' Li corrected him. 'There have always been demonstrations in China, but there have never been anything like so many people involved as in 1989, and it's all to do with information.'

'The government gives us Hong Kong and Taiwan television now,' Wang took up again. 'Always the films are supposed to show the countries in a bad way, like full of drugs and so on, but we're not stupid, we can see all those cars in the picture and we don't think they were all bought with drug money. More importantly, we see that Hong Kong and Taiwan are Chinese. We see what Chinese people can do. And so we ask ourselves, why isn't China like that? And the answer's clear – we have to change our political system.'

'Didn't you think to yourselves,' said Maria, her mind still on the drab black and white photos of Li and her friends in Tienanmen, 'that it would be nice to wear red or yellow or pink or green?'

With a sudden dawning of comprehension, my mind presented me with a recollection of a string of explosively gaudy hotel rooms.

Li laughed. '*No*! It's the same thing!' she said definitely. 'We had no information about the outside world. Nothing. We didn't even know what people looked like in other countries, let alone what they *wore*!'

So there it was. Without information, you cannot even form opinions.

'Was it difficult, being at school in those days?' Maria asked, lifting a piece of tofu with her chopsticks and dipping it in soy sauce.

'We were lucky,' replied Li. 'But many of our teachers were sent into the countryside. Many schools and universities closed completely. And there are people of my age who are illiterate now, because of the disruption. And of course a lot of our lessons were about Marx and Mao and the Party.'

'Does that still go on?' I asked.

Wang jumped up. 'I'll get you something!'

He went out and came back with a picture the little girl had done at nursery school. It was a duck on water. The duck was yellow, the sea was blue, the sun was orange. The big star at the top of the picture was red.

'You see,' he said drily, 'in China even ducks swim under red stars.'

'She *had* to draw the red star? In a little five-year old's picture?'

They were silent, as if words would only excuse the absurdity.

'When she's older,' said Wang eventually, 'we'll give her our own opinions.'

'Opinions!' Li virtually shouted, making us jump. Her vocal chords oiled by the beer, her cheeks were a little flushed. 'Westerners talk about opinions all the time,' she said. 'In my opinion this, in my opinion that . . . I'm not complaining, it's a good thing. I'm sorry to say that my country isn't rich in love and kindness outside our own families, and I think this is connected with our inexperience of many views. We're brought up to be intolerant by this insistence that there's only one right view. That's why democracy's so important. It's like a medicine for making people tolerant. For you it begins in your classrooms. But in China different opinions aren't easily permitted, and this too begins in school. In China the pupil *must* have the same opinions as the teacher.' She suddenly let the food between her chopsticks drop, and leant forward as to bestow a confidence, her voice turning to a whisper in the secret pride of a wrong she had committed. 'Last week,' she continued, 'my daughter came home from school saying the teacher had made her stand at the front of the class for laughing with another girl. She's only five years old – why shouldn't she laugh? It's a terrible thing to tell a five-year-old off for laughing. So I said to her, "She may be your teacher and you must respect her, *but that doesn't mean she's right!*"'

Li leant back again, the shimmer of excitement still showing, that this was a very *gauche* thing to have said about a teacher in China.

Wang sniffed. 'Like I said the other day, we're bound upon the wheel of history. The concerns of our ancient philosophers were all about social order and the fear of chaos, and it's the same today. I'm ashamed to say we haven't moved on for over two thousand years.' He poured some more beer and took a swig, the alcohol exorcising his intensity. 'Social order,' he repeated, sniffing again and leaning forward as if it were his turn to relay a witty piece of gossip. 'I'll tell you something about social order. You've noticed the fights and squabbles one sees every day on the streets?'

Awkwardly, we nodded. One could hardly miss it. Walking China's streets often seemed like weaving through a nexus of boxing rings.

'All Chinese complain about it,' he continued. 'Society's very chaotic now. In the Cultural Revolution, many good customs were lost. I tell you, before the Cultural Revolution people always queued for buses; now, they elbow each other. Before the Cultural Revolution, people would give up their seats for women and old people; now, they make them stand and think only of themselves. Before the Cultural Revolution, people spoke politely to each other; now, they're always fighting. But I tell you . . .' He pushed his glasses further over his nose to increase the effect of what was clearly a talking point for China's citizens. 'During the 1989 disturbances, which as you know went on for several weeks, people suddenly became polite again. Nobody fought in the streets. People said hello and smiled. If two people's bicycles crashed they'd make sure the other person was alright instead of hitting each other. Traffic drove more slowly, cars let pedestrians cross, and at junctions two cars would wait for ages insisting the other went first. Shopkeepers started letting people have food on credit. In Beijing, many, many people donated food to the students. All the time we were hearing story after story of people being kind to others. As soon as it was over of course, people got back to normal, pushing and swearing and being selfish again.'

'And how do you explain it?' Maria asked.

'The people had a sense of . . .' He reached for his dictionary. 'Collaboration. We were sharing the same hopes. We were all one group, one family, against the government.'

For a while we ate silently, digesting the image of people in China being nice to each other while their fate balanced on a razor blade.

The Politics of Sex and Power

IN 1993, THE CENTENARY OF Mao's birth was marked by revelations from his former physician that the 'Great Helmsman' and prophet of 'Socialist morality' was not only a concupiscent collector of concubines, but also an ardent company-man who required a regular supply of virginal country bumpkins for his personal initiation. Saturday night, it seems, was alright for bonking.

These stories are certainly true – Mao had numerous children by five marriages and nine known young mistresses – and they are certainly interesting. Sex in China always is, if only because it is more known there for its absence. There is the apocryphal story of a Chinese doctor, approached by a couple unable to have children after twelve years of trying. 'Tell me,' said the doctor, 'what do you do when you try?' 'Well,' said the couple, 'we take off all our clothes.' 'Yes . . . And then?' the doctor enquired, delicately. 'We go to bed,' they replied. 'Yes, yes, *and then*?' the doctor pushed. 'We hold hands,' said the couple, with nothing more to add.

Such anecdotes challenge our credulity because they knock on the head all we have come to believe about instinct. However, as Kazuyoshi Nishikura, of the Kyodo News Agency in Beijing told us, 'What is interesting about these stories is that they always concern people from the educated, professional class. People in the countryside have no problem knowing what to do, they can always watch the buffalo.' If this is true, it does suggest something is *interfering* with instinct in modern China, for those most affected are those most moulded by the system.

Many people new to China are struck by the profusion – and brevity

– of mini-skirts. Our introduction had been at Kunming, where ideas of fashion are untrammelled by more sophisticated influences from the developed East. There, what surprised us was not the waxy acreage of thigh on display, but the fact that *no man ever looked*. We even saw women using the top of their tights, rolled rather unaesthetically half-way up the thigh, as a place for keeping cash. When making a purchase in a busy street, they reached to it as nonchalantly as to a pocket. A matter of years ago, the entire nation was garbed in identical, shapeless and sexless 'Mao suits'. Now, the colour of every woman's underwear is on display, yet not a single male head turns. One feels entitled to ask why.

The answer, as does the clue to Mao's activity, lies in history. Confucius was himself a terrible prude who walked out of State banquets when the dancing girls were brought on, and had no time for equality either. It is not often realised that, right up until the Communist revolution, women's segregation in China was as extreme as anything found in the Islamic world. One Confucian document insisted that:

> *Men and women shall not go to the same well, nor to the same bathing place, shall not share the same sleeping mat, and shall not borrow each other's things, including articles of dress ... When a woman goes out she shall veil her face; if she goes outside at night she shall carry a lamp, if she has no lamp she shall stay inside. Walking in the street the men shall keep to the right, the women to the left.*

Such strict *mores* were propagated for the sake of social order, it being believed that – and here we come to the crux of the modern situation – *a castrated people are a powerless people. De-sex them, and they won't revolt.*

The emperors at the time hardly saw the need to abide by these restrictions themselves, any more than Mao did two millennia later. They were notoriously debauched, and equalled in their imaginative perversity anything that went on in Rome. While cynically foisting Confucianism upon the land they were actually *Taoist* themselves, and Taoism, already adrift from its sublime philosophical beginnings, was on its way to becoming extraordinarily licentious. The legendary Yellow Emperor Huang Ti was alleged to have achieved immortality as a result of having made love to twelve hundred women, and faced with advertising like that, across China people began to spurn Confucianism in favour of the new adaptation of Taoism, with a curious increase in the numbers of people taking holy orders.

By the end of the second century, Taoism surpassed Confucianism in popularity. In Sichuan, the ruler Chang Lu made Taoism the State religion, releasing criminals and imprisoning the sick. Elsewhere, the authorities were worried enough to outlaw Taoist gatherings. The result was the 'Revolt of the Yellow Turbans', when 300,000 people in 184 CE wound yellow ribbons (the colour of Taoism) around their heads and fought in the streets with government troops. Though the rebels were defeated in a horrendous slaughter, the government still fell, and China broke up into three kingdoms ruled by the military. Never had the ancient imperial belief that sexualised people were politically dangerous been so thoroughly vindicated. Following that incident Taoism was firmly repressed, and Confucianism instilled in the population with greater zest than before.

For the common people, for the best part of two millennia, certain things were not talked about, and were considered a 'male domain'. So it remains, really, today. For a brief period during the last civil war, monogamy was actually condemned by the Communists as a 'feudal structure', and free love was pursued as a matter of policy. It was known as the 'Glass of Water' principle – one made love, one drank a glass of water; it quenched the thirst, and wasn't worth getting hung up about. However, physical and emotional energies were soon deemed better directed towards defeating the Nationalists, and then to increasing productivity and serving the revolution. The pendulum swung back to how it had been under Confucianism. As a result, the Communist revolution may have put women behind the wheels of buses, it may have liberated them from the evils of footbinding, segregation and slavery, but that was as far as it went. The revolution did not, notably, allow women into government, and neither did it allow them many pleasures.

The Cultural Revolution finally put the nail in things. There was a campaign to eradicate kissing, on the grounds that it spread hepatitis. Even thoughts of marriage were discouraged. 'If one marries too early,' a *Handbook for Rural Cadres* advised, 'political and ideological progress will be affected. After a long time it may cause political backwardness.'

Today, these attitudes are little changed. In spite of the hard line on family planning, condoms are unavailable in shops and only obtainable on prescription, it being exceedingly embarrassing to ask for more than four a month, or any at all if one is over forty. Masturbation ('hand-lewdness', in Chinese) requires professional counselling and promiscuity, which can mean only one occasion of sex before marriage, is still a good enough reason for debarment from employment, exclusion from university, and occasionally incarceration in a psychiatric institution.

This is how the government wants it, and also why there are so many mini-skirts. They are no more than the latest fashion. No man looks, because no man knows he should. A castrated people are a pliable people. Ancient Chinese emperors offered transgressors a choice between death and castration, secure in the knowledge that any who chose the latter would be rendered as politically harmless as those who chose the former. In the same vein, during the First World War, it was realised that soldiers could be given bromide, not to dampen their ardour but to reduce their resistance to being sent back to the front. *A castrated people are a pliable people.* That was Mao's secret, passed down from his imperial ancestors in the mists of time. When we call China totalitarian, it goes that deep – deeper than ever was managed in the Soviet Union. In any country, and in any religion, the freedom of relationships and the empowerment of women have to be measures of its democracy.

2

MODERNITY HAS ITS OWN MOMENTUM that strains uncomfortably at the shackles of the past. It is natural for the child to replace the parents, for walls built long ago to crumble and fall, for the obsessions of the present to lose their grip with time. Ideas have a way of reincarnating, but to be reborn, they first have to die. That China is between death and birth has been evident since Mao passed away, and the opening of its doors in 1980 let in a stream of light that fell upon the leaves of its youth, their dazzled heads turning not only towards the sun of democracy, but to the fickle moon of consumerism.

Halfway between the Traffic Hotel and the bridge by the more expensive Jinjiang (which houses the American Consulate and which protestors tried to burn down in 1989 because of its association with Party privilege), past the point where the cobbled passage narrows into a pedestrians' obstacle course with bicycles and trees, the path widens again to accommodate the tourist-oriented restaurants. Several of them operate alongside each other, their tables picturesquely overlooking the Nanhe. From our arrival in Chengdu we had regularly dined there to chew over our strategies for entering Tibet. Selecting one at random from the rest, we now stopped again to eat. It was about six o'clock, and the hot Sichuan air was easing off into a comfortable, relaxing coolness. With the buildings on the other bank hidden by trees and a regular passage of vehicles over the bridge, the semblance to Paris was not unappreciated, although the water level was low enough for two fishermen to wade into the middle with their nets – something rather unthinkable in the Seine. While they fished in a timeless way, throwing their weighted nets square across the water and trawling them against the current, young student waitresses carried plates of food and bottles of beer here and there, stopping to practise their English, themselves enjoying the ambience of being amongst foreigners. We caught the eye of one, who came over with her notepad.

Sichuan women have the reputation of being the prettiest in China, and with her high cheek-bones, medium-length jet-black hair and fashionable denim shirt and skirt, the young woman who came to serve us certainly lived up to it. She also spoke an excellent if not perfect English, and easily fell into our jovial mood. Her name, she said, was Lucy, it being a fashionable thing for students of English to adopt an English name which is close in sound to their own. Her real name however, when we teased a literal translation out of her, was Paving Stone. She was born at the end of the Cultural Revolution, when her parents had been working on a project of demolishing a temple area and replacing it with a thoroughfare. They had been thinking of how useful paving stones were, of how so many people would be able to make use of them, and had named their daughter with the idea that she would somehow be 'a support to the masses'. In China, said Paving Stone, such political names were not uncommon, but even among her peers hers was a little unusual.

Paving Stone had been a student of classical Chinese literature (she liked Lao Tzu and Chuang Tzu the best), but had failed to get the right second-year grades. There was no second chance, and she was sent down. Now she worked by day as a factory secretary under, in her own words, 'a little woman with little brain and little power who thinks she has a lot of both'. In the evenings and at weekends she continued to work more enjoyably in the restaurants, as she had done since her student days, to improve her English. She also took Westerners to the opera. It was one of the services all the waitresses with better English offered for a little extra cash, the idea being that they can translate what would otherwise be a meaningless cacophony.

The following day we met Paving Stone by the waterfront. She arrived late, puffing and blowing excitedly on her bike and wearing another combination of the few clothes she possessed and constantly rotated. This afternoon it was jeans, which she had the rare fashion sense to wear tight rather than baggy, and a plain white shirt which set off the sultry blackness of her hair. Not for the first time of looking at her I considered that a Westerner would not have to be totally out of his mind to get her out by marrying her, were it legal.

'I've a friend who'd try that way!' she laughed when I ventured the possibility, cupping her hand over her mouth then turning away to hide an involuntary blaze of primness.

Recovering slightly, she came straight out with it: 'I haven't had a boyfriend yet. Relationships are too . . . complicated.'

'How old are you, Paving Stone?' Maria asked.

'Twenty-six,' she replied. 'I know, in the West people have relationships early, but in China it's different. Everyone's watching! Better get out of my factory, start a clothes stall, "be my own boss" as you say, then think about it.'

'But you'll be nearly thirty, Paving Stone.'

She shrugged. 'This is normal in China. Most people don't want problems before marriage.'

Being late in any regimented society may be a sign of mental health, but now it meant we had missed part of the opera. We pedalled fast behind her up the main People's Road to the giant statue of Mao, who waved to the bustling populace with an equally giant banner behind him, not now a red one praising the revolution, but a blue one saying simply, 'TAMPAX'. Tampons had been introduced only a few years previously, Paving Stone explained as we wheeled round underneath it, but many people were still getting used to sanitary towels, which were introduced only a few years before that, and the advertisers were having problems getting them to sell.

Past the grotesquely imposing Stalinist Sichuan Exhibition Centre we turned right towards the Post Office, left towards the Blind People's Massage Parlour, and with a further right and a left were soon lost in a maze of sidestreets with wooden houses. The opera house was in a market road that seemed to specialise in buckets of intestines, but it enclosed one of the most character-ridden tea houses we had seen. Tea houses, with bamboo chairs, low wooden tables and greenery, where you can sit for hours with eagle-eyed wandering waiters filling your cup as soon as it is half-empty, are a Chengdu speciality. Closed down across the country during the Cultural Revolution as breeding grounds for dissent, they opened again in Chengdu first – though not, for better or worse, in their previous dual role as 'flower houses' where men could go not merely for sex, but for the curiosity in a male-dominated world of women trained in music, dance and the art of conversation. Such flower-house courtesans were perhaps the most educated women in China, their ears often privy to a myriad of state secrets.

Now, in the tea house adjoining the opera, people just sat and played cards, slept or talked in the shade. Most of the clientele were old; glad, I supposed, to have their tradition back to this extent, even if it had now to be shared with their wives. The young, who had not known it at all before, eschewed it for the garish 'soda bars' in town and were conspicuous by their absence. Not for the first time one had the sense that the three generations of China were sharply demarcated by culture and ideas. There was no meeting point, little overlap, and hence little understanding between them. When one thinks of their respective experiences, it is perhaps no surprise. A seventy-five-year-old would have been born thirty years before 'Liberation'; they were the ones who propped up the old system, who were the revolution's victims and targets, who suffered the most terror. Their children, today's forty-five-year-olds, were their persecutors, who turned on their parents with all the ferocity of the Sons of Cronos and have since dealt with what they did in the classical way of Chinese psychology, by deflecting individual responsibility, by blaming 'orders', by scapegoating the 'Gang of Four'. Now their children, today's fifteen-year-olds, born with the birth of China's 'openness policy', know nothing of past privations. Both parents and grandparents complain that they have had it 'too easy', that they expect material comforts without the effort of earning them. The problem is compounded by the one-child policy, more easily understood in the West than in China where, with its attendant modes of enforcement such as the feared 'abortion squads', it is the single greatest source of discontent. The Chinese are quick to condemn the 'spoiling' that follows from an excess of undiluted parental devotion (there are even 'slimming camps' for adolescents, to cope with the new phenomenon of Chinese obesity), and both older generations agree that this new race of 'little emperors' is potentially the most dangerous of all.

Nowhere, perhaps, is the generation gulf quite so keenly embodied as in the opera. In the old days, opera was *the* form of artistic entertainment which stamped one as a participant in popular life. 'If you belong to the human race,' says a character in Chen Kaige's film *Farewell My Concubine*, 'you go to the opera. If you don't go to the opera, you're not a human being.' As Chen's film shows, a decline which had begun to set in with the 'modernism' of the 1920s was all but finished off by the Cultural Revolution. Ironically this was not because opera itself was seen as 'bourgeois', for actors and actresses in China as in Victorian Britain came from the lower levels of society. Rather it was because Mao's third and most dominant wife, Jiang Qing, was an actress who gave herself the role of wielding opera to serve the propaganda needs of the Party. Naturally, story-lines about production quotas and eradicating class enemies appealed to few people, and now that opera has been restored to its old self, only the old have returned to it. Inside, where the performance had begun, we considered ourselves to be the youngest present by at least fifty years – a fact which would hardly bode well for the future of anything. And yet, to tell the truth, the house was packed. Paving Stone had had to go that morning for tickets, and was lucky to get them.

We found our numbered, hard wooden seats amidst a dark sea of attentive, laughing faces, each kept cool by a flapping fan. We need not have worried that Paving Stone's translations would disturb people, for the entire audience talked all the way through, giving each other commentaries, falling into group silence only for the odd sung soliloquy, which would be followed by a little clap. According to Paving Stone, Chinese opera (of which this was the distinctive Sichuan variety) has a special language form adapted to singing which only old people can understand – rather like our Shakespeare, she suggested – and this necessitated her turning around every few minutes to be filled in on plot developments by the couple behind, an assistance eagerly and lengthily provided.

We saw four 'playlets' in all. The first involved a Han mother whose seven sons had all been killed in the Mongolian wars, and whose eighth and last son had now married a Mongolian. It was the story of how the son's wife won the mother over, and convinced her of the value of Han-Mongolian friendship. The second playlet concerned a young country girl of marriageable age who was left alone in the house while her mother went to temple. Bored, she naughtily decided to sit in the doorway of her house – in the days of segregation of women when they were supposed to hide themselves from public view – and duly fell in love with a passing young scholar. The outcome of this piece, ethereal by comparison with the stodgy Mongolian fare, was never known because the young actress, whose part involved much strenuous singing and dancing in the heat of the theatre, collapsed, and the curtain came suddenly down.

There were a few mumblings in the stalls and a brief apology from the stage, but not, according to Paving Stone, any mention of the well-being of the actress. And then we were on to the third play. For us, and seemingly for most of the audience who soon lost interest, fell asleep, read their newpapers or went out for a cup of tea, this one was a disaster. A forty-minute diatribe of anti-religious propaganda, it concerned a sixteen-year-old girl donated to the nunnery by her parents, who was now forcibly imprisoned by the evil Abbess under threat of 'dire punishment' should she try to leave. Alone in her cell she made fun of the Buddha and jumped up and down on the holy scriptures, eventually eloping with a handsome student she had venerated through her cell window. The play ended with the two happy lovers skipping away backstage, a cue for people to put down their newspapers, wake up or come back in for the fourth offering.

Completely different in style, this was a glorious farce in which a country bumpkin travelled to town to seek work as a servant. Negotiations with his would-be mistress go well until they agree on a wage, but not on his food. She offers a bowl of rice three times a day; he asks for twenty-four. She goes up to two bowls, then three; he agrees, but when she gives him some rice he complains about the size of the bowl. Ultimately maddened, she mixes corn pulp (used for fattening pigs) with the rice, and tells him it is egg-fried rice. He raises his eyebrows, wolfs down three bowls, and we think he's been had until, tipped by her from his sleep, he goes out to dig the garden. A hole here and a hole there.

'Why didn't you dig all of it?' she fumed.

'Why did you put corn in my rice?' came the triumphant reply and the audience cracked up, bubbling into the aisles in good enough spirits to last them the day, and encourage them to come again the next week.

'Aren't they going to tell us how the actress is?'

I was aching to know once the curtain had come down, but there appeared to have been no announcement. Perhaps collapsing on stage was a regular occurrence, given the heat. Paving Stone replied over her shoulder as we followed her up the aisle, but her answer was as unexpected as it was cutting.

'In the West perhaps they'd do so, but you're probably the only one who cares.'

Her disdain for her own people harrowed me. She had already complained about the sale on street corners of live crickets in round bamboo cages for children to use as footballs, and of the 'windmills' toddlers walked along with, which were made from two brown and cream flying beetles pasted live to a wheel on a stick. I wondered if she was picking up on foreigners' feelings about Chinese society, but her vehemence seemed to prove her sincerity.

Turning her head again, she continued as we shuffled along. 'Look, in my factory last week a man died who'd worked there thirty years. No-one even spoke of him the next day, but they all *knew*.'

I kept my peace, but could not help but wonder at the effect on a people of over two thousand years of Confucianism which encouraged them to rank their social concern according to family closeness, with the well-being of strangers, let alone non-Han, animals or insects, being beyond personal responsibility altogether. It seemed the complete opposite of the command to 'love thy neighbour as thyself'.

The geriatric crowd spewed slowly into the tea house, and we cast around for a table and chairs, fortunate to find some in a corner by a rubber plant as people put bags on the empty seats to reserve them for their friends. A waiter at once brought little clay cups and filled them with light, fragrant jasmine tea. Changing the subject, Maria enquired whether the third play was a modern one.

'No, they were all old – why do you ask?'

'Because it was anti-religious propaganda, I thought it more likely to be modern.'

Paving Stone's reply was blunt: 'No! It was fair enough! Why should parents give their children to a monastery? What does a child know about religion? What choices does it have in life?'

'Well,' Maria battled gamely, 'usually it's a sacrifice for the parents. If they're poor they need extra hands in the fields, which they're losing by giving the child to the monastery. And that child in the play could read and write, which the nuns had taught her to do.'

'Look, usually it isn't done for these noble reasons, but because the parents can't feed the extra mouth. And especially if it's a girl, they can avoid paying a dowry. They're not thinking of the girl, but of themselves.'

'But if the parents can't feed the child,' Maria pushed on, 'what else can they do? If they can't afford a dowry, what else can they do? The problem isn't the monasteries, but the social system that made a normal family life impossible.'

'I agree, of course. But you don't know how corrupt the monasteries were in China, how rich they were, how responsible they were for a lot of the rural poverty. Look, in India or somewhere else Buddhism may have been OK, but in China it was sick, and it's still sick now. Remember that play was written before the revolution.'

This we could hardly dispute. Largely because it was foreign,

Buddhism had been a target of vilification when it came to China, and never really stopped being one. Nowadays, when we consider the attitude of China towards Tibet, it is well to remember the historical attitude to Buddhism, especially to monks who do not work.

Maria was naked in the middle of the room when they came in. We had been soaked in a sudden summer rainfall, and having showered were fishing about for fresh clothes to put on before meeting Paving Stone again. On the way up we had reported our malfunctioning television to Reception, but had not seriously expected Chinese hotel service to be so efficient. Moreover, there was little we could do in our defence. We had no room keys. They stayed in the jealous possession of the surly, middle-aged woman who sat at the end of our corridor. When we arrived she would look at us, mentally match our faces to a number, let us in and walk away without a smile. There being no additional locking mechanism on the inside of the door, this woman had unrestricted access to our room whenever she wanted it, which included the right to walk in and replace our hot water thermoses at eight o'clock sharp every morning, whether they wanted replacing or not.

Squawking, Maria attempted evasive action by tugging at the pink bed-covers. The top sheet however was so expertly tucked under the mattress and laden with pillows (red, with yellow embroidered birds and flowers) that it refused to give. The television repair person accompanying the corridor-sitter was, thankfully, a woman, in blue overalls and carrying a cloth bag of tools. Since all Westerners in China soon become used to the direction of curiosity towards their feet and noses, in the common folklore that these are exceptionally developed, and Western women are additionally renowned for their (by Chinese standards) over-enlarged breasts, it was not surprising that our rude intruders, though barely interrupting their stride, could not resist a glance. With a disappointed look, they continued past her and stood before the dead television. I threw Maria a T-shirt.

'Why didn't you knock?' I asked the corridor-sitter, rapping on an invisible wall in the air in front of me.

The harridan curled her upper lip, let out a short, angry burst of Chinese and pointed at the cube of orange plastic next to the green curtains. I guessed it meant: 'We're repairing your set, aren't we? You should be grateful.' The repair woman meanwhile had pushed the 'on' button, and now uttered a resigned diagnosis with a shake of the head. The tube had gone. Between them they carried the cumbersome machine away, neither of them turning to apologise or even acknowledge us. Ten minutes later they entered again with a set from another room, connected it and walked out as if, with Maria's clothes, we had acquired invisibility. No matter how much we objected to the corridor-sitter's intrusions, we had to become used to them. She was queen of her fief, and had a free run of it regardless of its transient tenants. And perhaps she was right. We did after all have a functioning television again, although we wondered to ourselves whether it was worth it. There was so much blood on the screen every evening, even the toothpaste adverts ran with it, that when we got up to turn it off we half expected to find a great red pool of the stuff seeping into the carpet in front of the set.

With Maria dressed and recovered from her exposure, we set off as arranged for Paving Stone to take us to the cinema. It was her night off, but she had asked us to meet her at her restaurant and go on from there. By seven o'clock she was an hour late, and we were considering a third after-dinner beer when she arrived, pedalling along in her denim mini-skirt with a pair of unladdered black tights and a new white blouse with embroidered designs. She looked as if she had dressed up, which seemed strange if we were going to the cinema.

'Well, are we going?' Maria asked as she stood astride her bike at our table.

'I don't know.'

'You don't know?'

'There was a film last week, about the Emperor's servants, but it's finished now.'

'So what else is there?'

She pulled a newspaper from her bag, and named a few. All were action films, which meant guns, Kung Fu, and close-ups of glass entering jugular veins in slow motion.

'No romance?'

'We don't have many romantic films in China. There's an American film, *Scorpion*.'

'Sounds like an action film.'

'It is.'

'Any other ideas?'

'I was thinking . . . we could go to a . . . a dance?'

'Is it far?'

'No. Can my friend come?'

'Of course.'

I saw Maria look at her clothes and purse her lips, and the penny dropped with me also. They had planned this all along. Without more ado Paving Stone bounded over to her friend, who bounded back, and enthusiastically we set off through the leafy, wooden-housed backstreets in the old part of town. Her friend, Julia, was very short, under five-foot, but she was two years older than Paving Stone and a quieter, more complex type. I wondered if this was the same friend who would consider 'a bad way out'.

As we walked down the centre of the road, which was made only of earth and was churned up with holes here and piles there as if dug by the aggrieved labourer in the fourth act of the opera, the pair seemed in a markedly effervescent mood. This changed abruptly however when we arrived at the dance hall and an old matron came towards us, smiling, but waving her hand firmly.

'No foreigners,' she said simply, in English. We had half expected this, but our companions looked quite upset.

'Have you been here before with Westerners?' I asked.

The answer took us back. 'No. We've never been to a dance at all.'

'What, *never?*'

'Never,' confessed Paving Stone, humbly.

We looked at each other. Paving Stone was twenty-six and had been to university. Her friend was twenty-eight and was a teacher. How could they have got to that age and never been to a dance? Especially if it was something they *wanted* to do?

'OK,' I swallowed. 'Is there another place?'

'Yes. Around the corner. It is karaoke, but we can try.'

Inside we saw a few green armchairs and a bar, but nothing appeared to be happening. It was only eight o'clock, and perhaps we were a little early. We fumbled with our money and then the same thing happened. Evidently the authorities were still wary of too much inter-cultural mixing. When it happened again at a third place ten minutes later, we suggested adjourning to a soda bar.

'One more try!' Julia insisted, curiously tugging at her own hair with both hands.

Complaining loudly, they led us to a large, cavernous building off the main Dongfeng Road. A group of trendy ticket sellers sat on the pavement, drumming up custom.

'Four tickets, please,' said Julia.

The young man pointed at us and objected, but as we turned away his glamorous companion punched him on the shoulder and spoke into his ear. While I took in her clinging scarlet *cheongsam* split to the thigh, her black tights, high heels, heavy make-up and traffic-light lipstick, all of which made her seem more suited to the unrestrained decadence of the last days of Shanghai than to a modern Chinese boulevard, Julia cupped her hand over her mouth and whispered a quick translation: 'She said, "go on, let them in, there's no police tonight."'

We watched as they argued. 'We'll lose our licence,' the young man replied.

'But there's no police!' the dance-queen repeated. She was forceful, standing behind him and squeezing his biceps flirtatiously with both hands.

'Half an hour,' he relented. 'And they sit at the back in the dark.'

We did so, sending Julia to the bar with money for beers and colas – neither of them drank alcohol – while we hid in the shadows. Steadily, the place filled up. It looked modern enough, if not exactly sophisticated, and the light show was impressive. There was a live band, of which the drummer and the guitarist had collar-length hair swept back, and the latter kicked off with what could only be described as a pretty decent heavy metal riff. The girls sat there fascinated, looking around and taking everything in, whispering observations to each other while trying to look as if they came there every night. Alas the heavy metal proved to be a warm-up; when they began properly, most of the songs were an even-tempoed, traditional folksy pop.

We watched, equally fascinated if for different reasons. All were young, except for a solitary couple in their sixties who never left the floor all evening. There was little connection between music and steps, and couples danced as they were taken, so that to an ambitious Chinese version of Ike and Tina Turner's *River Deep, Mountain High*, one couple might be doing a fox-trot, another a waltz and another a tango, but most just held each other stiffly and moved around at a respectable distance. Moreover, girls tended to dance with girls, and boys with boys, with very few mixings. At the tables, too, the segregation held. Paving Stone, by whose standards all this was still very naughty, leaned over to me.

'There're *prostitutes* in here,' she hissed over the music, with the air of one confiding a salacious piece of gossip.

'Really? Where?' I asked, looking around and expecting her to point at some blatantly nefarious hussy.

'I don't know, but they're here,' she said. 'They used to be in front of the Jinjiang and everyone could see them, but last year there was a clean-up and they moved into the dance halls. It's easy, you see. They can make arrangements on the dance floor. They charge anything from twenty to a hundred *yuan*. Some girls even sell themselves to a man for a month at a time.'

'How do you know all this, Paving Stone?'

'We read the notice boards next to the Mao statue – everyone knows. Prostitution's one of the 'Six Harmfuls'.'

We knew about the 'Six Harmfuls' – Illicit sex (this included not only prostitution but also sex with foreigners and homosexuality), Pornography, Enslavement of Women, Drugs, Superstition (i.e. religion) and Gambling. It was interesting that the notice boards so openly admitted to the authorities' failure to contain them.

'Do you have a boyfriend, Julia?' Maria asked, exploiting the convivial spirit.

'I had one once,' she replied. 'It was very complicated . . .'

'She likes boys!' said Paving Stone, naughtily.

'But they're too much trouble!' her friend replied. 'In a society where it's accepted, like yours, it's good, it's easy, but China isn't ready yet. If people find out, if parents find out . . . oh!' She let out an exasperated sigh. 'It's hard to keep secrets in China. Too many people like to gossip, to make people . . . fall.'

Perceiving perhaps my intuition that she spoke from experience, she averted her eyes from my own. The song changed and conversation, led always by Paving Stone, ranged again from trade union rights to their wondering if Maria's legs itched when she wore tights, on the grounds of her hairy Western legs. Maria's reply that Western women shaved their legs sent them into paroxysms. And then, as two spiv-type youths waltzed woodenly but deliberately close to our table and away again, Paving Stone enquired:

'In your country, how many people are homosexual?'

'About ten per cent,' I said, refilling my glass.

'It's alright?'

'Some men and women face discrimination,' I replied honestly.

'Women!' Paving Stone's eyebrows shot up. 'I've heard some men are – gay, you say? – but never women!' She translated for Julia, and they jabbered excitedly in Chinese.

'In China,' she said turning back to us, it is an illness, treated with elastic bands.'

'Elastic bands?'

She made a motion of twanging one on her wrist. 'Family friend is a nurse, so I know,' she said. 'Have bad thoughts . . .' She twanged again.

'Opinion's divided, even in the West,' Maria said. 'But we think it's natural, like some people are born left-handed rather than right.'

'Well *I* think it's natural too!' Paving Stone spontaneously declared, finishing her drink.

Julia pouted. 'In China,' she added cynically, 'we make everyone right-handed!'

The song ended and the dancers milled around, some taking the floor, others leaving it. The two youths who had investigated our table during the last number took the opportunity to appear once more. Though they looked loutish they were polite, and like everyone else in the dance hall, had dressed their best. Yet they gave Paving Stone and Julia not a glance. Pretty as Paving Stone was, it was not she who had attracted them.

'Will you please dance?' the taller one invited Maria.

Like a shot she agreed. That left me.

'Would you like to dance?' The other youth spoke better English. As he loomed over me I caught the fumes of drunkenness and hesitated, wondering how not to cause offence.

'I'm sorry, I can't dance,' I said, hoping that would be the end of it.

It was not. Seizing the chance to practise his English instead, the shifty looking youth plumped down on Maria's seat and offered me a cigarette. I declined. He lit his own and swayed back against the chair, sending a swanky ring of smoke over Julia's head where it hovered like a misplaced halo before disappearing. The women looked at each other and frowned at the intrusion. He narrowed his eyes to focus on me, thinking of something to say. I took in his slicked-back hair, the up-turned collar of his jacket and pulled-back sleeves, and fought against the stereotype of a B-movie baddie.

'You have job?' he asked.

'Teacher,' I replied politely.

'In China?'

'No. England. And you?'

'I'm in forging.'

'Banknotes?'

'No. Steamhammers.'

'Ah . . .'

Mercifully Maria returned, having been told off by the management for dancing when we were supposed to be hiding, and our uninvited friends returned to dancing with each other. I sent Julia back to the bar for more drinks, and there was a change in tempo to 'real' disco dancing. For three songs the floor was packed with lines of bodies imitating swimmers limbering up before a race. It was the most popular spot, but perversely rationed. Three lively pop songs was all we were going to get, and after them the entry tickets were to be raffled. They called out the fourth prize, the third and the second, and with each number Julia became progressively more excited, to the disapproval of Paving Stone who gave her friend scornful looks as she hung expectantly on each number called. Then came the announcement of the first prize. Julia perched forward even further on her chair, her back arched upright, her ticket in her hand. There was a suitable silence, the number, a short pause, then a shriek, and Julia had won. She threw her hands in the air, jumped from her chair, ran over to the announcer and returned with a pair of silk slippers. She tried them on; they even fitted. She blubbered endlessly that she had never won anything before, never been to a dance before, and all the while Paving Stone sat quietly in judgement on her friend's undignified over-reaction. As the karaoke began, I suggested we went home.

'Do you have to be home by any time?' Maria asked when we were outside.

'Ten-thirty,' said Paving Stone, still a little subdued. 'She has to be in by eleven.'

I ruminated on the parental constraints inflicted on women of their age. Her friend meanwhile kept opening and closing her shoe box, taking them out, examining them, dropping them on the ground which was now wet from a little evening rain, trying them on and catching us up again. She reminded me of Eeyore, with his burst balloons and honey pots. It was interesting that the slippers meant so much. Paving Stone studiously ignored her.

'You're going to have to explain those tonight,' I said, half in jest. 'Your parents will want to know what his name is.'

Julia laughed. 'I'll tell them I bought them.'

'Would your parents mind if you'd been to a dance?'

'Yes they would,' said Paving Stone, still in a doleful mood as Julia fell behind again, examining the shoes in a stream of light from a window. 'It's one of those things that weren't around when they were young, and they attract a lot of bad people. There's a big generation gap in China, they're really suspicious of everything. But if they knew who I was going with, it would be OK.'

'If they knew you'd been with foreigners?'

'They wouldn't like it. They've never mixed with foreigners and have old ideas about them. They know I work in a restaurant, and they know I practise my English and take foreigners to the opera, but that's during the day-time, and kind of like work, so it's OK – it's not the same as being friends.'

We passed the plush Jinjiang Hotel, crossed the Nanhe and walked along the narrow, tree-lined path that led past their restaurant to our own hotel, its grim façade dimly lit by only one or two little street lights. It is not allowed for foreigners to take Chinese people into their hotel rooms, especially young women, so we had to say goodbye in the street. Having built up something of a bond, the parting was not borne easily. At first Paving Stone looked up with doleful eyes and bit her lower lip, then, managing an abrupt 'good luck', she turned sharply on her heels and sprinted into the night. Some yards behind her under the yellow glow of a streetlamp, a silk shoe cradled in her left hand, Julia turned her head in puzzlement at her disappearing friend.

Over the next few days the news was out that a private travel agent was undercutting CITS on tours to Tibet by three hundred dollars, for a minimum party of ten. We considered the option of five days in Lhasa for seven hundred dollars each minded by a guide, and then rejected it. There seemed something morally wrong with paying such sums to the jailers for a short, controlled stay in the world's largest prison camp. We thus resolved to go to Tibet under our own steam or not at all. This required getting ourselves to Golmud as quickly as possible, before the cold weather set in, and we asked a local tout to obtain Chinese-price tickets for us to Lanzhou the following day.

With our last afternoon in Chengdu, we decided to visit the temple of Wenshu. Our experience of Chinese temples so far was that they were too often shrines only to irreverence, and we went with no expectations. We had yet to see a temple that was only a temple, devoid of gimmicks and armies of pointers and laughers on a day out. Wenshu was no different, but for the first time these seemed to be balanced by the number of serious worshippers, many of whom were young. There were several shrine rooms, not exactly buzzing, but at least being used. In the temple of the Emerald Buddha in Bangkok we had found a collection of divination sticks, and watched a pious young mother kneeling before the Buddha, teaching her little girl how to use them, before having a go ourselves and collecting a fortune slip we had still not had translated. Here, although 'hell money' was burned outside, there was nothing remotely resembling divination, just incense to burn and, if you had it, money to place on a shrine.

Behind the door of another room however, we found the attentions of a number of people focused upon an old monk, an archetypal looking fellow with bald head, white wispy beard and black robes, seated on a chair. Three families were in a queue to see him, and we stood at the back and watched as the first family went forward. A young woman, her mother eagerly close, gave the monk some money. He, in return, reached into his sleeve for a piece of tightly folded paper, which he passed to her with a few words. The mother asked some questions, he answered briefly, and that was that. The same happened with the second and third families. Intrigued, we approached him.

'Do you speak English?' Maria asked.

His sight was not good and he had not seen us, so our presence surprised him. He looked up and nodded, perhaps more in greeting than the assertion we took it for.

'The mind is the Buddha,' he said, with seemingly practised sagacity.

'I was wondering if we could ask you something.'

'The mind is the Buddha,' he said, nodding wisely again.

'Only, we were wondering if our journey would be successful?'

'The mind is the Buddha.'

'I see.'

'The mind is the Buddha.'

'Oh well,' Maria concluded on the way out, 'if you can only speak five words of English, I can think of worse things to say.'

Religion and Resistance

HAN CHINA STOPS AT CHENGDU. It always was the edge of the Middle Kingdom, since the earliest times when it abutted the Bai Kingdom of Tien. In 119 BCE this area was so troublesome that Emperor Han Wu Ti sent the great historian Ssu Ma Ch'ien, then one of his chief secretaries, to oversee Tien's subjugation and open a trade corridor with India. This was only partially successful, since the puppet ruler they installed, Jen Kuo, an Indian and a Buddhist, had the impertinent habit of enquiring of all Han Wu Ti's messengers, 'whose kingdom is greatest – his or mine?'

The effects of the exercise of Han political power on the character and personality of the Han people are distinct. A Paving Stone, twenty-six years old with child-like naivety, innocence and sublimated instincts could not be produced in Tibet. That this is so questions what it can mean to call 'China's minorities' Chinese. National character is different. Language is different. History, beliefs and folklore are different. The only link is hegemonistic colonialism, where the Han are the colonisers, the 'minorities' the colonised. Neither are they viewed equally. A poster at the airport boasting that 'China's fifty-five minorities are good at singing and dancing', said it all.

Most of those 'fifty-five minorities' are found on China's western side. They tend to be either Buddhist or Muslim, the advent of Islam going back to the T'ang Dynasty, within a mere hundred and twenty years of Muhammad's death.

The T'ang Dynasty began well enough. Its first emperor, Kao Tsu (618–27), put an end to former Sui oppression and his son, T'ai Tsung

(627–50), who has been called 'the greatest monarch in China's history', built schools and libraries, allowed the first Christian (Nestorian) monastery to be built in China, and sympathetically received envoys from a variety of countries and religions. The trouble began when his ninth son, Emperor Kao Tsung (650–84), took one of his father's concubines into his own seraglio. Famous mistakes in history do not come much bigger, even if his father had already died, for this woman killed their own child and implicated Kao Tsung's wife as the murderess. In 690, after Kao Tsung had died of confusion, she proclaimed herself Empress and ruled with absolute power. Her first act was to amputate the hands and feet of Kao Tsung's wife and another rival, before throwing them into barrels of alcohol and personally, reportedly gleefully, watching them die.

Several convoluted assassinations later, Hsuan Tsung (713–57) ascended the throne. This man's mistake was to take his son's concubine for himself – the most famous beauty in Chinese history, Yang Kuei Fei. So besotted was he that he also made her brother Prime Minister, but the Prime Minister so angered another powerful courtier, An Lu Shan, that the latter revolted, taking the entire T'ang Dynasty down with him. In the end-game played out on a country road as Hsuan Tsung fled and An Lu Shan sacked the capital, the Emperor's own bodyguard mutinied and demanded the life of the Prime Minister. Hsuan Tsung gave them it. Then they demanded the head of the beautiful Yang Kuei Fei. Faced with a choice between his life and hers, he had her strangled by one of his eunuchs. And that is where the Muslims come in.

In a *hadith* of the Prophet, Muhammad reportedly advised his followers to 'seek learning, though it be as far away as China'. In the years following his death, Islam spread rapidly. The Qur'an had sanctioned war as a means of self-defence, and many Muslims felt it justifiable to advance the faith in the same way. So it was that the faith migrated, by the sword, through Bokhara, Samarkand and Turfan, turning Buddhist monasteries into mosques as it went, and found itself, in 751, on the Silk Road west of Dunhuang. The battle of the river Talas that followed was the first and only time that a Chinese and a Muslim army have met. Now considered one of the most important battles of world history, at the time it seemed insignificant to both sides.

The Chinese lost severely, with two results. The first was that through the capture of Chinese craftsmen in the battle, the technique of paper-making spread to the West. The second result was that not only

Han influence, but also Buddhist and Indo-European culture in the area was lost, and Central Asia became Muslim. With the rulers of T'ang busily enacting their own demise in a grand-scale family soap opera, affairs on the edge of the Middle Kingdom were not the concern they should have been, and it was not until the eighteenth century that Central Asia again came under the Chinese yoke. That year, 751, was actually a very bad year for them, for the Kingdom of Tien, now known as Nan Chao, was also victorious in a major battle and was not to succumb again until January 2nd 1254, when Kublai Khan, six years before his unification of China, personally bedded down with his troops in the gates of the capital, Dali. For the time being, Han China had been taught its limits.

The Muslim victory in Central Asia enabled Islam to establish itself in what is called China today. It has never been an easy relationship. Muslim rebellions in Yunnan between 1855 and 1873, and in Sinkiang between 1862 and 1877, led to deaths estimated in the millions. The worst perhaps came in the Cultural Revolution, when all religious practice was proscribed. In Dali a Muslim had told us of the letter box on the corner of the street, to be used by anyone to inform on a neighbour caught praying; how he had been forced to burn a Qur'an in public, and had been too afraid to even keep a copy beneath his floorboards, too afraid to even teach his son how to pray, or to admit to his own family that he remained a believer.

Only in 1979 were Muslims permitted to perform the pilgrimage to Mecca, a mere nineteen individuals from a Muslim population of twenty million being trusted to leave and return. Although the Hajj is no personal indulgence but an unarguable requirement of faith, numbers continue to be limited. There have been more uprisings recently, even if reports do tend to be hearsay. Rioting near Kashgar in 1989, apparently due to a refusal to build more mosques, led to the closure of the border with Pakistan. Since then, the province of Xinjiang has been subject to separatist bombings, selective assassinations of Party officials and retributive executions. In 1993, news reached the West of rioting in Xining involving thousands of Muslim demonstrators, with nine shot dead. This is not a problem that China can simply wish away.

The Buddhist problem, because of Tibet, is more well known. Not far from Xining is the monastery of Kumbum, where the Dalai Lama's elder brother, Thubten Norbu, held on for a year as Abbot when China invaded in 1950. The Chinese tried to play him off against his brother by sending him to Lhasa to persuade the Dalai Lama not to resist invasion or, failing that, to commit fratricide – with the promise of political power if he succeeded. Norbu feigned compliance but, on arrival in Lhasa, at once sped the Dalai Lama, together with Heinrich Harrer, over the border to India, then carried on to America where he won a pledge of diplomatic *and* military support from President Truman. For a while, from the early 1960s until Nixon introduced the present policy of appeasement, this was fulfilled: Tibetan fighters were flown to the United States for combat training and sent on some very successful incursion raids from a base in Mustang, Nepal. However, as the Dalai Lama realistically says in his autobiography, *Freedom in Exile*, this was 'not because they [the Americans] cared about Tibetan independence, but as part of their worldwide efforts to destabilise all Communist governments.'

Thubten's province of Kham bore the worst of the invasion. Accounts of it in John Avedon's book *In Exile from the Land of Snows*, make searing reading:

> *The obliteration of entire villages was compounded by hundreds of*
> *public executions, carried out to intimidate the surviving population.*
> *The methods employed included crucifixion, dismemberment, vivisection,*
> *beheading, burying, burning and scalding alive, dragging the victims to*
> *death behind galloping horses and pushing them from airplanes; children*
> *were forced to shoot their parents, disciples their religious teachers.*
> *Everywhere monasteries were prime targets. Monks were compelled*
> *to publicly copulate with nuns and desecrate sacred images before being*
> *sent to a growing number of labour camps ...*

In 1980 Norbu returned, and in *Tibet is my Country* writes about what he saw:

> *I went to see the village close to Kumbum where I was born. It*
> *was very sad; more than twenty of my relatives were dead. Only one*
> *cousin was still living ... When I asked her what happened to her*
> *father, she replied, 'He is dead.' When I asked her how and where,*
> *she did not know. Their farm had been taken, and their house torn*
> *down ... Others told me how their families and friends were killed,*
> *imprisoned, sent to labour camps, maimed and crippled. Some were*
> *beaten so severely over and over again with clubs and boards, that*
> *they lost their hearing or sight. Others had bodies that were bent or*

twisted from being forced to pull heavy carts, like animals. Many were
compelled to stand in public places while people were forced to pull
out their hair. Thousands died from exposure and starvation, unable to
survive on the worms, garbage, dead dog bones, pig food, etc., which
hunger drove them to eat. They told me that in 1959–60 all men
were rounded up, put in trucks and sent away to labour camps; that
the only people you saw then were women, children and the aged.

Subjecting the present to the light of the past, it would appear that, in over two thousand years of history, China has not moved on.

3

WE LEFT CHENGDU AT EIGHT the next evening, after the spiv we had taken a chance on delivered our Chinese-price 'Hard Sleeper' tickets with just one hour to go. Since the train departed five minutes early, it was as well he had not cut it any finer.

It was our first train journey in China. We found the carriage the same in style as in India, a row of green, hard-cushioned bunk berths, three-high and back to back, an uncarpeted passageway running at their feet, and only passengers with numbered tickets could sit there. Each bunk was covered by a straw mat. There was a dirty, unchanged pillow which came with a clean hand towel to put over it, and a larger towel, which appeared to function as a sheet. Between the bunks a small table folded down from the window, and below it on the floor stood two thermoses of hot water. The Chinese thermos is a heavenly idea only occasionally let down by human practice, when there is no hot water to fill them or the adjacent cups are too dirty and cracked from neglect to be used, but in this case they appeared welcomingly ready to be poured. Toilets however are another matter, and those on this train were already far worse than anything we had previously encountered.

The extra cost of a Hard Sleeper from simple Hard Seat was enough to ensure we were travelling with passengers a cut above the mass. Mostly men, they played cards, smoked and spat, ate nuts and drank beer, depositing everything unwanted on the floor around them. Shirts out and dirty, collars askew, their appearance fitted harmoniously into the mess they had made of their environment. Our immediate companions were more professional types, a couple in their sixties and two young businessmen in their thirties. When we spoke to them or offered them oranges they were pleasant enough, but initiated no communication themselves, even with each other. The younger pair read magazines, the older woman went straight to bed, and her husband sat on the fold-down seat in the aisle with a fruit-jar of tea and and a large bag of melon seeds which he worked through methodically, cracking them between his teeth and spitting the shells onto the floor.

For some time after our arrival in China, the poverty of communication bothered us. Even in hotels where people spoke English, engaging the staff in relaxed pleasantries was like drawing blood from a stone. There was, we sensed, a deliberate resistance. No-one so much as asked us our country, let alone anything about it, and with the exception of intellectuals such as Wang, Li and Paving Stone we began to consider our presence stiffly tolerated rather than welcomed. Hotel staff of course are trained to stay aloof from foreign guests, and a propaganda of suspicion may well have been to blame. On trains however a different answer suggested itself, for our companions did not even talk to each other. As in Japan there is a taboo on speaking to strangers, built up over many centuries, which means that two people may travel a thousand miles without exchanging a word. Simply put, in Confucian society friendship confers responsibility and duty; to make new friends is to create new responsibilities, new circles of duty. Naturally, people are reluctant to take new responsibilities on, will think carefully before beginning a new friendship, and in China there is not the distinction we would make between being friendly, and being a friend.

Now, when our travelling companions showed less interest in us than we might have expected, say, in India, we accepted it. It was not the case that they had no interest, but that their psychology did not permit them to investigate another person too closely without making a commitment. The older man who shared our sleeping space not only ignored us, he also ignored the younger businessmen and only sparingly spoke to his wife. The younger pair we at least persuaded to accept a copy of *Newsweek*, and they browsed through it together, absorbed in advertisements for cars.

At nine-thirty we were ourselves reading when the lights were abruptly turned out, and without exception the passengers obediently curled up with their blankets and towels. The carriage became not only pitch black but immediately, eerily silent, as if a curtain had come down at the end of an act, the scenery and players were magicked away, and all that was left was the gentle sway and the rhythmic, background noise of the wheels on the metal tracks. That they took their sleep seriously on this train was much to Maria's content. Feeling my way along the corridor I revisited the toilet and returned to find her similarly tucked up in her sheet-sleeping bag, wrapped in the larger towel, her baggage arranged around her for safety, her eyes already closed.

I had the top bunk and Maria the lower. These were regarded as the optimum places since the upper bunk is out of the way at night, and the lower is yours to sit on during the day. I climbed up and arranged my own bags, resting my feet on my rucksack, and using my shoulder bag as a pillow. Our Moroccan carpet-bag (the hardiest travelling implement I have ever known) which contained all our camera equipment, I wedged between my shoulder and the wall. My money and passport, which I was still carrying on my hip in a small leather wallet attached to my trouser-belt, I tied carefully around my bare waist. All this left, I found, little room for manoeuvre. I rested awkwardly on my left elbow, and watched aghast as the conductress came along with her torch, first sweeping the floor and then returning for a second run, obsessively placing everyone's shoes in a neat little line, moving some a centimetre forward and others a centimetre back, smiling in contentment that all their toes now nudged with precision the cleaned and emptied aisle.

Sleep came with difficulty. It was for one thing too early, for another too uncomfortable, and the sweaty Sichuan heat was unmitigated by any working fans. People snored, badly. I dosed and awoke, dosed and awoke, and at six o'clock, disturbed by the snores, I parted the curtains to witness the rising sun unveil a passage through winding mountains low-hung with cloud, with patches of ploughed earth carved out in seemingly inaccessible reaches. Not expecting such a sight, I swallowed and stared. On long train journeys it is often the moment of sunrise that rewards most. After travelling overnight at speed, having covered a lot of ground and leaving a familiar territory far behind, there is an element of surprise in that first glimpse of fresh surroundings, in the progressive revelation of the mysterious by the onset of the day. In those moments when human life has not yet stirred in the half-light, and the fields or the streets are naked of bustle, there is a sense of secretness, of intrusion, of stealing even, in that snatched perception of the world. I lingered over the stillness of the passing farming villages, curtain in hand as the train rattled through the dawn, with the feeling of someone parting a veil on a beautiful woman, who had risen but not yet dressed.

I let the curtain drop and lay on my back. Unable to sleep I considered the implications of a China in which everyone was rich. I had arrived at the prospect of one point two billion extra cars when my thoughts were derailed by the 'happy muzak' emanating from the train's speakers, so loud that even conversation was difficult. Above its volume, Maria swore. For her it belonged to the same category as the loudspeakers in the villages and small towns; it was an infliction, a way of telling the population they were unworthy of self-determination or choice. But to our companions I supposed it was like supermarket music, a little bit of noise to cheer you up. I rose and found my shoes, so punctiliously arranged by the conductress the night before, now kicked halfway down the corridor in the rush for the morning's ablutions.

In a country which throughout its history has had to cope with famine after famine, the most common greeting is not 'Good morning' or 'Nice day' but 'Have you eaten?' Eating is also the one pleasure which has not been interfered with by the state, and this has led to what even the most transient visitor to China cannot fail to notice is a national obsession with food. We thus turned not a hair when our companions' briefcases were opened to reveal not a single item of paperwork, but several jars of pears, tins of beer, packets of noodles, bowls of rice, bags of eggs and packets of sweetbread. For breakfast, noodles were made easily with hot water from the thermoses, and then four eggs passed in quick succession down the older man's throat while numerous dumplings, grabbed frantically from a platform seller during a brief halt, disappeared whole into his wife. The two businessmen opposite us slurped their noodles as if there were gold coins at the bottom of the jar, and all the way down the carriage the sounds were of chewing and smacking and crunching and slurping and spitting, the only thing missing being that it is impolite to belch. Twenty minutes later it was all over, the wrappings and debris bearing marks of finality as if Genghis Khan's warriors had just trampled a tiny settlement and carried on without stopping, the dead bones, bottles, tins and boxes being tipped unceremoniously out of the window. The uninhibited, almost hysterical orgy over, it was time for a smoke and the carriage settled down to its previous, if rather tenuous, hold on civilisation, the demons which had possessed it satisfied in their lust until lunch time.

Eating more slowly ourselves, we had not quite finished our own bread and bananas when we became aware of an unusually long pair of legs standing in the aisle at the end of our bunk, the head of their owner looking down at us with an ominously manic grin. We stared back. Behind his thick black spectacles the man's eyes were exceedingly narrow, and two gold teeth glinted prominently on either side of his mouth. He looked like a caricature of a Chinese, except for the remarkable length of his legs which suggested, as did the grin, that all was not quite well with him.

'You're American?' he asked, catching us both in mid-chew.

'No – British,' Maria replied.

With a jolt he sat down next to her and pressed the palms of his hands into the bunk besides his unnatural thighs, craning his head to look at us both as he spoke. 'Then you're knowing about our Lord Jesus Christ King of Kings Lord of Lords Saviour of Souls?'

'We are knowing,' Maria answered, carefully. The growth of evangelism in China was something we had heard about, though it was confined largely to the south-east and this was our first experience of it. Undoubtedly China needed some moral system, for the discrediting of Buddhism, Confucianism and now Communism had left a void in people's lives which the baser American Churches were now rushing to fill, placing China at the top of their 'hitlist' of countries with conversion targets to reach by 2000. Even Sun Myung Moon's nefarious Korean Unification Church, or 'Moonies', were given permission to proselytise in China in exchange for setting up a car production plant in Guangdong, and the Chinese people, denied their old religions and alienated from the Party, were fair game. I fancied them sold by a cheapskate Madam in a bordello, letting her captive assets go for any price. When the proselytisation of foreign religions was proscribed by law in 1994 – another echo from China's past – the news was ill-received abroad, but we could understand the need. In a country which had excised analysis and criticism from its education system, how could people be equipped to make informed choices in the matter of religion? That religious zealotry could replace the political in China seemed uncomfortably feasible. I thought I detected an American accent, and listened for it as the fellow continued, virtually without any pause for breath.

'He came to teach us this world hell this world ruled by Satan next world is heaven ruled by God is permanent and everlasting this world temporary best think of next world believe in our Lord Jesus Christ and be saved from this world hell when you kick bucket.'

Relieved at his evident harmlessness, we smiled. Our other companions were staring at him, and making slight faces at each other. Even without knowing the language, the mental imbalance was clear.

'Yes,' I said, thinking that any Chinese person could justifiably consider this world hell after their recent history.

He continued, still talking at the same, rabid, speed. 'I evangelical American Baptist Church imprisoned in hospital five times teaching about our Lord Jesus Christ government say only priests can teach teaching on streets against security hospital say I mad believe things aren't true see things aren't there I don't care I say only law I follow God's law like St Peter.'

'They send you to hospital?' asked Maria, with less surprise than she showed.

'Yes five times hospital first they send me jail in jail they break my legs.'

'That's terrible!' we exclaimed together, genuinely sorry for him.

'Yes not nice people they do it laughing I lie down crying well done now in jail attack body in hospital attack mind they say I mad I say I sane everyone else mad since ten year I become Christian in Guangzhou God say to me I teach Jesus on street in China.'

'That's very brave of you,' I volunteered.

'No no brave no God always help me God always there you know Chinese people heathen people Confucian Buddhist Taoist Maoist people no know God only know Buddha or Mao no help there I was Buddhist have demon go Buddhist temple pray demon still there I go church pray demon go and demon go I become Christian power of our Lord Jesus Christ now I layin' on of hands I cure man have goitre by layin' on three years there now gone other man have thirty-five years stomach ache I layin' on now gone woman have cancer I layin' on now gone cancer go power of Lord Jesus Christ.'

'Very good.' It was so difficult trying to follow the man's words that it was hard to know what to say when he eventually stopped. I tore off another mouthful of bread and banana and waited for him to begin again.

'You were having Margaret Thatcher?' He suddenly changed tack.

'Yes,' I said. 'You know about her?'

'I know yes I know I have radio I listen BBC England World Service.'

'What do you know about her?'

'She wear same clothes as Chinese people.'

Instinctively, we looked about us. The old woman sitting on the aisle seat, as hypnotised as we were by the conversation she could not understand, was wearing flared green nylon slacks with bright red socks and a dirty white shirt which was barely tucked in. Somehow, I doubted the claim. Neither, thankfully, could I long maintain the image of our unbeloved ex-Leader in the equally typical Chinese mode of a mini-skirt, with her stockings rolled half-way up her thighs and some loose change tucked into the fold.

'Really?' Maria said, puzzled as to what he meant.

'She always wear blue Ha! Ha! Ha! Ha! Ha!' The man slapped his hands up and down on the bunk, and rocked backwards and forwards. We groaned, feeling ourselves the recipients of some awful Chinese joke.

'What do you *think* about her?' I asked, pressing for some of the intelligence that was undoubtedly in there, sluicing around with all the other mental spaghetti.

'In America they say anyone become President even lousy actor in UK same thing Thatcher she live in shop later become Prime Minister.'

'Yes well, even democracy has its handicaps,' Maria replied ruefully.

'Democracy one day come China not now wait long time this world hell until then China very hell indeed so I much work to do openness policy backfire people have no job people sleep on street people very poor China very hell indeed so I much work to do God's work power of Lord Jesus Christ work through me well bye-bye.'

He stood up as suddenly as he had sat down.

'Wait . . .' Maria put her hand on his sleeve, feeling as I did that there were jewels in there somewhere, if only we could get at them. He sat down again, looking suddenly very confused. 'What's your name?'

'My name Hua,' he said, and put out his hand for us to shake.

'Thankyou for talking to us Hua,' I said. 'Where're you going?'

'I go Lanzhou visit family ten days come back Chengdu teach Chinese people God.'

'Do you have much success,' Maria asked, 'teaching God to Chinese people?'

'Lots success but sometimes no success God tells me be patient all things come in the end not my fault people not listen their fault I do my best if I do my best I go Heaven meet Jesus dance in the field of the Lord.'

'What do you do in Chengdu, Hua?' I wanted to know, trying to tie him down.

'I work in hospital help make people better help doctors by power of layin' on hands —'

'The doctors let you do this?' I interrupted.

'Some they know others they don't know best not say I go now read Bible back seat bye-bye.'

He stood up again, evidently anxious to escape the questioning. I surmised that this was because, even if he did not admit it to himself, his stay in the Chengdu hospital was less voluntary than the 'work' he suggested.

'Before you go, Hua,' said Maria, shoving a piece of paper towards him, 'tell us what this says.'

I looked at it. It was the slip we had received from the temple in Bangkok after shaking the lucky sticks. Maria had been using it as a bookmark, and we had not yet had it translated. Still standing, Hua grabbed it from her and held it tightly in both hands.

'This heathen matter!' he said, laughing. 'It say good success in all things very lucky what you try will come to you number sixteen best number you see one and six is seven and also it is two times eight all good numbers so success and lucky but only joke not believe in superstition you believe in Jesus Christ instead he bring you everything if you pray you may want in this world hell but in next world you want for nothing bye-bye.'

This time we let him go, pivoting around on his left foot and swinging his gangly legs back the way he had come.

'It makes you wonder whether they put him in hospital because he won't shut up about religion, or because he really is mad,' I mused.

'But look at our prediction,' said Maria, waving the piece of paper happily. 'Success in all things! I believe we'll get to Tibet after all!'

For the rest of the journey we turned our attention to the window. In the glare of mid-day, the long, green diesel-pulled train carried us from Sichuan to Gansu, bringing as it did a change of scenery more dramatic than any we had yet seen. In China's western provinces, the deep, iron-rich red, dragon's blood earth of Yunnan gave way to the easy greenery of Sichuan, and now the land was transformed again into something light brown, and largely barren. What was cultivated here was an effort. The grass-tufted, wind-sculpted, conically undulating hills were mostly home to mountain sheep and even, here, a few cows. The heavily overcast skies which had plagued us with summer rain for the last two days in Chengdu seemed unlikely to wander this far north. These were desert skies, cloudless, under a ruthless sun. Habitation was becoming mud-walled. In the small towns, the houses were plastered in greys and browns, as if to blend in with the earth. In the wilds between the towns the round faces of unkempt urchins who peered at the speeding train from the safety of their doorways also matched the environment, their skin tanned into hues of russet by the sun and wind. Old shepherds who squatted immobile in the fields with their staves were wizened, showing their age more readily than the Han, who usually manage to look youthful even in dotage. The women who sold their food through the windows when the train stopped wore delicate little veils, and the pitta bread we bought from them signalled another cultural shift. We felt as if we were leaving China behind. Gansu, a long, thin corridor from far in the north-west to almost the centre of the Middle Kingdom, has long been a funnel into which Muslims, Tibetans and Mongolians – three peoples uniquely renowned for the tenacity with which they have defended or exported their identities – have historically poured themselves. In the villages and small towns that we passed their tale of migration could readily be seen, but Lanzhou when we arrived there was just another faceless and functional Han city, devoid of charm, a 'new town' scraped from the soil on the edge of the empire to cater for their own population overspill.

The botanist Joseph Rock called Lanzhou in the 1940s 'the dirtiest Chinese city I have ever seen'. The problem now is not dirt but the opposite almost, the loss of character in nondescript modernity. Every road was the same: wide, with cloned concrete buildings hiding behind evenly spaced trees. Thinking there could be no city in the world of less interest, we returned at once to the station and bought tickets to Xining for the next morning – with some trepidation as only the cheapest Hard Seat tickets were left.

The five-hour journey turned out however to be an excellent introduc- tion to Hard Seat travel without the rigours of excessive endurance. People were poorer than in Hard Sleeper, but being a daytime train were at least not drunk or otherwise too boisterous. It was memorable only for the policeman who sat opposite, his face cold and severe behind dark glasses, his uniform crisp and clean, and, as if to preserve it that way, he held himself tautly in the same position the whole journey, moving only to relieve his bile in the aisle. And then our eyes moved down to his feet, which were sheathed in pretty, transparent, blue nylon socks and plastic, high-heeled sandals. This was common footwear in a land where leather was at a premium, most available earth being used for crops. 'In China,' a Chinese businessman had told us, 'if you want to know someone's social position you look at their feet.' Policemen, evidently, were not highly paid.

Arriving in Xining, we moved directly to the bus station. It was enough to see that we were not truly in China anymore. Xining was strongly Islamic, its Hui inhabitants obvious from their white beards and hats. As with other non-Han areas, people smiled to see us in the street, and when the bus we needed was full the Muslim passengers urged us to get on anyway, and sat on top of each other in their eagerness to give us room. Some had blue eyes, and throughout the short journey they gazed at us warmly, their natural impulse to communicate a complete contrast to the Han instinct, to isolate themselves from outsiders.

We received the same effusive welcome on reaching the goal of our journey, the small town of Huangzhong. At first sight it too appeared predominantly Hui. There was a single mosque, far too small for the religiosity of its inhabitants who poured in and out of it with their white beards and hats while the women, sporting men's suits and black veils which encircled rather than covered the face, were left to run the small stalls and businesses. In the short course of our stay we would deem Huangzhong a showpiece of Islamic possibility where, to our admittedly superficial gaze, men and women appeared to mix freely and in modesty but without the sexual suspicion which has spread from Arabia to subvert cultures elsewhere. Yet Huangzhong is not entirely, or even mainly, Muslim. A donkey and cart took us up the steep connecting hill to where the Tibetan shops began and, at the top, to the beginnings of the Kumbum monastic complex.

For the first time we had the sense of being in Tibet proper, a feeling enhanced by the open grassland beyond the monastery that rose steadily towards the abrupt irruption of the Amne Machin mountain range. Indeed this *had* been the Tibetan province of Amdo. Tsong Khapa, the greatest scholar in Tibet's history, had been born here, and so had the present Dalai Lama, and neither considered it part of China.

'You mustn't speak to the monks!'
The old Han in the hotel office waved his finger viciously as he spoke. It was not a good beginning. The hotel was located inside the monastic complex,

monks were all around us and we had merely enquired as to the times of the *pujas*. We snarled but held our peace, and brooded as the younger Han took us to our room.

The 'hotel' had been an old lama residence, and in earlier times would have housed several lamas with their attendants. The two-storied wooden structure had been built around a flagstoned courtyard, but where it would once have been decorated with exquisite *thangkas*, *Your Country Needs You* posters glorifying the PLA and the *Wu Jing* – the armed police – were now plastered everywhere on its walls. It seemed deliberate salt in the wound, but following the young boy up the stairs to the first floor verandah, we began to cheer up; the rooms were original after all, with thick beams, and were painted Tibetan-style in warm oranges, blackcurrants, reds, yellows and greens. There was an ante-room with sofas, table and thermos, and with minimal effort we found ourselves looking past the posters at the historical atmosphere and thinking that, whatever happened next, to all intents and purposes we were in Tibet, living in the rooms of one of the most important old monasteries. Even if we did not get to Lhasa, in a sense we had already made it, and no-one could take that away.

We put down our bags and chatted to the boy. He was friendly enough, an English student from Lanzhou, and probably knew less than us the turmoil of the past. On the wall by the door were the hotel rules.

He pointed at them and said: 'I write. Is good?'

We read the little poster.

It is not allowed to smuggle, dance or disturb the others during or after drinking.

'Very good,' said Maria. 'Don't change a thing.'

He smiled proudly and led us to the single outside toilet. The tiny, doorless 'room' was reached by crossing a patch of grass which contained a fiercely barking but tethered (we gratefully noticed) dog. We peered inside. There were three large holes, close enough for three people to rub shoulders in a friendly joint crap, and below them one could see an original eight-foot drop now reduced to five by years of such communal shitting.

'That's alright then,' I said. 'Is there any water?'

He took us back to the office, from where we had to obtain the key to the mud-brick outhouse with a hot water boiler. Maria would have to lock herself in, but in the evenings I could join in with the monks who trekked from their dormitories to perform a curious method of scrubbing their backs with a stretched wet towel, to avoid water dripping uncomfortably into their underwear.

After resting, we went out to visit the little town. Until July 1949, there were nearly four thousand monks here. Now their numbers were limited to five hundred, but the Tibetan presence was still strongly felt, not only from the monks, the shopkeepers and the stallholders, but from the merchants and nomads blown in from remoter regions to combine pilgrimage with trade. People here were as different as liquorice allsorts, but we especially noticed the Khampas, Tibet's legendary fighters from the adjacent province of Kham. Frequently over six and a half feet they are statue-like and muscle bound, yet their hair is worn in a single pigtail wound around the head, enmeshed with strands of red silk and fastened with turquoise. With their thick lips and wide mouths, the overall effect is quite androgynous, an impression further enhanced by knee-high leather boots and massive animal skin coats cut diagonally to the waist, where the hilt of a traditional *tri*, a not-purely-ceremonial long-knife, juts from its scabbard, laterally hung for quick access. A race more different from the Han you could not find by sticking a pin in the globe, and the image of these men nonchalantly de-capping beer bottles with their teeth would stay with us. Through Maria I also understood their legendary status with Western women, not a few of whom have confessed to following them dreamily around the bazaars.

We returned again to the square of sand where the bottom of the monastery met the top of the town. In the square were eight large, white *chortens*, containing the relics of previous high lamas. In the heat of the day and at this altitude they reflected powerfully the ultra-violet glare of the sun; now, as dusk was falling, they were gentle, more bearable to look at. The tape and clothing stalls on the perimeter were closing down, and in the morning would be joined by stalls selling buns and yoghurt. There was a soft but gusty wind, and here and there it picked up the sand and dust in little whirling pockets and set it down again, as if a dozen invisible hands were mischievously at work. The sad and ghostly strains of the *erhu*, the traditional violin-like instrument of the blind beggar in China, seemed mournfully at one with the movements of the wind and emanated from a family of three such beggars, father, mother and a young son, each of them blind, wretched and scabied, who had entered the square holding each other's coat-tails until sitting down and beginning to play. Around them a mad boy ran about as if he could see the demons responsible for the swirling sand, stopping suddenly and shouting into space, clapping his hands as if to grasp the eerie wind-borne notes, then running on again, displacing more sand with his calloused and naked feet. A few of the current five hundred monks were coming and going, their daily duties over, maroon robes flung over bare arms and flapping in the wind like wings. The odd dog, which neither Muslim nor Tibetan would eat (the one because they were dirty, the other because they were holy), ran about on the scavenge. A few locals hung around like cowboys in the Wild West with the saloon closed on a Sunday afternoon and nothing particular to do. This, outside the door of the hotel, was a Kumbum sunset.

And then, as dots in the distance becoming clearer, a large family of nomads, as dirty and engrimed as it must be possible to become, laboured to the top of the hill. The first to arrive almost staggered to the wall of the hotel, and waited until the rest had caught up. Two of the women slid down, their backs against the bricks. Compulsively, and against all will of politeness, we gawped. Above reels of tangled amulets and layered necklaces of turquoise and coral, the women's faces were greased with yak butter which still glistened beneath the dirt that had stuck to it. Each wore a heavy overcoat, tied with a cord at the waist and thrown off the shoulders to function as a back-bag for their rolled-up possessions. Over this and beneath Bolivian style hats, they wore their hair in a hundred-and-eight intricate plaits, tied at the waist by clasps of silver and turquoise or bronze and lapis lazuli and silk. Centrally parted, meticulously braided, perhaps for the pilgrimage, and swinging in lines of freedom as they moved while remaining gathered at the backside by the clasps, such hair worthily demanded admiration, the hair of the men who were not wearing hats even more so. One young boy, about ten or eleven, was completely shaven save for several Rasta twists springing randomly from his skull, and two of the men had their heads shaved front and sides only, their hair at the back hanging like a sparse collection of limp, stretched coils. Both men and women had pierced ears – that Han aversion – the women with dangling silver and turquoise, the men with smaller studs. Both wore the same calf-length, colourful leather boots with upward-pointing toes, and both went for the rounded Bolivian style hats of felt or leather.

They were, we guessed, Goloks, 'those who turn their heads away' (i.e. reject authority), the nomadic inhabitants of Amdo with a reputation for banditry, whose presence barred the way of anyone, Tibetan, Chinese or Westerner, who would have walked placidly from here to Lhasa. Early explorers in the area all gave the Goloks a wide berth, and were well justified in their caution. It was with Goloks in mind that Peter Goullart, whose own wanderings in the region brought him into friendship with David-Neel, commented in his moving testament to the threatened Nakhi people, *Forgotten Kingdom*:

> *Personally, I would rather deal with a Chinese or a Nakhi robber*
> *than a Tibetan one. A Chinese or a Nakhi robber seldom kills*
> *his victim. He robs you, but he does it with a degree of finesse and*
> *delicacy, and at least leaves you your underwear to enable you to reach*
> *the nearest village with a modicum of decency.*

We, however, felt no need to worry. To a person they bore a Dalai Lama badge pinned to their coats, and each carried a *mala*, a string of mantra-beads wound around their wrists. These they now slipped off, and began as one unit to prostrate around the *chortens*. They raised their hands, palms together, to the top of heads, to lips, to chests, pushing tired bodies flat out on the sand, touching foreheads to the ground, hands again outstretched on tops of heads. And then they stood up, took one step to the left and repeated it all, again and again and again, exhausted as they already were after walking goodness knows how far in the heat of the sun, until their circle of the *chortens* was complete. Only then did they enter the hotel for food, water and rest.

Involuntarily almost, we followed them, and for both parties there occurred what anthropologists would call an encounter with the *other*. Had we green hair and purple skin the effect would have been no different on people who had never seen fair hair and pink skin before, but the fascination was equally ours. In the West we are programmed from childhood that it is rude to stare, but for once we were helpless in the face of a stimulus stronger than our own conditioning. Since they were gazing at us however, we reasoned safely that no offence could be taken in our gazing at them, and eventually everyone repaired to the restaurant where, by mutual consent, we gazed at each other all evening.

The 'restaurant', housed in a second courtyard across from the boiler room, befitted the hotel. No more than a shack with six wonky tables and numerous broken chairs, it was run by two exceptionally large Mongolian brothers. They were invariably drunk, and the wife of the elder one gave from her kitchen a good impression of a tubercular death-bed. Her husband, who attempted with miserable failure to cultivate the sophisticated aura of a pipe-smoker would, when adequately inebriated and the restaurant sufficiently crowded as to make it inadvisable if not impossible, chase his wife around the tables in an attempt to demonstrate that he really was the master of his house. Finally bent over whichever table she was caught at by his great left arm, she would add to its occupant's meal at point-blank range the benefit of her heaving, helpless cough. But the food, as they say, was good.

The wind earlier that evening must have suggested a storm, for the atmosphere was soon enhanced by rolls of thunder and torrential rain, falling rippingly on windows, walls and roof, lightning flashes outside spasmodically alleviating the internal gloom and smokiness. Surrounded by a mixture of monks, merchants and pilgrim nomads, we perhaps unkindly fancied ourselves in the restaurant at the end of the universe, or the *Star Wars* bar with Chewbacca in one corner and several unidentifiables in the other. We eyed each other constantly, while we ate with chopsticks daintily, and they hunched and slurped. Their greatcoats of coarse black yak wool had brightly striped hems and cuffs, one or both shoulders still shrugged off to hold their bundles while they ate. Underneath were the filthiest, once bright shirts and skirts and jumpers, and numerous scarves that began and ended somewhere around the middle, and again the amulets of silver, the beads of coral and turquoise that suggested, Indian style, that whatever wealth they had went into their jewellery. Closer now and seated, we could take in their details, the white and gold of their teeth and bright white eyes that gleamed like jewels, their high and rugged cheekbones so dark and shiny with the yak butter, each one with a thousand lines. The women we noticed were prone to hunches, the elder ones in particular permanently stooped from a lifetime of infant and load carrying. For their part without exception they could not concentrate on what was probably their first hot meal for days, and stared at us wide-eyed and open-mouthed, as if we were ghosts that refused to disappear.

Even before their meal was finished the prayer beads were off and the deep hum of *aum mani padme hum* began to reverberate under the thunder from different corners of the room. We were two opposite ends of the human spectrum, yet in many ways mirrored each other. We had bought *malas* ourselves from one of the stalls in the bazaar, and that Westerners should possess them was a major object of fascination. Probably, we surmised, they lacked the education to make us fit their mental jig-saw of the world. Presumably they knew the Dalai Lama had fled to India, and that many lamas had gone to a place called America, wherever that was, so it should not have been inconceivable to them that their religion had spread. Moreover, when they were used to being treated like animals by the Chinese and considered way down the scale of social, intellectual, political and even genetic evolution, the fact that others could look at them respectfully and share their religion gave them and it a credibility, a seal of approval in the face of official attacks.

Our *malas* now became a bridge to communication, as one of the visiting monks pointed at them and stuck up his thumb. We smiled, returning the acknowledgement. Then, followed by his monk friends, he came over for a closer look, fingering it and purring approval of the quality. To keep the communication going, we showed them Stephen Batchelor's wonderful *The Tibet Guide*. Turning the pages, we came to a picture of the Dalai Lama.

'Dalai Lama,' said Maria, pointing.

With a start, one of the monks jumped backwards like a frightened kitten. He looked around anxiously and quickly, waved his hand as if to say 'No, no!' and put his finger to his lips. There could well have been plainclothes policemen or informers in the packed restaurant. They may all have worn Dalai Lama badges, but that was a different matter from sitting around talking about him. The fine line between His Holiness's role as a religious and as a political figurehead was institutionalised as paranoia in Chinese law, where it was legal to possess one photo of the Dalai Lama but illegal to possess two; it was legal to buy or sell a photo of His Holiness but illegal to give one away. This inconsistency was removed in 1995 when, as part of sweeping new restrictions on religious practice, it became illegal to possess a picture of the Dalai Lama at all. In May 1996 this was enforced by mass searches of private homes by armed soldiers in several cities, leading to the largest riots since 1989, widespread monastic strikes, the sealing off of monasteries by troops and the complete closure of the famous Ganden monastery after the shooting there of several monks forced the rest to take to the hills, while in Lhasa truckloads of dead and injured Tibetans were witnessed by foreigners being delivered to the central hospital. This was, China later announced, the first implementation of a 15–year plan to eradicate the Dalai Lama as a recognisable figure in Tibet, a policy as absurd, and hopefully as impossible, as trying to eliminate pictures of the Pope in Ireland. With the exception of one small group accused of cult-like tendencies, His Holiness the fourteenth Dalai Lama has the unswerving support of all Tibetans both in Tibet and in exile.

When it comes to secret police states, few countries can outdo occupied Tibet. But the man recovered himself well, and having ascertained that all was safe he took the picture and placed it delicately on his head, murmuring *aum mani padme hum* while he gave himself its blessing. The book was then passed to the next monk, who passed it to the next, who passed it to the Goloks, and we sat in awed bemusement as our guide book was passed reverently from head to head around the restaurant, while the thunder roared and the lightning flashed outside, and the large Mongolian chef remained determinedly above it all, stoking his pipe and pretending to be otherwise thoughtfully engaged.

Moved by the evening and the sense of place, when the storm had passed we went out and pressed our foreheads to each of the *chortens*. As we finished the last one an old lady with a basket passed deliberately close by, squeezed our arms and spoke without interrupting her stride, the arm that held the basket revealing a surreptitious, upturned thumb as she disappeared quickly into the night.

'When you're oppressed,' said Maria in judgement on the evening, 'it's nice to know you have friends.'

Our three projected days here turned into seven. Well, Mme Alexandra David-Neel (1867–1968), one of the greatest travellers of all time, stayed for two years, from 1918–20, and then only left with the greatest reluctance. True, she did have a special temple built just for her, but even without that we could see the fascination Kumbum must have exerted in previous days of freedom, when the monastery would have thronged with greater crowds of pilgrims than our small troupe of Goloks.

Today, we had to purchase expensive foreigner-price tickets for the monastery from the disagreeable Han in the hotel office. Ignoring the coachloads of drunken Chinese soldiers dressing up in Tibetan clothes to have sarcastic pictures taken, we visited those parts of the monastery – only ten of the fifty-two temples remain – which are now cold museums. The fact that it had been made a protected monument in 1961 had saved some of its external walls, but obviously not its treasures, for most images of worth, especially the tantric ones, were long ago destroyed. The Chinese particularly targeted the tantric images because such open depictions of sexuality seemed both primitive and immoral, and indeed confirmed Tibetan culture, in their eyes, as a delinquent faith. But Tibetan Buddhism *is* Tantric Buddhism, and to take this aspect away is absolutely no different from forbidding representations of Mary to the Catholic Church. Any Tibetan *gompa* in Ladakh, Sikkim or Bhutan will have its depictions of deities in copulation. They are tools for meditation, symbols of the co-incident opposites at the heart of a dream-like universe, the coming together of the form and emptiness of the mind and the world, of the intrinsic wisdom and compassionate action of personal being. Yet at Kumbum, all this is erased. Even in the Tantric Institute itself, the walls are now covered with identical, 'clean' pictures of Tsong Khapa, 'the man from the onion country' who was born here, and who founded the Geluk school to which the Dalai Lama belongs.

Away from prying eyes however, in the seclusion of the main courtyard, the daily debate classes were unpolluted. Here, one young monk in each group would sit and answer questions from another playing the examiner. Walking away when building an argument, walking towards when delivering the consequence, the questioner would raise his hand above his head and, *mala* flying, slap it loudly onto his other hand as he delivered his philosophical thrusts, the forearm smash signifying something like 'Ha! Get out of that one!' When they got enthusiastic, the red robes and *malas* would really fly. It amused us that while the government wrestled with its redundant propaganda, these monks were once again immersing themselves in more time-honoured problems of the universe.

'If things are void of inherent existence, how can there be a world of forms? If things do possess inherent existence, how can there be a world of change? Ha! Get out of that one!'

Indeed, the situation at Kumbum could be worse.

The Problem of Existence

IT ALL BEGAN WITH SVETAKETU, an Indian youth in the Hindu Upaniṣads who asked his father to explain to him the nature of reality.

> *'Put this piece of salt in the water and come to me tomorrow morning.'*
> *Svetaketu did as he was told.*
> *'Would you please sip it at this end? What is it like?'*
> *'Salt,' said Svetaketu.*
> *'Sip it in the middle. What is it like?'*
> *'Salt,' said Svetaketu.*
> *'Now sip it at the far end. What is it like?'*
> *'Salt,' said Svetaketu.*
> *'My dear child, so it is with the highest reality, the finest essence which the whole universe has as its Self. That is the Real: That is the Self: That art thou, Svetaketu!'*

'*Wrong,*' said the Buddha, a thousand years later. There is no continuous, unchanging identity at the heart of the universe. Both we and all compounded things are like onions, centreless, devoid of any ultimate being. Behind the transient pleasures and inevitable sufferings of old age, sickness and death, lies nothing but constantly changing appearances. There is no rock of God on which the world rests, no eternal soul that resides within the flesh. All things are unsatisfactory, marked by impermanence and empty of inherent existence. We are such stuff as dreams are made on – literally.

As an illusion, a dream or a castle in the air built by fairies,
Just so should we consider birth, duration and death.

So said Nagarjuna, the greatest ever Buddhist scholar. There are those who may consider this depressing. The Buddha himself had to correct people who thought his teaching nihilistic:

Those, Kasyapa, who misunderstand the teaching of emptiness as a
negative thing, I consider forlorn, irrevocably lost . . .
Better it is to be an out-and-out realist than be a nihilist.

The correct view, according to Nagarjuna's famous 'four-cornered argument', is that:

Things do not exist, nor not-exist, nor both exist and not-exist, nor do
they neither exist nor not exist.

Buddhist philosophy from the word go has revolved around the question of existence. It is not easy to grasp the 'correct' view on 'reality', but when it does click and things do fall into place, that is when one is said to be 'enlightened'. Enlightenment was not the prerogative of the Buddha, but something open to everyone, especially in the Northern or Mahayana school of Buddhism found in China and Tibet. Hui Neng, the famous Sixth Patriarch of the Ch'an (*Zen*, in Japanese) School, became enlightened on hearing simply that 'all things are unsupported'. When the Buddha held up a flower but did not speak, and everyone else just scratched their heads, the alleged first member of the Zen school, Kasyapa, became enlightened. Enlightenment is the philosophically correct understanding of reality, and when attained it can be expressed in both behaviour and in words.

An example of the former can be found in the life of the First Patriarch of Zen in China. The beginnings of Zen are shrouded in myth, but it seems certain that a man called Bodhidharma arrived at Guangzhou by sea around 470 and travelled north to Lo Yang, where he spent nine years sitting in front of a wall. The accretions of myth inform us that he met the religious Emperor Wu of Liang who asked him: 'How much merit have I acquired from building pagodas and other good works?' 'No merit at all,' was Bodhidharma's reply, which promptly got him banished. Equally mythical are the ideas that Bodhidharma's nine years of wall-gazing were uninterrupted by visits to the bathroom, bedroom and dining room, so that when his disciples eventually lifted him up, his legs fell off; that he cut his eyelids off to prevent himself falling asleep, or that his disciple, Hui K'o, cut off his own arm as proof of his sincerity. These anecdotes do however point to the pain and suffering which are often emphasised in the school, for Zen deliberately works with physical discomfort – rigid postures have to be maintained for long hours of meditation, for example – as a tool to shift the mind beyond its normal perception of the world.

The most famous example of enlightenment in words comes from Hui Neng, an illiterate son from a poor family. When the Fifth Patriarch had to decide his succession, he announced a poetry competition. One candidate, Shen Hsiu, rose at midnight and wrote his verse on a monastery wall:

> *The body is the bodhi-tree,*
> *The mind a mirror bright;*
> *Take care to polish it all the time*
> *And let no dust alight.*

The next day, the monastery was abuzz with the crisp expression of Shen Hsiu's insight. That night Hui Neng dictated to a friend a reply to be graffitied next to it:

> *There never was a bodhi-tree,*
> *Nor any mirror bright;*
> *Since fundamentally not one thing exists*
> *On what can dust alight?*

Fearful that the other, jealous, monks might harm him, the Fifth Patriarch passed Hui Neng the robes and the lineage in secret, then advised him to flee.

Buddhism arrived in China before it came to Tibet. It did not have a good start. It was attacked for lacking filial piety (being a monk meant leaving home), drinking urine (a habit of some of the Indian monks) and encouraging begging. Moreover, most Chinese could only comprehend it in terms of Taoism, and the belief arose that Buddhism really was Taoism, that the great Lao Tzu had gone to India instead of dying, and Buddhism was really Taoism returning home again. (Ironically, the truth was almost the opposite, the genesis of Taoism probably lying in Indian yoga teachings filtering into China through the land of Tien.) To cap it all, stories spread of the Buddha as an Immortal, able to fly, shape-shift and drink the dew.

Unfortunately, the early monks in China, who were really meditation teachers, colluded with this in order to stay and win acceptance, and great distortions of Buddhist teachings began to be established. The Chinese could not comprehend the idea of no soul, especially as they traditionally accepted not one but two souls – a good soul (*hun*) and a bad soul (*p'o*). Therefore they ascribed Buddhism a permanent soul (*shen ling*), and furthermore, the teaching on karma eluding them, they imagined rebirth as being in various paradises. Buddhism in China looked set to become mutant as a result. 'Pure Land' Buddhism, an immortals-in-Paradise cult offering instant rebirth in Amitabha's heaven to all who believed, seems to have grown out of this mire. At one point mere recitation of the name 'Amitabha', even without belief, was thought enough to bring salvation. One man, Shao Kang, regularly gathered crowds beneath his balcony, got them to shout 'Amitabha!', then showered them with coins. It was perhaps the Nichiren Shoshu of its day, offering great rewards for little effort and no understanding to people attracted by the glamour of something new but lacking the mental capacity to assimilate anything more subtle.

However, all was not quite lost. Into this desperate situation in 401 walked a man who was without doubt the saviour of Buddhism in China, Kumarajiva. Born in Kucha on the Silk Road, of Central Asian royal stock, Kumarajiva was educated and astute enough to untangle the confusion of doctrines. Yet his arrival in China was involuntary, being captured by an invasion of Kucha. A prisoner virtually all his life, he lamented: 'In the land of Ch'in the profoundly intelligent are rare. My wings are broken here, and I can't have a decent conversation with anyone.' The Emperor tried to improve his mood by giving him a string of concubines. Kumarajiva protested histrionically: 'Alas, I am a lotus growing in dirt!' But he accepted them, nonetheless. Concubines apart, Kumarajiva applied himself to his work, and without him the truly great forms of Chinese Buddhism, such as Zen or Hua Yen, could never have arisen.

In 845 however, what accomplished Zen masters China had produced were sent scurrying into the hills when Emperor Wu Tsang, coldly presaging twentieth-century Marxist terminology, made this proclamation:

Only since the Han and Wei has this idolatrous religion come to flourish. In recent times its strange ways have become so customary and all pervasive as to have slowly and unconsciously corrupted the morals of our land. The hearts of our people have been seduced by it and the masses all the more led astray. From the mountains and wastes of the whole land to the walled palaces of the two capitals, the Buddhist monks daily increase in number, and their monasteries daily increase in glory. In exhausting men's strengths in construction work, in robbing men for their own golden and jewelled adornments, in forsaking ruler and kin to support their teachers, in abandoning their mates for monastic rules, in flouting the laws and in harming the people, nothing is worse than this religion.

Now, when one man does not farm, others suffer hunger, and when one woman does not weave, others suffer from the cold. At present the monks and nuns of the empire are numberless, but they all depend on agriculture for their food and on sericulture for their clothing. The monasteries and temples are beyond count, but they are all lofty and beautifully decorated, daring to rival palaces in grandeur ... Why then should this insignificant western religion compete with us? ... It is most proper that we regulate the Buddhist Church ... in aiding the people and benefitting the masses.

More than 4,600 monasteries are being destroyed throughout the empire; more than 260,500 monks and nuns are being returned to lay life and being subjected to double tax; more than 40,000 temples and shrines are being destroyed; several tens of millions of ch'ing of fertile lands and fine fields are being confiscated ... Monks and nuns are to be placed under the jurisdiction of the Bureau of Guests, to indicate clearly that Buddhism is a foreign religion. We are returning more than 3,000 Nestorians and Zoroastrians to lay life, so that they will not adulterate the customs of China.

There would be revivals, but the apogee of Chinese Buddhism was already past. There would never be another Kumarajiva, another Bodhidharma, or another Hui Neng, and the contribution of historical attitudes to the modern Chinese policy on Tibet is as clear as a falling rock.

4

LEAVING KUMBUM FOR XINING WE found only Hard Seat or Soft Sleeper available for the twenty-one hour journey to Golmud, the latter at fifty pounds each, foreigner-price. We opted for the former, with a foreboding which turned out to be entirely justified the moment we set foot in the cavernous waiting room.

Arriving an hour early, we located the characters for Golmud on a little metal post, and trawled the packed benches behind it for somewhere to sit. This was no easy matter, since even the floor was covered in the bodies of prostrate peasants leaning against their sacks, the slightly better off using rough mail bags to keep their own bags clean. Some passengers were already drinking, most were incautiously hawking and spitting, and here and there the stomach-wrenching smell of vomit rose from steaming pools on the floor to mix with heavy wreaths of smoke in the air. Near the front all eyes were turned in mute observance of a maximum-decibel shouting match between a woman and a man who had squared up face to face, their respective families pitching in from behind. We skipped unseen through the impromptu theatre of anger and found two seats in a corner at the back. Placing our rucksacks carefully between plots of green sputum we leant on them, and made a mental note to acquire mail bags at the first opportunity.

Things did not improve. The fat, five-year-old boy opposite who had been occupied for half an hour dipping his hands into a kilo of pure sugar, now pissed all over his seat. As the spreading puddle reached the trousers of the man next to him, the man got up and sat next to a six-year-old girl, who was equally fat and sucking on a bottle of milk. The man on my left, drunk, pointed at the boy, who reclined uncomplaining in his urine as if nothing had happened, while his blank-faced mother stared emptily ahead. The boy dipped his fist again into the bag of sugar, which spilled and stuck to his face, fingers and urine-soaked trousers, the pure white crystals turning yellow before disappearing.

Lurching forward as he did so, the drunk spoke to me: 'China no good.'

We looked at him, unsure how to respond. He pointed again, this time at the boy's mother, who was ignoring her son's plight completely.

'China madam no good.' He jerked himself back against the seat with an effort, and almost as quickly lurched forward again, swaying as he tried to twist sideways. Pointing at Maria, he said musically, 'English madam, very good.'

He had, from listening to us, guessed our nationality correctly. We smiled, and said thank you. Meanwhile a stretcher arrived in the next row, bearing a corpse destined for Lanzhou accompanied by a mournful family, dabbing their eyes with their handkerchieves. In a far corner, another loud and heated argument began. The man leaned over me again, pointing in its direction.

'China people no good . . . always . . .' He made conflict signs with his fingers.

'Arguing,' I suggested. It was hardly something we had failed to notice, and while disputes were usually broken up by others, sometimes they did become physical. In Chengdu we had even seen a middle-aged woman march out of her optician's shop and hit a passing youth over the head with a wooden chair.

'Argument, thank you, argument. China people always.'

'Are you Hui?' Maria leaned across me to ask him; to me he looked Chinese, and I had thought he was, in his maudlin state, berating his own people.

'Yes. Hui. I Hui,' he replied jovially, beaming at his recognition.

It was the turn of the six-year-old girl to piss on the seat, and the man who had moved next to her to escape the boy sighed huffily and stalked off to stand next to the wall. In the next row the corpse sat up, revealing itself to be merely a sick young woman, for some reason covered completely by a sheet while awaiting the train to Lanzhou.

Our tickets carried no reservations, and the result was a scrum which began when a uniformed woman official barked the arrival of the train. At this, the two hundred or so peasants around us picked up their sacks and elbowed their way to the front, until the official barked loudly again and they froze, obediently allowing another woman official to cajole them into twin files, a process which seemed little different from playground control in a primary school. When everyone was quiet the first official led off, the long double queue following, still kept in check by her watchful assistant. We walked up stairs and down underpasses, seemingly all around the station, until we came almost to the platform, and a thick white line painted across the concrete. The leading lady stopped and pointed at the line, making the double queue stand behind it; then she stepped aside and it was everyone for themselves.

We found a carriage with seats and sat in them quickly. It was a strongly male affair, and a tight fit in facing rows of three. Maria had the window seat, I was next to her, with a man in his forties next to me. Uncomfortably, we knocked knees with two ragged youths opposite who stared at us through mistrustful eyes. The youth beside them, only slightly better dressed, fiddled unhappily with a non-functioning walkman. Across the aisle, a man in brown suit, brown jumper and straw hat was the spitting image of the Dalai Lama, but incongruously swilled beer and laughed raucously with his army friend. The man next to me suffered the pandemic Chinese nervous habit of tapping his heel on the ground, his right knee bobbing up and down incessantly, irritatingly intruding on my vision and reminding me that Chinese blood pressure levels (apparently due to excess salt in the diet) are reportedly the highest in the world. Occasionally, he accompanied his anti-social condition by whistling the rhythm of the train. All around was aggravating movement and noise, constant competition for too little leg room and nowhere to lay one's head. Our nerves were frayed to breaking point just half an hour out with another twenty to go. It was not going to be an easy night.

For a while we turned our attention to the scenery. It had a curious beauty, beguiling, yet ultimately unkind. Mountains rose and fell abruptly like herds of camels kneeling on the grass, with little space between; here, isolated families of farmers lived in craggily intimidating valleys, where the heat of the sun could not be felt until hours after its true rising, only to be deprived of it again too early at night, and the distance to the next valley, though short in terms of miles, must be measured instead in heights and depths. Sometime after leaving Xining, these mountains gave on to gentler grasslands, and great green expanses of emptiness suggested only greater vastnesses beyond. Brooks and streams burbled idyllically by, gleaming blue in the low sun which would remain fierce until the moment of its final disappearance. At a quarter to eight one of the two youths opposite pursed his lips and clucked at the opposite window. Lake Kokonor had come into sight and it hung, calm and silvery clear, like a perfect mirror in a frame of gentle brown hills, with sloping grassland leading down to it from the train.

In not so ancient times this side had been Mongolia, the other, Tibet. The shore of Kokonor was where, in the sixteenth century, in a ceremonial affirmation of the priest-patron relationship between Tibet and Mongolia, Altan Khan, descendant of Genghis and Kublai, bestowed upon Sonam Gyatso the title of Dalai (Mongolian, *Ta Le*) Lama, acknowledging him as both spiritual and temporal ruler of Tibet. We followed the lake, lost it and picked it up again several times. In contrast to the train, all outside was peace, and not an animal, person or movement could be seen. Only a solitary line of unconnected telegraph poles, ending mysteriously at the water's edge (I imagined someone putting them in, getting to the water, looking at their map and scratching their head), abused the image of open virginity. The lake looked a pure oval, preternatural, the stuff Excalibur-like legends are made of. Day-dreaming, I wondered about the exact spot where Sonam Gyatso and Altan Khan had met and imagined being present at the time, the horses, the finery, the tents, the gifts, the pomp and ceremony . . . and then, after only forty minutes, we lost the lake for good, and soon after, it got dark.

The impact of darkness was a signal for the total degeneration of the carriage, which was already very drunken. Groups of loutish youths ran up and down the aisle, drinking, shouting and mock-brawling. A party of six males nearby incessantly played the popular game of 'scissors-paper-stone-water', screaming rather than shouting as they jerked out their arms thrice for every round and the losers knocked back more drinks. Qinghai, formerly the Tibetan province of Amdo and only opened to foreigners in 1980, is China's most desolate province and home to most of its prison camps. Many of the people on the train would be coming here because they were unable to find work elsewhere in China, with criminal records perhaps, but the prison camps which once held them would take them back for a small wage. They could not have looked forward to it, if they knew where they were going. The police presence in the carriage was strong, but they also drank too much and were disinclined to intervene. This human mess, the constant knocking of knees, the inability to change position, the continual, anxious heel-tapping of the man next to us, was all making us shattered and frayed. We were contemplating how to combine nodding off with keeping an eye on our bags on the rack, sleeping in shifts perhaps, when relief came in the form of an angel, disguised as a conductress.

'We have Hard Sleeper. You want?' she asked beneficently.

We paid up the calculated difference in Foreign Exchange Certificates, the crazy parallel currency which foreigners were supposed to use all the time but ordinary Chinese weren't allowed to touch. (There was such a black market in FECs that ordinary Chinese rabidly collected them and foreigners were only too pleased to sell them for regular *renminbi*. Mercifully, the system was abolished in 1994.) Following her the length of the train however, it was evident that even in the Hard Sleeper carriages the situation was much the same: all male, and everywhere drunk. The constant sound accompanying the rattling train and the devilish laughter of inebriated conversations was the smash! smash! smash! of glass breaking on the tracks, as bottle after bottle was thrown from the open windows. Still, at least we could now lie down. This time we both had top bunks, and hauled ourselves up to rest in the middle of a cloud of putrid smoke from the four over-zealous card-playing policemen beneath us, swearing venemously as they drunkenly slapped down their trumps, hand after hand as if wages, homes, sisters and wives or even souls were at stake in this mobile casino of hell. There was no point in trying to sleep. Sleep was not taken seriously on this train; in fact, it was not taken at all, and soon we found out why. Somewhere between midnight and dawn the train stopped, and half-emptied. In the middle of nowhere.

'*Laogai*,' Maria hissed, lifting herself onto her elbow. 'Labour camps. China's bloody Siberia.'

In the morning we even slept an hour or two through the loud, jazzy music, until it culminated in the aural torture of a Chinese version of *Yankee Doodle Dandy*. When we woke properly it was to the additional sound, and feel, of an icy wind. I looked at my watch. It was just nine. The sky was bright, and down through the window I could see flashes of sand. We dismounted and looked out properly, to an unbroken, infinite line of horizon where pale orange met life-threatening blue. For miles and miles the single railway track was accompanied by lines of straw grown in half-metre squares, and behind that were straw fences, the purpose of both being to keep the sand from forming dunes upon the track, such a soul-numbing task as could only be performed by prison labour.

We walked along the carriage, which we now had almost to ourselves, closed all the windows, cleaned our teeth, made some tea and sat down, still shivering in the new wintry chill. We had some stale buns left from Xining; the diet seemed to befit the view. We passed several identical settlements in the desert, square, concrete compounds with rows of tiny rooms and the inevitable basketball pitch. And then, a line of men in regulation grey, hoes over shoulders, heads of lank hair unenthusiastically hung, being marched towards the squares of straw. It seemed strange that these *gulags* should be so public, but then the railway was what they were here for, and it, too, served them. Indeed, the very track we were on had been built in this way, when the original intention had been to extend it all the way to Lhasa. We gazed out as the hours went by, and camp after camp went past. Eventually the sand transformed into salt, and salt extraction as a task replaced the lines of straw, but still the compounds remained soullessly the same.

Up to ten million people were reportedly held in these camps, which held eighty per cent of China's prison population and existed all over China. Indeed, over thirty million people are estimated to have disappeared through China's *gulags* since 1949. Fox Butterfield's all-too-valid critique that when a dissident was sent to a prison camp in the Soviet Union it was headline news, but when it happened in China no-one cared, came instantly to mind. The former Soviet Union was for years subjected by the West to the propaganda attacks of the Cold War while China, though worse in many ways than the USSR, remained a curiosity shop on the edge of the universe. It is changing a little now, but names such as Wei Jingsheng and Phuntsok Nyidron (a Tibetan nun serving nine years for demonstrating, whose sentence was increased by a further eight years in 1994 for singing a song of independence while in jail) do not yet trip so easily from the tongue as Sakharov and Solzhenitsyn, and China remains a blind spot in the eyes of the West, visible only when it comes to trade. Chinese troops can kill hundreds of pro-democracy demonstrators either in Lhasa or the centre of their own capital, live on television with running commentary, yet 'favoured nation' trading status is not withdrawn by the United States, and British towns twin happily with Chinese cities in a way that would have been unthinkable with the Soviet Union or South Africa a decade before. This is all apart from the evidence linking Western companies with the export of precision-made torture instruments to China, none of which have been prosecuted. It is curious to think that the adults involved in such decisions, presidents and prime ministers included, who are themselves instrumental in perpetuating the worst excesses of totalitarianism this planet has yet produced, would be horrified should their child return home from school having been told that the Holocaust was a good thing.

We stared at the passing, traipsing lines of grey, the taste of dry stale bread in our mouths. They were living ghosts, human beings with pasts but no present, who suffered and lived but like the dead could not imprint their existence on the world. The real irony was, as Butterfield also points out, that 'unlike many regular civilian factories and farms, which are mismanaged and operate in the red, the labour camp factories and farms all earn a profit.' This is a point stressed by ex-inmate and *laogai* campaigner Harry Wu, and is chillingly evident in Kate Saunders' compelling exposé of the *laogai* system, *Eighteen Layers of Hell*.

We arrived in Golmud and spilled off the train to find not one but several army units on the platform. The route to the hotel revealed a sprawling town with few citizens but roads large enough for any number of tank convoys to organise themselves. Golmud is the base for military operations in Tibet, and it should not have been surprising to see truckloads of troops everywhere. In reality the whole town is one vast garrison, bleak, concrete and dusty, and perhaps in a hundred years its inhabitants will have sixty words for 'grey'. But it was here that we would learn whether we would make it to Lhasa, or have to turn north to Dunhuang. We checked into the decrepit Municipal Guest House, and set off to cash some travellers' cheques.

At the bank we met Hal, a small, plump Californian in his late fifties who was given to wearing a large Bolivian-style Tibetan hat, smoking more moderately sized but still showy cigars, and to placing a portable computer on the counter when he wished to change money.

'I like to show 'em what they're missing,' he hissed with a sidelong smirk, drawing pleasure from our own surprise while the clerks remained admirably unimpressed.

'Spread a little discontent,' he continued, taking out the cigar and winking conspiratorially. 'Make 'em wish for a better life. Know what I mean?'

He finished his transaction and Maria signed her cheques, smiling at the young clerk.

'Going to Tibet?'

'We hope so. And you?'

'That's the idea. Just got to work out the system. Different every time.'

'You've been before?'

Hal, it transpired, had been to Tibet on numerous occasions and seemed to see himself as an unpaid intelligence agent for the Tibetans. On his last visit he had been able to simply leave the train, get on the bus and get off in Lhasa, all in one go. Admittedly, he said, he was assisted in this by being on a bus loaded with illegal workers and a rogue driver who drove around several checkpoints, paid off others, and drove at night when most were closed. Now, unless we could find such a bus again, it was not going to be so easy. Hal's manner suggested a person who should be taken with a large pinch of salt, but his experience in getting to Tibet was indubitably useful, even if things were a little exaggerated in the retelling. We decided therefore to throw our lot in with his, at least in the initial stages of investigation, and after a late lunch we went to the bus station together, thinking we should try the easy things first.

'No.' The girl behind the counter was friendly but her answer was flat. 'You need permit. Then we give you ticket.'

At least this suggested permits existed, so we went to the PSB, the Public Security Bureau. We had heard two rumours about them: one, that they were bribable, the other, that they could be pressurised into issuing permits by turning up in their office every day for a fortnight. Both smacked of unfounded travellers' lore. We entered a little concrete room inside the compound gate. It was uncarpeted and dusty, with chairs on three sides and a man behind a desk on the fourth.

'No. Cannot go Lhasa.' He had said it almost before we asked, as if he were tired of streams of the same request. He was final and abrupt, but spoke little English, and went out at once to fetch his boss. When she appeared she was young and quite pretty, and hardly seemed suited to her stiff uniform.

'We're not allowed to give permits for Lhasa,' she explained in good English. 'Lhasa is in Tibet and Golmud is in Qinghai. We can give permits for Qinghai, but no other places.'

'But in Chengdu they give permits and Chengdu's in Sichuan.' Hal automatically assumed the role of questioner.

'No they don't.' She contradicted him firmly.

'But many people go from Chengdu.'

'Only on tours.'

'But they do give permits.'

'Only for groups.'

'We are a group.'

'You must be on a tour.'

'We are on a tour. We're three people.'

'Tours must be official. You must go to CITS.'

'Then you are allowed to give permits?'

'No. CITS do it. PSB are not allowed to give permits for other regions.'

'But Chengdu PSB give permits.'

'Chengdu is Chengdu, Golmud is Golmud. We can give you permits for anywhere in Qinghai.'

'But I met someone who got a permit from you.'

'When?'

'Two years ago.'

'We've been criticized in the past for giving permits. We can't do it now.'

As if to indicate the matter was closed, she went outside. I doubted there was much point in continuing these circular arguments. They had their orders and that was that. Hal on the other hand, who had more experience of Chinese officialdom, evidently believed in the theory of attrition. Maria wondered whether bribery would work, and when the woman came back in, we tried it.

'How much is a permit?' Maria asked.

'No money! No money! We're not allowed!' She seemed neither amused nor taken aback. Hal returned to the plaintive.

'Look, we've come all this way from America and Britain to go to Lhasa, and people are going from Chengdu, and we *know* people are going from here too. What can we do? Please give us some advice.'

'Go to CITS. Take a tour.'

'CITS are thieves,' said Hal. 'You know they're charging 2,500 FEC just for a bus ticket? And where does the money go? Into their pockets!'

'We don't care about this.'

Her English was not so good; she meant there was nothing she could do. She walked out of the office again and stood in the car park, her foot up on a wall, picking at grass. For now, we had to accept we had drawn a blank, but somehow all three of us had the feeling she knew more than she was saying. As we left I approached her to apologise for Hal's persistence. I was surprised to find her genuinely upset by his interrogation, but resisted the urge to put my hand on a policewoman's back.

Our next stop was CITS. Compared with the bare PSB office, theirs was plush. Situated in Golmud's best hotel it was large, luxuriously carpeted and contained three big, polished wooden desks behind which two suave types in expensive suits and a snooty young woman were doing nothing but swivelling in their comfy chairs. We hated them on sight.

'How much is a tour to Tibet?' We addressed the one who seemed to be in charge.

'Five thousand FEC,' he said, dismissively.

That winded us. In a matter of weeks it had doubled. Maria got out her calculator. The pound had gone up to 8.88. That made it £568.18. It frustrated all of us to know that from some people they would get it, and that these spiralling fees were the direct result of such people making things difficult for the rest of us.

'I see,' I said. 'And what do we get for that?'

'A five day tour.'

'Five days in Lhasa?'

'No. Two days to get there by bus, three days and two nights in Lhasa, and a flight out wherever you want to go.'

'London, for that price.'

'No. Chengdu or Kathmandu.'

'Can't we do it any cheaper?'

'No. You want to go to Lhasa, you pay the money. Don't argue with us. It's the only way you'll get there.'

They were smiling, cocky. Maria and I looked at each other in grim resignation, already beginning to consider our next step. Hal, however, was not about to leave it there. Ostentatiously lighting one of his cigars and blowing a plume of smoke towards the ceiling, he stepped into the middle of the room.

'Where does the money go?' he enquired, naturally.

'What do you mean, where does the money go?'

'You want five thousand FEC from each of us. That's fifteen thousand FEC for two nights in Lhasa. Where do we stay – honeymoon suite at the Holiday Inn?'

'No. The Yak Hotel.'

'The Yak Hotel is fifteen *renminbi* a night,' Hal retorted instantly.

'Don't argue with us. That's the price.' The woman had butted in, and waved her hand disparagingly.

'You get a guide for two and a half days' said the boss, as if that made it acceptable.

'And how much is he paid?'

'That's none of your business.'

'Suppose I don't want to fly out ,' suggested Hal. 'Can you reduce it by the cost of the flight?'

'Yes. The cheapest we can do then is four thousand one hundred FEC.'

'So you're charging nine hundred FEC for a flight to Chengdu, that I can get for five hundred FEC by walking across the street to CAAC? Where does the extra four hundred go?'

'Service charges.'

'Over three months' wages service charges? You mean into your pockets!'

'Don't argue with us,' repeated the parrot. Every time she said that, it made Hal more determined to do so.

'How much is the bus?' he persisted.

'I'm not telling you any more. Stop arguing.'

Nervously, I detected Hal's face beginning to redden. Beneath the thinning ginger hair which his hat disguised, his freckled complexion was an easy barometer of his moods.

'You're charging us five thousand FEC to get to Lhasa, a place which does not even belong to you, and a Chinese or a Tibetan can go there for sixty *renminbi*. And you deny that is going into your pockets? Where does this nice suit come from?'

Suddenly, Hal blew smoke all over it. I swallowed, unsure as to the amount of self-control he possessed. Later he would report the calculations going through his brain, that if he turned their office upside down and made a good job of it, it may result in a policy review being imposed on them from above, but he would probably get deported, and not via Lhasa. In the event, thankfully, he affected a great openness:

'Look, tell me honestly, do you think it's a good price?'

The man swivelled in his chair, looked at his friend, and laughed uncomfortably. Hal directed a cloud of cigar smoke past his face. The official winced now, and said nothing. I could see from the smile on

Hal's lips that a kind of victory blow was about to be inflicted, and instinctively put out a restraining arm. Hal shrugged me off, indicating with a downward wave of his hand that he was not about to do anything stupid.

'Come on,' he repeated seductively. 'Do *you* think it's a good price? I'm asking you for your *personal* opinion.'

I saw the man try to hold Hal's eyes, but was unable to stop his own from shifting.

'Yes', he said, committing himself to whatever was coming. 'I think it's a *very* good price.'

Hal took his cigar out of his mouth. He walked calmly around to the other side of the desk, and leant over the deserving victim until their noses were centimetres apart.

'Then you're sick in the head, a thief, and I hope that when this country has a decent revolution you'll be first against the wall!'

Understandably, the man paled. Probably, he had expected Hal to hit him, and the thought had crossed our minds, too. As Hal proceeded to grab the man's lapels I strode forward and put one hand on Hal's right arm, the other round his waist, and pulled hard. He let the fellow go, and walked out of the room. The other two officials, rooted to the spot like pillars of salt, looked at us in pure bewilderment. The man who had been on the receiving end of this whirlwind of wrath gathered himself, and spluttered:

'Your friend is sick!'

But we were all justifiably angry and aggrieved, and Hal was really only returning the superior, dismissive attitudes they had shown us the moment we walked in. Refusing to show sympathy, Maria turned on her heels and I followed her out of the office to where Hal was waiting for us on the steps, chewing his cigar in the sun.

'Sorry about that,' he said with a smile and a shrug, 'but it just wouldn't be right for people to abuse their positions of power without receiving some discomfort in return.'

We returned to our rooms to rest, and ruminated over the next step. While sympathetic to many of the Western tantrums we witnessed in the face of Chinese officialdom, there were too many question marks over Hal's personality to leave us comfortable with the decision to tie our own attempts at reaching Lhasa to his. Moreover, having exhausted the legal ropes, only the illegal were left. What to do? I had the idea of returning to the bus station, and trying to find the same girl we had spoken to before. She had been friendly, a student type, and was probably well placed to give us some advice. Without telling Hal we slipped out by ourselves, and by luck she was still there.

'Hi!' she said, smiling. 'You have permit?'

'No, that's the problem. The PSB say no permits for Tibet. We believe some people have gone by bus, but we don't know how. Can you help us?'

'Ha!' she laughed. 'Permit for Tibet, no. CITS only, very expensive. You get permit for Tibet *border*!'

Well why had she not told us that the first time, I thought.

'And then?' we asked.

'And then, up to you. Some people stay on bus, have good luck OK, no problem, have bad luck, come back. Some people' – she stuck out her thumb – 'hitch-hitch.'

Hope returned, rushing up my spine. I felt as if an ignition key was turned.

'And what's the name of the town on the border?'

'Tuo Tuo He.' She wrote it down. 'Yangtze is there.'

'Of course!' Maria exclaimed. 'The source of the Yangtze! What a wonderful reason to go to Tuo Tuo He!'

I turned back to the girl. 'And what time does the bus arrive there?'

'There are two buses. One arrives at eight pm, the other at ten-thirty.'

We thanked her, and, because she had knowingly colluded in our crime, we gave her some money. A firm plan now presented itself. We would return to the PSB and ask for a permit to Tuo Tuo He. We would get the later bus, since then it would be dark when we arrived, and easier to covertly find a truck that was willing to take us. It was, we knew, illegal for Westerners to ride non-public transport in China, but it would be the driver, not us, that got into trouble. Consequently we would have to pay them enough to make it worth the risk. We needed a couple of days to get hold of sufficient provisions and warm clothes, and then we would be ready to go.

Even had we wanted to, it would have been difficult to have avoided Hal since we were staying at the same hotel and there were few other

Westerners in town. We were as good as thrown together by fate, and whatever our misgivings there seemed little we could do about it. Back at one of the restaurants outside the hotel, we found him in conversation with a Japanese returning from Lhasa, having gone there by precisely the method we had just been advised to use. The checkpoints could be a problem he was saying; you have to either lie down and cover yourself with blankets, or get out and walk around them. Some people made it, some people failed, but if we could get to Lhasa, we should be alright. When the Japanese had gone to his room to sleep off the journey, over a hopeful meal and several beers Hal explained to us the curious conundrum of why it is alright to be in Lhasa, but not alright to go there. He seemed to have calmed down, and to be in sensible mood.

'There are two authorities,' he said simply. 'The TAR (Tibet Autonomous Region) Authority which governs Tibet as a whole, and the city authorities, such as Lhasa or Shigatse. The TAR is linked to Beijing, and generally disapproves of *anyone* going to Tibet except on expensive package tours, which are limited in time and make sure you are 'minded'. The city authorities on the other hand take a different view. They see that individual travellers put money into the community by spending it at local shops, restaurants and hotels, in a way that people on expensive tours at the Holiday Inn don't. The loophole for us is that the two authorities tend not to tread on each other's toes. So, we are not allowed *into* Tibet, because that is under the control of the TAR, but if we can get to Lhasa, that would be like making a home run, and the city authorities would leave us alone. It's the same if we were to travel between two cities: if the TAR picked us up we could be sent out, but if we made it to the next city, say Shigatse, we should be OK again.'

'A bit like cat and mouse,' I offered.

'And we are the mice,' he said.

'But don't your repeated visits arouse suspicion?' asked Maria.

'You bet,' Hal replied, visibly warming to the question. 'I've been arrested twice, my mother in the States has received phone calls from Chinese people when I was over here. When I came into the country at Hong Kong, a guy pretending to be a preacher kept talking to me about Tibet without me even telling him I was coming here – he just kept saying 'don't go there, don't go there . . .' That was weird. In Tibet, the plainclothes police are everywhere, they follow you and listen in on your conversations, but at least they're obvious because they wear leather jackets and swagger about. This was something else. This was *high level*.' Hal paused for effect, then threw up his hands in a mixture of complaint and bewilderment. 'I mean, dammit, the Chinese ought to be damned grateful to me for spending my time persuading people *not* to demonstrate – especially those stupid sixteen-year-old nuns who keep getting themselves arrested, but for what?' He paused again, thinking to himself, then gave us some telephone numbers. 'These are in the event of my disappearance,' he continued. 'I tell you, there was a guy woke up in his room in Lhasa with a two week memory loss. Yup, every visit will be more dangerous than the last.'

He searched our faces, looking for reactions. We were blank. It was his manner that made him untrustworthy. Uncomfortable with the silence, he rambled a bit more until we finished our drinks, made our excuses and left.

Back in our hotel room we wondered again what to make of the man. There was no reason to doubt the general drift regarding Chinese persecution, and anyone who had spent a fair time there must have some knowledge. Yet Hal's rejoicing in drama made us question his motivation – was it for the Tibetans, or for his own ego? He had taken such delight in telling us how he had run around road blocks at night that we felt he was living out a James Bond role, and part and parcel of that condition could have been the amplification or manipulation of 'facts' to fit a picture – like his mother receiving phone calls, and the man with a two week memory loss. Could we really believe those things?

'Self-analysis is very difficult when you travel alone,' Maria reminded me. 'And he's been keeping it up for years. He's also in his fifties, and his personality is probably permanently fossilised by now.'

'If you ask me,' I said before we went to sleep, 'he comes over like a fervent evangelical Christian, except that he believes in the Tibetan cause instead. Not that there's anything wrong with that of course. The Tibetans need all the help they can get. But I'm not sure how long he could travel with anyone before arguing with them. It's often the case with these single-minded, driven personalities that they have to be on top all the time, and consequently end up quite lonely.'

The next morning we found ourselves again at the PSB office. The lady officer looked at us dubiously, but lightened when we said we wanted to go to Tuo Tuo He. Her colleague gave us the permits immediately, in the full knowledge of what we were doing. When we told them that the CITS fare had gone up to five thousand FEC, they both visibly fell back in their chairs. I made motions of putting my hands in my pockets. They laughed, and did not contradict.

'But if they're thieves, and you know they're thieves, why don't you do something?' Maria asked them.

'We don't care anything about this,' said the woman in her unfortunate English, meaning, they were powerless.

She grimaced and shrugged, as if tacitly indicating her sympathy. It must have been hard for them, I thought. They, as police, had come through a very conservative political education and may well have been exceptionally moral and conscious of the public good as a result. CITS officials however came to their positions through the world of Chinese business which is lubricated by corruption and deception. The PSB pair in front of us probably received the normal monthly wage, with a few small top-ups here and there, and survived on it, well aware that the smooth operators of CITS were oiling their pockets astronomically by comparison.

Permits in hand, we went to the bus station together and saw the same girl.

'Three tickets to Tuo Tuo He please,' I said, flourishing the precious pieces of paper. 'For the day after tomorrow, on the later bus.'

'Of course,' replied our friend.

'Er – would it be possible to have front seats?'

'Sorry, no allowed.'

'Pardon?' I would have understood 'sold out', but not 'no allowed'.

'Front seats Chinese only. My boss say. Foreigners at back.'

'But we pay more than Chinese!'

'Sorry. Boss say.' She did look apologetic; there was no point in biting her ear off.

'Monks are always at the back when you see them on buses,' said Hal. 'And police are always at the front. Makes me sick.'

Nevertheless, with our tickets tucked reassuringly in our wallets we returned to the hotel, where Hal and I got excited and Maria started to look up altitude sickness in her medical books.

Above – Getting granny about town in the Barkor. Carpet weaving is an important local skill, but also a task for profitable prison labour.
Left – Pilgrim with prayer wheel and mala circumambulating the Jokhang.
Below – Traders talk at the corner of the Jokhang. On the wall behind is the auspicious Tibetan symbol, The Knot of Eternity

Above – Ganden monastery – the slow beginnings of reconstruction.
Left – Nomad mother and child © *Irene Kristalis/Tibet Image Bank*
Below – Desecration unrepaired – the Sera package tourists
don't see.

Above – Traditional Tibetan architecture, now very much threatened.
Right – Making new images, in straw and clay, at Samye. Sacred texts and mantras are added before baking.
Below – Lama dancing at Tashilhunpo, Shigatse.

Above – Jokhang Square seen from the roof, with prostrators below and a circle of circumambulating pilgrims.
Below – Images in the Lingkhor wall surrounding the Potala, attract stones as offerings. Worshippers press heads to the base of images to obtain blessings.

Above – Inside the Jokhang – monks venerate Guru Rinpoche (Padmasambhava) and keep the butter lamps burning.
Below – Inside Palhalupuk cave, an image of Palden Lhamo is flanked by Buddhas. A bottle of alcohol is offered.

Above — Potala Palace with scaffolding, seen from Kyichu River.
Below — Maria and humorous children en route to Sakya.
Travelling companion Ted Yoshioka looks on.

Above – Nomad encampment on Lhasa plateau.
Below left – The road to Lhasa – our drivers take a rest behind the injured truck.
Below right – Poor Khampa man near Reting
© *John Miles/Tibet Image Bank*

"Jowo" Buddha statue in the Jokhang
© Robin Bath/Tibet Image Bank

Part 2

THE 'AUTONOMOUS REGION'

The 'Autonomous Region' is less than it is made out to be, too.

Not only does it only contain a third of the true number of Tibetans, two million rather than six in a truncated Tibet the rest of which has been hived off into the provinces of Yunnan, Sichuan, Gansu and Qinghai, but it is also anything but autonomous.

The Dalai Lama, from his base in exile in Dharamsala, India, has for thirty-five years been calling for autonomy, not independence, for his people.

If China looked after Tibet's defence and foreign policy and the Tibetan people could democratically elect their own government, such conditions would be sufficient for his return.

But the Chinese have offered no dialogue.

'If the Chinese had only been nice to the Tibetans,' said a tourist simply, 'they would not be making a fuss.'

Now, the Chinese are losing control over their own provinces, and the unrest of Tibet has spread to Xinjiang, Gansu and Chinese Mongolia.

Perhaps the Special Economic Zones will be next. For their refusal to talk to anyone, the future may suddenly hold freedom for all.

Where we had thought to travel outward, we shall come to the centre of our own existence; where we had thought to be alone, we shall be with all the world.

JOSEPH CAMPBELL

Travellers Past

THE ROADS TO LHASA ARE little, but famously, travelled. In much earlier times, Lhasa had been reached by a variety of Jesuit, Capuchin and Franciscan missionaries, their task of converting Tibetans, already more religious than most of their own countrymen, a fairly hopeless one. The first known Western visitors to Lhasa – assuming Friar Oderic's visit in 1325 is merely legend – were Fathers Grueber and d'Orville, who stayed for two months in 1661. Fathers Desideri and Freyre arrived in 1715, Desideri's thirteen-year sojourn remaining the record for a personal stay. The Capuchins operated a mission in Lhasa from 1719 to 1740, when they were expelled, and the first layman to visit was van der Putte, in 1720. The first Englishman was Thomas Manning, who stayed for four months in 1811, not long before Fathers Huc and Gabet arrived in 1846. They were the last before, with the British in India, a Chinese *amban* (envoy) in Lhasa and Russia increasingly seeking to expand its influence in Asia, Tibet became the centre of what came to be called the 'Great Game'.

During this time the roads to Lhasa were open season for a medley of spies, missionaries and independent explorers, few of whom were sane, none of whom was invited, but each of whom was bent on finding his own way to the forbidden citadel – even, whether by capture or falling victim to the ravages of the journey, at pain of death. Their stories are captivatingly told in Peter Hopkirk's masterly *Trespassers on the Roof of the World*.

The Russian soldier Przewalsky (after whom the little Mongolian horses are named), made numerous attempts to get to Lhasa. When he most looked like making it (being taken for a wandering saint) he ran out of money, and returned again prepared to shoot his way through, but knowledge of his intentions reached Lhasa before him. He tried once more, and died of typhoid.

Disguise and force were popular methods. William Rockhill, an American diplomat who spoke both Chinese and Tibetan, tried twice hoping to be taken for a Chinese minority. At first attempt he got within four hundred miles of Lhasa, and the second time within a hundred and ten, before being unmasked and forced to return. In 1890 a Frenchman, Gabriel Bonvalot, attempted to storm Lhasa with hostages. He reduced the distance to ninety-five miles and was lucky to leave with his life.

In 1892 a Presbyterian Englishwoman, Annie Taylor, driven by God to convert the Dalai Lama himself, entered Amdo disguised as a Tibetan. For four months she endured the most extreme weather conditions, deaths of servants, the loss of most of her possessions and horses to bandits, and still got to within three days of Lhasa before being betrayed by her own resentful guide. Three years later she was bettered by a much odder assault – the thoroughly unpleasant Littledale family, Mr, Mrs, 6'3" blond Oxford-blue nephew and dog. Their sepoys, Mr Littledale boasted, 'knew what fighting meant [and were] ready to face hopeless odds simply because their *sahib* ordered them.' They were within one day's march of Lhasa when Mrs Littledale's illness forced them to back down in a stand-off on a high pass. In the usual fashion they were allowed to leave, and the dog was made a member of the Royal Geographical Society.

Most harrowing were the adventures of the Rijnharts, Mr, Mrs, dog and year-old baby. Intent on spreading the gospel, they spent some time at Kumbum before heading to Lhasa in disguise. They passed through rain, wind and bandits until the baby died. Burying it in the tent, they pressed on. Turned back near Lhasa, they were attacked by bandits. Seeking help, Mr Rijnhart crossed a river and was never seen again, probably having approached the very bandits who had attacked them. Undeterred, Mrs Rijnhart went home to Canada, married another missionary and returned to Tibet, only to die there herself after childbirth. Far from evoking sympathy, their tale recalls a comment by Joseph Rock, that the more outlying the place, the less intelligent the missionary. Thus, the century ended with not a single Westerner having made it to Lhasa.

As soon as the century turned however, someone did make it, disguised as a Chinese doctor, and he lived there, maintaining this pretence and even having frequent meetings with the Dalai Lama, for over a year. While there he was joined by a fellow countryman, a real spy, although neither seemed aware of the other's presence. However, since Ekai Kawaguchi and Narita Yasuteru were Japanese and possessed the natural disguise of Asiatic appearance, credit is not given to them for 'winning the race', and for the next twenty years powerful political developments precluded any further individual attempts.

In 1904 the Younghusband expedition, trawling a retinue of British tabloid journalists, blasted its way in. It incurred over a thousand Tibetan deaths and as many injuries to a mere handful on the English side, a bill for £562,000 in 'expenses' being presented to the Tibetan government on arrival in Lhasa. The Dalai Lama fled into exile in Ulan Bator, but no sooner had he returned than he was forced out again in 1910 by a Chinese occupation several thousand strong. Their behaviour was worse even than that of the British, and this time it was in British India that the Dalai Lama sought refuge, unable to return until the Chinese had been forced out by popular revolts in 1913.

It was yet another decade before the next individual attempt, when Dr McGovern of the School of Oriental and African Studies penetrated Lhasa disguised as a caravan trader and, consequently, had to live like one. A predictable dose of dysentery forced him to reveal his presence, and while angry crowds stoned his house (amusingly, he joined in after escaping by a side door) the authorities were more benign, allowing him to recover before escorting him back to India. It is Dr McGovern therefore who should be given the credit for 'winning the race' and, since Britain had now assumed control of Tibetan immigration, he had to beat his own government, too. Shortly before, the more famous Mme Alexandra David-Neel had her presence discovered at Shigatse. When she left, the British resident there saw fit to fine the villagers with whom she had been staying two hundred *rupees* for failing to inform him of her departure. He gave her fourteen days notice to leave the country when she appeared again to complain.

Not surprisingly, David-Neel conceived what she called a 'witty revenge' against the British, and her real journey to Lhasa, when she made it, was largely motivated as an anti-British snub. Only a year after McGovern, Mme David-Neel, fluent in Tibetan, disguised as a beggar down to darkened skin and hair and with a young Sikkimese friend, Yongden, posing as her son (he later became her adopted son in France), set out from Kumbum at the age of fifty-five. After four months of the usual hardships they made it. Her story is told in *My Journey to Lhasa*.

In a review of this book Younghusband paid tribute to 'a very courageous and a very difficult feat in travelling to Lhasa from China in disguise. Those who know the terrible cold and disgusting dirt of Tibet can best appreciate the endurance it must have required to live as she did for months in Tibetan houses of the poorest type and among the lowest classes. The filth of the food alone would be sufficient to deter most travellers.' They lived as natives in Lhasa for two months until called to testify in court regarding a fight they had witnessed. Afraid their secret would come out, discretion got the better of their valour and they exited, via Gyantse, to India.

In all, David-Neel spent fifteen years in Tibet, travelling on foot or by yak, making her last journey there at the age of eighty. (When this remarkable woman reached a hundred, she applied to have her passport renewed. Did she intend to die there?) So totally immersed was she in Tibetan language, culture and religion, she was granted the title of *lama* – not something given lightly. Yet she was such a fierce critic of British policy that her extraordinary achievements were belittled here. Younghusband criticised her for 'a strong anti-British sentiment . . . She speaks of the Dalai Lama being under British suzerainty . . . [and] seems to think that it is through the British that he refuses permission to explorers, savants, missionaries, scholars . . . [but] the Dalai Lama is as independent of Great Britain as is the President of the French Republic'. Since the British refused Sven Hedin permission to enter in 1906, turned Gertrude Benham back from Gyantse in 1925, and deported Aina Cederblom with a fine of fifty *rupees* in 1937, all at the legacy of his own invasion, this was disingenuous of Younghusband to say the least. Moreover, when David-Neel proclaimed 'what decided me to go to Lhasa was . . . the absurd prohibition which closes Tibet', we recognised her motivation in our own.

5

THE FOLLOWING DAY WE SPENT shopping in Golmud for supplies: not only food but also gloves, woolly hats, T-shirts, woollen tights that threatened to itch like mad and a large blanket each, all to keep out the cold. It crossed our minds that our denim jackets could, together with the hats, help us be mistaken for Chinese if we were lying face-down, but the blankets could be thrown over us completely. For good measure we purchased a couple of mailbags, more now to disguise our rucksacks than to keep them clean.

At noon on our fourth day in Golmud we found ourselves joined on the bus by a Japanese student named Akio. Though he had some English and bore a perpetual smile, he rarely spoke, and possessed a humility that tended to render him invisible, so much so that when he was with us in a group we could easily forget he was there. He took the seat next to Hal and in front of us, for most of the journey absorbing silently the stock of diatribes we would otherwise have received. We were all of course at the back, in the company of several Tibetan monks. At the front sat only Chinese, with the exception of a high-ranking Tibetan policeman who had the best seat by the door.

The bus pulled out into the wide, dusty road, and headed out of town. The young monks were friendly, warm and playful, and messed around with each other constantly when they were not being thrown against the roof of the vehicle, which was driven too fast for the poor condition of the road. Ahead was the eastern edge of the Kun Lun mountain range, jagged but with low formations of rock rising like giant shards from a desert of sand and gravel. The lower slopes were shored up with sand blown about by the wind, and the higher reaches were a pastel grey under the brightness of a tent-like sky. I felt as if we were in a little glass dome that children play with, and if someone picked us up and shook us it would snow.

Two checkpoints came and went in the first hour, and our permits held. After four hours the mountains right and left were snow-covered, but the gravelly desert gave way to patchy tufts of grass. We saw our first shaggy yaks, and a mother and baby Tibetan antelope – an endangered species – frightened by our noise. Part of the effect of the thin air was that things which were distant seemed very near, and everything glistened with clarity – the icy mountain streams, the granite poking from the ground. A marker giving our altitude as 4767 metres (Hal predictably had an altitudometer built into his watch, but it had given up at over 4000 metres) explained our headaches, but most of the Chinese seemed worse affected, and put their heads down.

After five hours we hit a long, wide plateau, and the mountains receded into the far distance. The impression of space was overwhelming; not a place for an agoraphobic, thought Maria. A solitary eagle, perched on a telegraph pole, was the only living thing for miles, until we hit military supply depots, a giant water pipe construction scheme, and at the end of the plateau, quarries and mines. Xizang, the Chinese name for Tibet, means 'western treasure house' and also suggests why they wanted it. Tibet is rich in uranium, gold and all manner of minerals, and its rape began here. Further on, another plateau, and encampments of nomadic yak herders dotted the scenery with modern, white cotton tents until, after eleven hours on the bus and still on the plateau, we rolled into Tuo Tuo He in complete darkness and a torrential rain that thudded on our jackets and beat on our scalps, soaking us through before we had taken a step.

The bus deposited us in the drive of a rundown hotel, muddy and becoming muddier by the second. As luck would have it, the last filling station in China was next door, though we did not at first see it in the darkness. A little further on was a line of trucks, pointing towards Lhasa. By the cab of the first truck two Chinese drivers were huddled, talking under an umbrella.

'Lhasa?' I said.

'Lhasa!' they agreed.

We pointed at ourselves and at the hotel, held up four fingers and said, 'Lhasa' again. I got out a hundred FEC note and pointed once more, each person, one hundred FEC. This was a month's wages, total overkill – we wanted no messing around with haggling. Their eyes visibly bulged. Completely speechless, a mere glance at each other was enough and they nodded vehemently, waving at us to get in.

There were three drivers, and we were to be in a convoy. Allowing them to direct us, Maria and I got the brand new Mitsubishi, while Hal and Akio got the older Isuzu behind. Both were massive, articulated affairs, but surprisingly uncomfortable inside. I gave Maria the window seat, leaving myself the harder one over the gear box, my hips twisting as I was forced to sit with my left leg over my right. We put our rucksacks the other side of the curtain behind our heads, and prepared for a possible forty-eight hours of limited movement. The third truck was smaller, probably Chinese, its load bound with ropes under a tarpaulin. It was also apparently damaged, the load considerably slewn off its chassis, and perhaps for this reason it went in front.

The road immediately climbed, and with the quick gain in altitude the rain turned to sleet, and then to snow. Soon the headlights revealed several inches of settled snow on the road itself. We climbed and climbed, then after a sharp bend began to descend. We went slowly, in low gear. Ahead of us on the right, a truck just as big as ours had left the road and lay several metres below on its side. Its driver ran in the field towards our headlights, waving his arms like a windmill to get us to stop but we kept going, leaving him there to his snowy fate. It was not because of us. It was the law of the road to look after oneself, rather than others. Though we had seen it many times, in these conditions it seemed a custom of exceptional cruelty. The man would be lucky not to have frozen to death by morning.

An hour later we pulled off the road. The driver motioned with his hands that we were to go to the other cab to sleep. With the engine off however the temperature plummeted, and with our clothes still wet-through the four of us had to hunch together to keep warm.

At half-past five we were still freezing and sleepless, though the dryness of the air at this height had, in spite of the cold, absorbed the dampness from our clothes. Hal climbed out and began stamping up and down impatiently, his hands in his coat pockets.

'They're supposed to drive at night and sleep by day,' he called out. 'The biggest bloody checkpoint of all is just two hours away. What are they doing? Waiting for the damned thing to open?'

'Maybe they don't know we're illegal cargo,' I suggested unhelpfully.

He glared at me, but we certainly doubted our drivers' wisdom. For all we knew this could have been their first run to Lhasa and they may have been completely unfamiliar with the checkpoints, let alone the strictures on importing deviant Westerners. But there was nothing we could do. We were in their hands and that was that. At six the other engine came on; we warmed up for ten minutes and were off again, the wounded truck slowly in the lead. At a quarter to eight we went through the major checkpoint for entering the TAR. It was closed, its barriers pointing upwards and still, and we sat back and smiled in relief.

Hal and Akio's driver was relaxed, friendly and humorous. Ours was tense and uncommunicative, and with a tight grip on the wheel stared silently ahead the whole journey. We offered him bread, nuts and cans of honeyed-orange *Jianlibao*, all of which he brushed aside with a strong arm, saying nothing. He put the radio on. There was only crackle, and for an hour and a half we listened to crackle. But his driving was good, and the pan-Chinese habit of switching the engine off when going downhill to save petrol was thankfully not his, at least in the snow. We wondered what on earth would happen to him if he pranged a brand new Mitsubishi. Accepting his terms of mutual ignorance, we concentrated instead on the ethereal, snowy mounds that resembled upturned rice bowls in the half-light. And then we began to climb again.

Not for nothing is Tibet called 'the roof of the world'. This was the highest civilian road on earth – higher, even, than the Karakoram. The peak of the pass was something of a plateau, mountains rising again about a mile to our left, the downward curve just evident in the road ahead. Nothing grew at this height, neither grass nor weeds, and we had long ago left the tree-line behind. The highest point was marked by a monument at which our drivers stopped, and we dismounted to pay our respects. The road had been built by the army on normal wages, and their efforts on behalf of the 'motherland' were commemorated by a hideous representation of a PLA roadworker, half a dozen rough blocks of stone unevenly piled on top of each other, the highest sculpted into a head. Behind a concrete slab bearing the name of the pass and the height – 5231 metres – a solitary string of prayer flags was mixed up with the telegraph wires. There was no traditional cairn of stones. It was a forlorn, depressing place – a sterile, spiritual waste.

Sharing his cigars with the drivers, Hal conveyed he felt easier about them after discovering they were carrying goods for the Holiday Inn.

'I'm sure half this stuff's contraband,' he said. 'The Holiday Inn manager told me I'd be surprised at the things he can get delivered. They won't be wanting to get checked. And don't forget half the reason for becoming a truck driver in China is for what you can make on the side.'

Mentally, we threw a little salt over our shoulders. Distilling the essence of fact from Hal's James Bond optimism left us somewhere in the no-man's-land between reassurance and apprehension, with grounds for both. We had yet to encounter our first road blocks, and had no idea how our driver would deal with them when they came. We got back into the cab feeling there was a long way yet between here and the Potala, the palace of the Dalai Lamas that dominated Lhasa like a basilica in Lilliput.

We descended slowly. Sleet came, and fizzled out. Below the snow-line nomad tents made of black yak wool appeared, and the yaks themselves, truly hardy creatures, seemed as happy to graze on the snowy bits as on the grass. Soon it was all gentle hills and green pastures again, nomad communities and warmth. We made a toilet stop, and the children of an encampment of tents ran screaming towards us, their fascination when they got up close freezing them as if the music had stopped in a party game. From the edge of the road we watched them, little statues of snotty brown faces, big, big eyes and layers of rags, and the actuality of our presence in Tibet began slowly to sink in. It was as if the presence of real people was necessary to dispel the romantic image of Tibet we still carried in our heads, of a spiritual fantasy land of levitating monks, visions of gods and magic spells.

Such stories are often what first brings Tibet to Western attention, and of course they do begin here, and travel by repute. To the Chinese, these mountains were the legendary home of the 'Queen Mother of the West', who could bestow immortality on those she favoured. Emperor Han Wu Ti (141–87 BCE) reportedly met her, but was not judged sufficiently pure. For Tibetans, these mountains hid the mythical kingdom of Shambhala, from which the forces of light will one day ride to defeat the forces of evil (a not very Buddhist idea which came from co-habiting with Manichaeans in Central Asia). In the West, too, we have a legend connected with Kun Lun, for it was here, not in the more romanticised Himalayas, that James Hilton, reworking the Shambhala myth, set his fabled Shangri-La. Sadly, the twentieth century has visited on this land the grimmest of realities, and we could not imagine a Shangri⁄la or Shambhala lying anywhere off this road.

Suddenly, as if in confirmation of our thoughts, on the hill ahead of us and coming down, a long line of green army vehicles appeared, a convoy of over fifty trucks. We met in the dip, and as they whizzed past and upwards again our nerves resurfaced. Rhythmically they went by, twenty⁄one, twenty⁄two, twenty⁄three – and then, the truck in front of us which was injured and slewing about, clipped an army truck with its wonky load and came to a halt.

We watched as the driver in front got out and nervously fingered his ropes a few yards ahead. From the left an officer walked up behind him, spun him around and followed through with a right hook to his cheek. The hapless driver staggered, and fell backwards against his vehicle. With his left hand the officer grabbed the driver's hair, pulling his head viciously around, slapping him repeatedly about the face with his right. The man could do nothing but accept and hope it would pass. So many soldiers had seen us we had not bothered to bury ourselves into our seats, and now sat mesmerised by the scene unfolding in front of our window. More punches went in until, mid⁄assault, the officer looked up straight into my eyes. My stomach turned. This, I thought, was the end of the line. For a few thought⁄moments we stared at each other, then the officer grabbed the man by the hair again and thrust him round to the rear of the truck. Only then did our driver get out to mediate. In the silence of the road on top of the world, we waited. Other army drivers and passengers were laughing in their cabs, their eyes straying constantly in our direction. For them, the incident was a bit of light relief on a long journey, and perhaps their officer had thrown his weight around for their benefit. Some strolled about, fingering the awkward load and laughing at it. After five minutes, they began hooting their impatience. Our driver returned, and with a few more hoots the convoy began to roll again.

I pointed at the truck in front. 'Is he OK?'

Our driver tilted his head briefly to one side in answer. Perhaps some financial settlement had been reached. But we were safe; as Hal was to say later, it was just not the army's job. The police would be a different matter.

Once again the scenery became one long plateau, though long⁄haired and Tibetan blue sheep now joined the herds of yaks and dzos on the vast plain of emptiness. I could not recall seeing a tree since leaving Golmud, and the unrelenting sameness around us made the journey seem interminable. The wounded truck was slowing us down, and by checking the milestones I calculated we were averaging forty kilometres an hour, at which rate we would need a second unwelcome night in the cab. The milestones themselves were a masterpiece of colonial perversion, telling us not how *near* we were getting to Lhasa, but rather how *far* we were getting from Beijing.

As the day wore on the situation declined, and we began throwing in twenty-kilometre hours with frequent stoppages to check tyres and the slipping load, to stretch and drink tea. At six we reached Nakcho, the major source of employment in which is its infamous prison. This was also the second major checkpoint after the TAR border, where several Westerners had previously been caught, and we knew that if we got past here we had a good chance of going all the way. We buried ourselves in preparation into our seats, keeping well below the window line. Our driver slowed to fifteen kilometres per hour. The poles of the first road block at the beginning of town were raised upwards, and we simply drove through. Unable to resist, we raised our heads above the dashboard and saw a town teeming with life, the prison which dominated it clearly visible from the road, Tibetans in their natural dress far outnumbered by Chinese soldiers and police in uniform and not a truck or car that was not military. Surely, I thought, this had to be one of the worst places for a Tibetan to live, so surrounded by the arrogant intimidation of the occupying forces. Ahead, we could see the second road block was also up, but we ducked below the window again until our driver indicated it was safe with a restoration of the radio to its crackling half-life.

At ten we stopped at a small row of shacks to eat our evening meal. Travelling now for thirty-four hours without sleep at high altitude, our tolerance was perhaps wearing thin. Our drivers sat as usual with other drivers, and Maria went to point at some vegetarian food. Hal mentioned the difficulty of being vegetarian in Tibet and I agreed, mentioning that we had got this far and hoped we would be able to continue.

Suddenly, Hal flipped as if in the grip of something; his face became reddened, and with a peculiar, unconscious clenching and unclenching of his fists he launched into a tirade against vegetarians, who were dishonest if they wore leather shoes, were hung up on piety and used it as an excuse to think they were doing enough for a suffering cosmos. It was more than as if a shadow were cast over him; he had become a raincloud, and spat lightning.

'Why are you talking like this when you know we're vegetarian? Are you including us?' I asked nervously.

'I've never met one that was different, and I've unfortunately met hundreds,' came the reply.

Seeing another of Hal's confrontations brewing, this time with ourselves, Maria flashed me a nervous glance. I looked at Akio. Dimly visible, it seemed as if he were there, smiling away, the uneasy current in the air apparently passing him by.

'Well,' I began calmly, 'I wear leather shoes. Some people eat fish but not meat. Some people go the whole way and avoid dairy produce. It's important to find a level you're comfortable at . . .'

'I don't accept that. If you start something you should go the whole way or you're dishonest . . .'

He spoke with venom, without even the social skills to say, 'I don't mean you but often . . .' I have these conversations in class with fourteen-year-olds, I thought to myself, who are too young to have developed abstract thought. They can be forgiven for thinking in the black-and-white terms of childhood, but this fellow was in his fifties.

'. . . and they're so fucking pious,' he concluded.

'It needn't have anything to do with piety or personal purity,' I persisted. 'It's a stance based on the logic of supply and demand. If you—'

'Supply and demand doesn't mean that,' he interrupted.

'Doesn't mean what?'

'What you said it meant.'

'I didn't say what it meant. I just used it—'

'Look, it's no good bringing out cute philosophical concepts. People have got to be consistent. I've never killed a mosquito or a cockroach but I've got a gun at home and if a burglar came into my house I'd shoot him dead.'

Unavoidably riled now, I lashed back. 'Isn't it rather fascist to insist that only *you* know how to think, and the way other people struggle to make sense of life renders them dishonest?'

'Fascist?!' He reddened even more with anger, banging his fist so hard on the table that Akio's cup jumped and spilled its tea. Across the room, the drivers' table went quiet.

Instinctively Maria stood up, spreading her hands with finality through the air. 'Look! I've had enough of conversations where the only aim's to put people down because one of them has an outsize ego and constantly needs to prove himself in verbal combat. That's it. Finished. I've had enough!'

Still scarlet and breathing through clenched teeth, Hal strode into the night leaving us to pay for his meal. Maria went to the counter while I sat there apologising to the faceless Akio, who had now gathered something was amiss and was no doubt wondering in his Japanese way whether Western self-expression was less virtue than vice. Returning to the trucks, I looked for Hal and found him smoking in the dark beside his cab.

'Look, I'll put it down to exhaustion and altitude if you will,' I offered.

I waited a moment. There was no reply, just an intense focusing on the smouldering end of his cigar in the night. I returned to our own cab, knowing that from now on we would keep our distance. Perhaps it was better, I mused, having an excuse to do so.

'Hell, I don't know why I allow myself to get sucked into these things,' I complained to Maria when we were moving again. 'Why can't I just keep quiet?'

Maria was fuming. 'It wouldn't help him if you did. It's what I said before about self-analysis being difficult when you're alone, and he's been travelling alone for years, probably because he can't hold down relationships at home since no-one could put up with his ego. Now he's living out a James Bond archetype precisely to avoid the really challenging things in life, like getting on with people. And as for that bit about the gun — no, I'm glad you used the word fascist.'

With a reassuring squeeze of my knee we travelled on in silence, apart from the crackle of the radio which the driver again put on in order to drown the sudden, unwelcome spate of conversation.

Almost at once we came to another checkpoint in a small village. This time, it looked serious. Outside our windows, the visible world consisted of little that loomed out of the darkness beyond a long line of tarpaulined trucks piled up in a lonely road in the middle of a vast nowhere, all throbbing engines and diesel fumes, short, barked bursts of speech and moving uniforms, as military police inspected every load intimately, their torches running over everything like swords. We took our place in the queue and the driver turned off the engine, waiting for them to come to him. We put on our hats and curled up on the seat, our faces pressed into the cushion, the blankets drawn over us. I was aware of every laboured breath, my heartbeat a persistent hammering in the chest. In the paranoid play of my mind the argument with Hal acquired the guise of a bad omen, a divinatory signal of the end of our spell of good fortune.

After five minutes they came to the door and the driver wound down the window. The policeman barked a question. The driver answered, accompanied by a rustling of papers. There was a silence while they were read, then we heard them being passed back again and placed on the dashboard. Another sharp question. Another answer. And again. The check was hardly friendly. And then, the door opened. The beam of a powerful torch shone into the cab; I felt it go over our bodies slowly, investigating us like an ice-cold tentacle. Another question. Another answer, and the driver got out. Silence. I heard a sound at the back of the truck and realised it was being opened. With the door left open we remained frozen, in both senses. I wondered why these checks were so thorough. Had they been looking for people I assured myself, they would have had us out at once. But could the trade in contraband really be enough to merit this? There were more footsteps. The driver got in, closing the door behind him, and started the engine. Excitement pulsed as we felt ourselves move off, and when the familiar crackle reappeared we sat up, smiling at each other in the blackness of the night.

It seemed as if the last push towards Lhasa had begun. Finally leaving it to fend for itself, we overtook the wounded truck and increased our speed to sixty, rattling over the Tibetan plateau in moonlight. I felt the land haunted by the ghosts of travellers in times gone by, when the scenery may have looked the same but for the long and tortuous tarmac that now seemed, in this wild beauty, a swathe in pure flesh. Even when Tibet ruled itself it was suspicious of the outside world. We were, given its history, entering Tibet in a time-honoured way. It pleased me to think that our travelling to Lhasa in subterfuge was, after all, the traditional way to do it.

It was not totally pitch now that the clouds had allowed the moon to come out. It had been full a few days before, and its light allowed us to discern faint forms of scenery. There were, I realised, trees again. A white owl with brown wings, surprised by the truck, took flight ahead of us, the light of the moon shining on its soft body. It headed for the safety of another tree, behind the silhouette of a *chorten*.

'It *is* a magical place,' said Maria. 'In a landscape like this you *have* to believe in the supernatural, in spirits of nature and supernormal powers. Perhaps it's because, in places like this, they do exist.'

I smiled, recalling something else David-Neel had said: '"I would not have been very startled had I suddenly surprised some elfs seated on sun rays . . ."'

About seventy kilometres out of Lhasa, the long plateau which had supported us for sixteen hours ended. We entered a valley and followed a river whose full beauty in the light of day we could only imagine. Our headlights picked out willowy grasses, and primitive, mud-brick whitewashed compounds festooned with prayer flags which we at first took for ruins. (They were, we later elicited, communes, which persist in Tibet as a mode of social control.) In darkness Tibet was no less fascinating than in daylight, but for the next hour we had to closely watch our driver whose head was dropping worryingly often. A crash here at sixty kilometres an hour with pure glass in front of us and no seat-belts was not an attractive prospect to muse on. Yet he seemed to be aware of the problem, scratching his head repeatedly, breathing deeply, shifting position, opening the window and turning on the radio, all techniques culled from experience. And when he turned on the radio this time it was no longer crackle, but the bouncy melody of Indian songs, transmitted somehow over the Himalayas.

'It's like a welcome home,' said Maria, so familiar were we with Indian music. I smiled in agreement, and then found myself caught by a double-take of what she had said, and looked at her wonderingly. Had we been here before?

There was lightning over Lhasa the first time we saw it.

'Lhasa! Lhasa!' said our driver, in his first and only unsolicited communication in twenty-eight hours.

The first lights, when we reached them, must have belonged to the only isolated farmhouses in the world which could be said to constitute a suburb, and it was several miles further on before we hit the city proper, and a sudden blaze of highway lights. David-Neel had first seen the Potala at dawn, after a fortuitous sandstorm had concealed her entry past the then Tibetan-manned checkpoints. Now, with the roads flooded by yellow streetlamps, it was like a last run through a tight gauntlet. We drove down one long street, turned into another equally long, and at the end of it a figure with a torch appeared from the shadows, waving us down. The driver saw him late and screeched his brakes. We ducked quickly, not having time to pull the blankets over us. Of all our journey's terrors we felt this one the worst, to be so near, and yet so far. Our muscles and minds went taut again as we followed the footsteps. The policeman came to the cab, and opened the door. I assured myself we could not be seen unless he climbed up. The driver put on the light. Papers rustled. Fears raced. A conversation followed, interrogative and responsive. The interrogator's tone was normal, not sharp as the last time. The papers rustled again as they were handed over, again as they were handed back, again as they were returned to the dashboard. Silence. Too long. We felt ourselves studied. There were a few more words and then, the door closed.

We stayed down as he drove off, only sitting up again when the Indian pop music returned. I looked at the driver, for signs of whether he had felt it a close call, but he could have been watching snow melt. Later Hal told us their driver had nearly shat himself when he saw the uniforms, and was of the opinion that we had been seen.

'He *must* have seen us,' said Hal. 'It must mean that Lhasa city police have a policy of accepting a trickle of tourists without a permit. After all, if they didn't, they could clean out Lhasa tomorrow. Mind you,' he added, 'he could still have fined the drivers for carrying us and pocketed the money . . .'

In the event, it was the last checkpoint and we were through. We turned left at the end of the long road and there was the Potala, the moon in drifting clouds above it, a mountain in its own right, lost in its own thoughts. For us, it was also the victory tape at the end of a marathon. Involuntarily I felt a great well of excitement burst up my spine; my cells pulsed like a crowd rushing forward, my fists clenched themselves in triumph on my thighs. Like the initial frantic, joyous grasping of the Golden Fleece or the ecstatic sighting of the Gardens of the Hesperides, it signalled the achievement of a journey as much mythological as geographical, a journey as much made on the inside as out. It was a divine moment, that first sight of the Potala, a transformative, initiatory crossing of a meridian in personal history that would always be recalled, and visited in dreams.

Of Goats and Bodhisattvas

THE HOLIEST PLACE IN TIBETAN Buddhism is the Jokhang – 'House of the Jowo'. 'Jowo' is an affectionate term meaning 'Lord', 'Master' or 'elder brother', and the statue concerned is an image of the Buddha which legend attributes to Vishvakarman, a sixth century Indian artist whose work was so sublime he was later considered a god.

The Jokhang was built in the seventh century, on the site of the heart of the demoness which was Tibet. It was not an easy task, for the queen's diviners had located the heart at the bottom of a lake, which then had to be filled. Herds of goats laboured day and night, carrying logs and buckets of earth, until the lake was no more and the temple could be built. The demoness gave no more trouble, Tibet became Buddhist, and Songsten Gampo, the thirty-third king who had already unified the country, ruled wisely and well.

Contrary to Tibetan tradition, there is no evidence that Songsten Gampo personally converted to Buddhism, although he was certainly liberal towards it. The statue and the temple came as dowry gifts from the two wives he had received as tributes from lesser powers. The Chinese princess Wen Cheng brought the Jowo, which had been a gift to her father from the King of Bengal. The Nepali princess Bhrikuti Trisun had the Jokhang – then called the Trulnang ('place of miraculous appearance') – constructed by craftsmen from Nepal. As the town of Lhasa grew it took the Jokhang as its centre, and the temple was fated to be an ever-present backdrop on the stage of Tibetan history.

When the Chinese explain their claim to Tibet today, they never fail to mention Wen Cheng, as if the very fact of their marriage was evidence of political unity. This was not the Chinese understanding at the time. Following Songsten Gampo, subsequent Tibetan kings continued to expand militarily while allowing Buddhism to spread at home. By the time King Ralpachen (c.800–38) ascended the throne in 815 however, China had grown in strength to the north and east, and in 832 a treaty specifically recognising the separateness and integrity of both nations was carved onto a stele and erected in front of the Jokhang where it still stands today. It reads:

> Tibet and China shall abide by the frontiers of which they are now in occupation. All to the East is the country of Great China; and all to the West is, without question, the country of Great Tibet. Henceforth on neither side shall there be waging of war nor seizing of territory. If any person incurs suspicion he shall be arrested; his business shall be inquired into and he shall be escorted back.

To enter the Jokhang today is to enter a spiritual *axis mundi*, not entirely removed from the time of its creation. There is a sense of being at the labyrinthine centre of things, in the bowels of the earth, in a place that is so *real* that anything can be true. Behind thick wreaths of butter lamp and incense smoke, a thousand images of deities, peaceful and wrathful, loom in the gloaming, their golden feet touched by the mantra-murmuring heads of the faithful. In front of the Jowo himself, whole bodies slide in supplication.

David-Neel, for all her Tibetan sympathies, actually complained about this:

> I felt saddened at beholding the procession of worshippers, lost in superstition and exactly following the path that was condemned by the very one whose memory they worship. 'Beings led by ignorance, who tramp for fathomless ages the sorrowful road to renewed births and deaths,' as the Buddhist scriptures say.

In saying this, she was attempting to side with monastic intellectualism, rather than the simple faith of the masses. In his autobiography, *Freedom in Exile*, the Dalai Lama explains:

Part of [my meditation] involves what is termed 'deity yoga', lha'i naljor, during which I use different mandalas to visualise myself as a succession of different 'deities'. This should not, however, be taken to imply belief in independent external beings.

So what are the Buddhist 'deities'? Do they exist or not, and do they belong in a religion that is determinedly atheistic?

Although the Buddha disagreed with the idea of Brahman, the world soul, or that there could be any single 'entity' looking over us, he never condemned the notion of the many Hindu gods, in part because even in Hinduism they were not eternal, nor free from the changes and sufferings of the rest of us. When Northern (Mahayana) Buddhism separated out from Southern (Theravada) Buddhism in northern India around the 2nd century BCE, there arose the concept of the *bodhisattva* (literally, 'enlightenment being'). The *bodhisattva* was essentially anyone who was on the path to Buddhahood, who may well have reached such attainments as controlling their own rebirth, and whose compassion was such that they would never enter the final peace of *nirvana* so long as suffering beings remained behind to save. This was the total opposite of the *arhat*, the highest ideal in Theravada, where a monk meditates himself into oblivion, and the doctrine was a major contribution to the split. The Mahayana had discovered total selflessness, and the sense is well expressed by the Buddhist poet, Santideva:

May I be the doctor and the medicine,
And may I be the nurse
For all sick beings in the world
Until everyone is healed.

May a rain of food and drink descend
To clear away the pain of thirst and hunger
And during the aeon of famine
May I myself change into food and drink.

May I become an inexhaustible treasure
For those who are poor and destitute;
May I turn into all the things they could need
And may these be placed close beside them.

Buddhist 'deities', in theory, are simply *bodhisattvas* of the highest attainment.

Among the most famous is Chenrezig (Avalokiteshvara), the 'Lord of the World', whose thousand eyes and arms indicate his all-seeingness and omnipotence. The story goes that Chenrezig was about to enter *nirvana*, but turned around for one last look at the earth. Alas, the sight of so many suffering beings made him check himself, and decide to stay. A tear that fell from his eyes landed upon the earth, and from it the female *bodhisattva* Droma (Tara) was born. Together, this pair hold a popular place in Tibetan lore. Chenrezig is the *bodhisattva* of compassion who strives ceaselessly to develop kindness in human hearts; Droma is the 'goddess' one turns to when there is an obstacle to be overcome, to help us with which she has twenty-one forms to turn into. (Her mantra is said to be particularly useful for mending things.) There are, also, the protectors, native spirits of the old religion of Bon perhaps, who were won over to the Buddhist cause and now protect it from attack, and the wrathful *bodhisattvas* whose fearsome guise makes them useful for waging war on our own baser moods of greed, hatred and ignorance.

To most lamas including the present Dalai – himself theoretically an emanation of Chenrezig – these are only *symbols*, of wisdom, compassion or even anger perhaps, which function as meditational aids, rather than truly existent beings flitting around in space. But this is not the understanding of the masses, which is why David-Neel experienced her moment of self-righteousness.

And yet, I would support the faith of the common people. Religion for the masses can serve a need even if it is blind, stimulating abstract thought and imagination, prompting self-improvement, confirming a sense of place in the scheme of things and offering reassurance in times of despair. At this level, the issue of truth is subordinate to religion's psychological value. And when religious dogma is taken away, often other dogmas are imbibed in its stead – there is no liberation in that. When it is done on a mass scale, as in China, the result speaks for itself.

6

FOLLOWING FORTY-FOUR HOURS WITHOUT sleep, we slept for six hours, woke at eleven, and miraculously felt fine. The drivers, ecstatic with a sizeable bonus, had driven off hooting up a street with both 'no entry' and 'no horn' signs. After that, we were surprised that our banging on the heavy wooden doors of the Yak Hotel was necessary to wake the six staff, who slept fully clothed and huddled under blankets in the office.

We had been given a small room at first – and a flask of our first Tibetan yak's butter tea as a welcome – but now, on waking, we were transferred to a larger, brighter room with a long, shared balcony that blinked white in the powerful sun. While two young Tibetan maids attempted to clear our room of flies – a long process of ushering them out like sheep in preference to killing them – we stood on the balcony, taking in the view. In the distance to the left, further along the same street, two rifle-toting sentries stood guard on the flat roof of one of the many police stations built within fifty yards of the central shrine. Across the hotel courtyard was a large house, and from its back windows, faces stared at us.

'Spies,' said Hal, venturing from the room next door on hearing our voices.

We laughed at first, taking it for a gross exaggeration, and he shrugged his shoulders, as if by the end of the day we would be more inclined to believe him.

At the far end of the balcony, acknowledging us with nods but keeping themselves to themselves, was a clutch of Nepali businessmen. From the maids' broken English, we established that our arrival had taken the number of Westerners in the Yak to seven. The Nepalis, at eleven, outnumbered us, as did the Japanese and Hong Kong contingent who, passing easily for Chinese, combined at twelve. There were one or two Westerners at other small hotels, everyone else in Lhasa being on expensive package tours at the Holiday Inn. These statistics went home. They made us appreciate our fortune and favour, just to be setting foot in Lhasa at all.

'You missed the parade,' said Hal.

I detected condescension. 'What parade?'

'Oh, only about sixty troop trucks trundling up and down Dekyi Shar Lam.'

The maids nodded. It had happened.

'I thought you'd just got up.'

'No, I'll sleep later. I like to go out early, before the police get up. Go to the Jokhang, get breakfast, that kind of thing. It's best to lie low during the day.'

'What was the parade for?'

'Just showing off their strength, their weapons. Intimidating the Tibetans. We're coming up to September 27th and October 1st, the anniversary dates of the 1987 independence demonstrations.' Shielding his eyes from the sun, he looked across at the sentries and added blithely: 'They always get edgy, this time of year.'

Hal was noticeably cool towards us. He blamed us for the argument the previous evening and had not yet forgiven us. He had taken it as a challenge, and regular references to our ignorance were intended to shore up his superiority. Something inside us had slammed shut towards him, too. We were adult enough to continue talking to each other, but it was a prickly experience for both parties.

'Can you recommend anywhere to eat?'

Given the nature of the previous night's argument, it was perhaps not the best of questions. He raised his eyebrows, tilted his head back, and looked down his nose at us.

'Well since you're *vegetarian*,' he said, placing a sarcastic emphasis on the word, 'don't be tempted by the rice and dhal place the Nepalis go to. That's a *collaborators'* restaurant, and you'll find it full of Chinese police. Last time I was there the proprietor kicked his dog. And Tibetan Buddhists,' he added forcefully, 'Tibetan *Buddhists* don't kick dogs."

The dogs, in fact, were our first impression of the city as we left the hotel and walked onto the street. Running in packs by the score they scampered, for the most part playfully, all over the city. And they were good-natured, unlike the infamous Tibetan mastiffs used by nomads to guard their tents. They were so good-natured because they were fed and looked after to the extent that puppies, when found alone, would be taken in and pampered until they had grown a bit. Our hotel had one of these, a doleful-eyed creature, in size and effect like a small rag doll, which the maids perpetually fussed and carried around. Occasionally, we would see a Tibetan throwing scraps of food to a gathered pack, much as someone in the West might walk down to a lake to feed the ducks. There is a tale which doubtless some Tibetans believe, that Lhasa's dogs are reincarnations of dead monks, denied human birth by their karma but with the will to at least be reborn near their monasteries. To the Chinese, who view dogs much as the West views pigs, as obnoxiously dirty while living but good food when dead, the Tibetans' love for dogs is indicative only of their hopelessly primitive state.

Our first port of call was the Jokhang, Tibet's Holy of Holies, the most important temple of the faith which, according to Hal, was open for worship three days a week, subject to political temperatures. A large, brown and white, banner-fronted building, its inner chapels becoming progressively taller towards the centre, it looked over a great square of which Paving Stone's parents would have been proud, while from the nearest, lowest roof, the Buddhist symbol of the eight-spoked wheel flanked by two kneeling deer glinted beyond another police station in the direction of the Potala, half a mile away. Clearly, traditional Tibetan houses had once stood here for the Jokhang had been the centre of the old town, but now these had been removed to make room to swing tanks. A Chinese flag flew imposingly above us on a stark pole, and outside the police station a squad of rookies ate tuna from cans, leaning haphazardly against the wall, rifles propped at their sides. On benches in front of them bemused old Tibetans rested, their sad eyes disbelieving still, after all these years. By the Jokhang's main doorway, between two concrete crucibles of fragrant burning juniper, centuries of perpetually prostrating pilgrims had worn the flagstones into a series of smooth ruts. We turned our backs on the soldiers, and watched instead the dozens of bodies that rose, fell and slid in the ultimate offering of the self to the Buddha. Turning our eyes from one to the other, the image of the lone student with a carrier bag trying to halt a column of tanks in Tienanmen came immediately to mind. One may as well have held a candle to deny the dusk, but such contrasts are now Tibet's nature, the fate of a land indignant of its malevolent occupation.

Approaching the great building from the stele of independence, we collected a thermos of liquid butter and travelled with a queue of worshippers through a dark, narrow canal. To left and right in their own chapels loomed large, protective spirits, the wrathful *rakshas* on the left, the gentle snake-spirit *nagas* on the right. They were the powerful keepers of the doorway, to whom one made the first and last offerings of butter, pouring it into lamps that kept them bathed in a yellow glow.

And then, we were through the canal and into the womb, a vast, cavernous space, a well-spring from which emanated all the elements of the Tibetan Buddhist faith. Gigantic, golden figures of Padmasambhava, the future Buddha Maitreya, the thousand-armed, peace-bestowing, all-seeing Chenrezig, all newly made after the hiatus of destruction, towered in the centre as if nourished to their giant size by the butter offerings below, the pungent smell of which at first knocked us back. All else was dark. The room seemed pregnant with the barely visible, and at the edges people were swallowed by the permanent night.

We went forward carefully. In some places we could not see our own shoes. There were a series of ante-chambers, caves, more like, and caves within caves; we banged our heads, bumped into pillars, felt our way with our feet and trod on people's heels. Prayer beads clicked, mantras were recited aloud, and all about was hum and murmur. Incense mixed with the butter smoke, so rich and penetrating it was breathed through the nose and tasted on the tongue. The smoke could not escape and clad us like a cloak, yet comforted rather than oppressed. The queue wove through the chapels like an endless, slow-moving serpent and, as it twisted and turned, one and then another sun-worn pilgrim face, peeking from coats that looked straight off the animals' backs, ears stretched with silver and turquoise, veered in the light of the lamps and was gone. When they saw us, the reception accorded a respectful foreigner was almost that of a hero. People stepped aside, bowed heads, stuck out tongues, smiled, beamed or just nodded knowingly, before returning again to shuffling introspection.

Approaching the Jowo himself, heads were touched on the copious yellow silk robes covering his giant thighs and, since anything that touches him is automatically blessed, *malas* were flung across his lap and withdrawn. Prostrated before him, handfuls of blessed barley grains and ladles of blessed water were given and received, drunk and wiped on hair. Elsewhere, worshippers touched their foreheads mindfully to the thrones of a thousand wrathful and peaceful deities; the road to personal transformation they represented was the root message of Tibetan Buddhism which the simplest peasant would receive.

In the midst of it all, a handful of unarmed *Wu Jing* riot police ambled beneath the gaze of the Jowo like rubbernecking tourists, bemused by the behaviour of worshippers they were evidently seeing for the first time. Their presence in the temple reminded us of the Jokhang's more recent history, of how ten thousand women and children seeking refuge behind its doors had been mercilessly slaughtered in a single afternoon on March 22nd 1959, and the floor on which we stood had been an execution ground on several occasions since. Now, leaving the Jokhang for the bright of the day, we noticed several more groups of *Wu Jing* sightseeing in the square, and correctly deduced the ominous arrival of a contingent of reinforcements, in advance of the approaching anniversary of the 1987 riots.

Ignoring the troops, we immersed ourselves in the surrounding Barkhor or 'inner wheel', a bustling, circular walkway lined on both sides with double-storeyed white, inwardly-leaning walls, each window painted with a surround of black, and hung above with green, red, yellow and blue striped bunting which fluttered in the breeze. Both the cloth and the paint, Maria noted, would in normal circumstances have lent Lhasa a festive air. In front of the houses on both sides were stalls, and at one stall we browsed over statues, coins, masks and thigh-bone trumpets. As Maria picked up an ornate wooden *tsampa* (barley flour) bowl to admire, a woman alongside her, quite old and poor in dress, spoke.

'For many years, those weren't allowed.'

We looked up, surprised to hear such good English from an old woman. Looking into her face, we could see traces of nobility which contradicted her present appearance. She was tall, thick-set, her hair was braided, she wore an old *chuba* with a traditional Tibetan rainbow apron, and her face was deeply lined. She spoke a little hoarsely, and allowed herself the slightest of smiles.

'Nor dress, nor prayer wheels, nor *malas*. Nothing to do with our culture, not even the food bowls. And these stalls weren't here. The Barkhor was empty.'

'Where did you learn . . .' Maria began to speak, but already the woman had excused herself and walked away, as if afraid to talk as freely as she wished. We let her go. Her two plaits joined at her back by a green ribbon, her head hanging heavily, she melted into the crowd.

We walked on. Everywhere in the Barkhor monks and children were begging. One urchin, unwashed since birth and clearly malnourished, grabbed Maria's hand and refused to let go even after I gave her some money. It was a signal for two others to come and cling to the same arm, a situation resolved only by the intervention of several adults. The monks usually begged in groups and sat chanting scriptures on the floor, their collection boxes in front of them. As monks they begged not for themselves, but for funds to run and restore their monasteries, since the Chinese government which destroyed them brick by brick in the first place remains loath to fund repairs except on the most touristed routes, and even then is limited in what it gives. It seemed perverse that the Buddhist food round should be unacceptable to Communist theory, while the monks were forced to take to the streets anyway to beg for money, contrary to their own religious laws.

Further on, as Maria fiddled with some curious articles on another stall, a man very innocently began playing with her hand, reaching out for it and giggling every time she reached out for various objects. We were already aware of certain salient features in Tibetan humour, that it was strongly spontaneous with a large element of physical teasing, and this fitted the established pattern. Maria looked up at him and smiled.

'I am Khampa,' he said proudly, though his hair was short and without the plaits wound tight on the head and run through with red silk that would normally have identified him as such.

'Then where's your hair?' asked Maria, jocularly.

With the speed of a bubble bursting his smile vanished, and he looked down.

'The Chinese cut it,' he replied. 'I was arrested. In demonstration. I'm sorry.'

And with that apology, the mood having changed to sadness in a moment, he too went away, becoming lost in the circle of pilgrims.

Towards the end of the circuit, workmen were pulling down several centuries-old Tibetan-style houses in order to build a department store. This was what Hal had been speaking about – a plan to transform Lhasa from a Tibetan to a Chinese city by the year 2000. The destruction and construction was largely ignored by the crowd, perhaps because it had been going on for months. And then, as we stood and stared at this unrequested imposition, the most obscene impression of all forced itself into view. Thirty armed and jackbooted *Wu Jing*, the Chinese military police responsible for all Tibet's massacres, appeared stamping deliberately and determinedly in the opposite direction, three abreast and ten deep, rifles held diagonally across their chests, forcing the Tibetans to the sides. This, we thought, had to be the ultimate symbol of Tibet's occupation, the fully intentional counter-clockwise circumambulation by armed troops of its holiest shrine.

We stared open-mouthed at the sight, and at the Tibetans. One may have expected more visible anger. With armed police pointing rifles at them from rooftops and stamping the wrong way around their holiest shrine just to antagonise, with their own city being repopulated with Chinese to the extent that the Tibetans are a minority in their own land, with their own houses being dismantled before their eyes in order to build department stores to serve the Chinese with Chinese goods, with their own living area being reduced to a 'quarter' in their own capital, never mind the enormity of the past and the regularity of present arrests, tortures and disappearances, it would have been surprising to say the least had the atmosphere been remotely good. Things had moved on since the window of liberalisation in the early 1980s, when tourists had first been allowed in. Things then had been all simmering, under-the-surface resentment. Since then there had been the disturbances of 1987-9, the demonstrations which still continued, the programme of demolition; things were more open now, old wounds were raw again. Yet to say one could have cut the atmosphere with a knife would suggest that it was highly charged. The peculiar thing is that it was not. Rather, a blunt heaviness hung over Lhasa like a pall. People, we felt, were not resigned to a future like this, but they were resigned to the present – it was just that the time had not yet come. A whole tidal wave of emotion lay waiting a breach in the dam.

And we felt – numb. The numbness was a way of dealing with what we were seeing. Perhaps the Tibetans felt numb, too. It was, I supposed, a state of permanent shock. When we tried to dispel the numbness, it was anger that appeared. We looked at the current of devoted pilgrims, the platoon of troops cleaving a passage against their flow, and there came the intimation that we were witnessing nothing less than the very nakedness of the human spirit. We had seen the human spirit naked before, in pictures of course, but never before our eyes. Jesus on the cross was one, Auschwitz survivors another. And the stories! We had heard so many of them but the real subject matter, the real nature of what we were hearing, had never sunk in until now – prisoners of conscience, victims of tribal wars, South America's 'disappeared' . . . Everywhere there is oppression, the human spirit is without clothes, and perhaps that is why we look away.

Informed by the hotel staff that we were in time for the Autumn Bathing Festival, we made a diversion through the small maze of side-streets to the Kyichu river, the Brahmaputra tributary that runs across the south of the city. We arrived at a bridge, and over it the southern banks and little sand-islands of the Kyichu contained hundreds of picnicking Tibetan families, sheets spread out on the ground beneath them, some strung up as shades to deflect the heat of the sun. The Tibetan love of picnicking is legendary and, as we threaded our way through to a spot at the water's edge, no-one ignored us, everyone looked up and smiled, and returned our *tashi deleks*. In the river itself, naked children splashed and played. Young and old women ritually bathed, the old careless of their exposure as if, while younger ladies guarded their bodies like jewels, the older ones knew their depreciated value and no longer bothered with false modesties. Two topless old ladies near us, laughing as if quite alone, wrung out their long black hair. Half a dozen children, their bronze bodies gleaming in the water, jumped and dived and fell from logs, and smiled to catch our eyes.

But there was no getting away from the oppression, even here on a festival day. Prominently, in the middle of the river in a boat, three uniformed policemen sat and ostentatiously fished. To Tibetans, the Kyichu river itself is holy, and on the grounds that eating fish requires the taking of many lives whereas the eating of yaks requires fewer, eating fish is especially contrary to religious sensitivities. To us this seemed not clumsy ignorance, but a deliberate flaunting of power.

'The Chinese have been in Tibet long enough to know what upsets the Tibetans,' Maria reflected, sadly. 'Upsetting them can only be done by design, not by accident.'

To make matters worse, we had a tail already. A young Tibetan in jeans and black leather jacket was squatting on the other side of a bush, about three yards from us, looking at us periodically, chewing gum. Born after the annexation, he would not have known any other Tibet. Perhaps he was from the countryside, one of many brought in to spy on the townsfolk by the lure of cash and privilege. We glared at him. He remained cocky, chewing. He was the only person there alone.

Unperturbed by his presence, or perhaps not seeing him, a family on the other side of us, smiling constantly in our direction, sent their little boy over to give us a piece of cheese. We had heard about Tibetan cheese. Hovering excitedly, the child gave us each a square. It looked like thousand-year-old camembert.

'*Thukjichay*,' we said, and put it in our mouths.

The boy giggled, and ran back. The cheese he had left us with was rock hard, literally. We wondered what to do with it, and sucked with difficulty on its large and awkward shape. Here was contrast again. Tibetan bathers, Chinese anglers. On one side the plain-clothes policeman, on the other, the friendly family. Innocent of the tragic play in its embrace, the air was soft, comfortable and warm. We were still aware of how its thinness seemed to accentuate the light, made objects stand out, the air itself seem bright. In front of us the sun refracted on the frolicking children and the river's gentle waves like mirrors in a desert. We sucked away at the cheese, as unsuccessfully as on a stone. From the corners of our eyes we became aware of the family speaking to their child, cajoling him jokingly into further action. He returned and stood between us and the river, fidgeting with his fingers, embarrassed but trying to be brave. We looked up at him, smiling our own encouragement. His mouth twitched as he looked to us, his parents and back again, until eventually he got out his lines, the strange words his parents had given him to say.

'I – like – you,' he said in a measured and monotone English. And before his shyness finally overcame him and drove him back to his parents at a rush, he found the courage to say the words again: '*I like you!*'

Nakedness of spirit, it seemed, was all around, and it was not a trick of the air.

Returning to the Barkhor, the flirtatious trinket-sellers were there to cheer us up. Extraordinarily extrovert by nature, these Khammo, or women from Kham, wear the most eye-catching turquoise head-dresses, and cover their *chubas* with necklaces, brooches and bangles of silver, turquoise and coral. Like their Khampa menfolk they are strikingly good-looking, but turn their backs upon sight of a camera. Because it is done with humour, not with the purely mercantile intensity of hawkers elsewhere in Asia, it is a pleasure to be clustered around and followed for yards as they repeatedly yell, 'How much this?' while thrusting first one thing and then another under one's nose. Even when they know they will not make a sale they continue, making of it one big game. Now, as we were busily shaking our heads, one of the Khammo, pretending to lose patience, cupped her hand under one of her breasts and thrust it towards me.

'How much this?' she asked wickedly, causing her companions to roar with laughter.

I raised my eyebrows, stroked my chin and examined the item closely.

'Oh – two thousand dollars,' I assured her, with all the seriousness I could muster.

'Two thousand dollars!' she exclaimed, taken aback, then quickly put her other hand under her other breast and thrust them both in my direction.

'Take two!' she exclaimed again.

The contrast of such playfulness with our inner sense of foreboding, with platoons of fresh-faced, freshly arrived troops wandering aimlessly around trying to make sense of their new location, was acutely felt. It did take us aback to find the Tibetans so humorous, when their circumstances were so dire. We were to learn that humour is their way of dealing with suffering, yet it is also evidence of a great strength of spirit and the main reason why they have not been crushed. It did not seem a coincidence that the Tibetans, the Vietnamese and the Jews, who between them have had more than their share of the world's suffering, should all share this quality of humour. That it was expressed so warmly towards us was also a sign of the value they attribute to the Western presence, for so long as we are there, they are neither forgotten, nor invisible to the outside world.

Longing for the Landlord's Daughter

SEEN FROM THE FOOT OF the muddy slopes of Red Hill, the red and white, inwardly leaning walls of the Potala loom as sharply as the cliffs of Dover – only seemingly higher, more definitively awesome, as if they were designed to house a god, the switchback stairways to heaven leading to someone who lived in the clouds and need never come down. A thousand-roomed wonder of the world, built without a nail in a country without the wheel, the Potala is one of the greatest achievements of human architectural endeavour.

Construction had begun during the reign of the 'Great Fifth' Dalai Lama, Ngawang Lobsang Gyatso (1617–82), who was great not only in his writings and scholarship, but in his politics too. By adroitly using Mongolian patronisation of his Geluk school, he managed to keep the Chinese Manchu Dynasty at bay and win acceptance of his authority from all the other Tibetan schools – something which remains unchallenged today. When he died in 1682 however, the Potala was far from complete, and the chain of events that followed was nothing short of bizarre.

His regent, Sangye Gyatso, concealed the news of his death to ensure the will remained to complete the work. Announcing that the Dalai Lama had entered a prolonged retreat, he managed to maintain this deceit, using a monk as a double to stand in at state receptions and make appropriately ritualistic noises in the meditation chamber, for a full thirteen years. Due to his own considerable political acumen, Sangye Gyatso not only survived after revealing the truth to a startled nation, but continued to hold the reins of power for some time to come.

If not all the Dalai Lamas had been Buddha-like, it was Sangye Gyatso's ward, the sixth Dalai Lama Rinchen Tsangyang Gyatso, who was the most obvious exception in his unsuitability for the office. Selected and reared in secret by Sangye Gyatso, who of necessity had been unable to observe the proper procedural formalities of the search or to make full provisions for an appropriate education, the sixth Dalai Lama developed into a lonely prisoner of a figure who grew his hair long and renounced his monastic vows, but was unable by dint of birth to resign his position. Yet the education he received did bequeath him the ability to write, and his poems are among few examples in Tibet of literature being turned to artistic rather than religious purposes. The standard is perhaps not that of the best Chinese or Indian poets, but he certainly had an eye for imagery:

> Over the eastern hill rises
> The smiling face of the moon.
> In my mind forms
> The smiling face of my beloved.

Yet it was hardly the subject matter one would expect to flow from a Dalai Lama's pen:

> People gossip about me.
> I am sorry for what I have done.
> I have taken three thin steps
> And landed myself in the tavern of my mistress.

Most of the time it seems he was destined to be frustrated, for he wrote frequently of unrequited love (or lust):

> Longing for the landlord's daughter,
> Blossoming in youthful beauty,
> Is like pining for peaches
> Ripening on the highest branches.

And well might he have written:

If I could meditate upon the dharma
As intensely as I muse on my beloved,
I would certainly attain enlightenment
In this lifetime.

One could almost imagine his tutors giving him that one as 'lines' to write after classes. I can certainly imagine him looking wistfully over the village of Shol from the windows of his darkened rooms, writing romantic, even erotic poetry about the women he met on the occasions when he managed to sneak out in disguise. Neither was there any secret about his activities, for the prostitutes of Lhasa and Shol sang songs about his visits. Sangye Gyatso despaired of him, and once attempted to assassinate his drinking partner in a bid to stifle his habits. The attempt failed when, during a tavern crawl with a servant, they all swapped clothes and it was the servant who got killed.

As if recognising himself as a political disaster, Tsanyang Gyatso surrendered to the latest wave of Mongolian militarism and died being taken out of Tibet. A wealth of mythologies (he was a tantric master, who did not really die) has arisen from attempts to explain his behaviour, and it must be said that the present Dalai Lama has vouched for his authenticity. As for the regent, he was a master survivor, but he eventually fell foul of the Qoshot Mongolians, who executed him in 1705.

From this time onwards Chinese meddling in Tibetan affairs becomes much more noticeable. The office of the Panchen Lama in Shigatse was cultivated and played against the Lhasa court, while the ninth, tenth, eleventh and twelfth Dalai Lamas all mysteriously died before their majorities. The 'Great Thirteenth' Dalai Lama, Thubten Gyatso (1876–1933), had to expel his own regent to be rid of Chinese interference at court, and went on to guide Tibet through the 'Great Game', the Younghusband disaster (1904), a Chinese invasion (1910) and two resultant exiles, and still had to put up with a foreign power, Britain, taking charge of his foreign affairs.

The reign of the present Dalai Lama, Tenzin Gyatso, who was born in 1935, is the most widely known. When China invaded his homeland in 1950 the law had to be changed to allow him to take office three years early. Just one month later came exile in India, while the collaborator Ngawang Jigme Ngapo, using false government seals forged for the purpose in Beijing, rescinded Tibet's independence in the infamous '17–point Agreement'. Hoping to compromise, Tenzin Gyatso returned to Lhasa in August 1951, but in March 1959, things came to a head.

When word got round that he had been invited to a theatrical performance in an army camp but told to leave his bodyguards behind, thirty thousand Lhasa citizens gathered outside the Summer Palace to prevent his going or being taken. Artillery was drawn up and pointed at them. The Dalai Lama urged them to disperse. They stayed. Two hours before midnight on March 17th, following two contingents of his family who had left an hour or two before him, Tenzin Gyatso took off his glasses, put on layman's clothes, placed a *thangka* of his *yidam* (personal protectress) Palden Lhamo in his backpack, borrowed a rifle from a guard, and slipped unseen through the southern wall of the Norbulingka. At two in the morning on March 20th, believing him still to be inside, the Chinese shelled the Norbulingka, slaughtering the Tibetan infantry and citizens who remained there to protect him. The massacres continued for three days, with the Potala, the Jokhang, Sera monastery and other religious places where people had gathered for refuge being heavily hit. The driving of armoured cars through the ancient doors of the Jokhang and the massacre of the monks, women and children inside finished off the resistance. In three days of fighting, 84,000 people, by Chinese statistics, were killed. In the Norbulingka, bodies were turned over individually to identify the Dalai Lama. In the afternoon of March 31st, suffering from dysentery, he crossed the border into India.

Now, from his base in Dharamsala, India, the Dalai Lama negotiates patiently the terms which may allow him to return to the Potala. It is a one-way negotiation. The Chinese say as they have always said that he is welcome to return to the 'motherland' and live in Beijing. Willingness to accept autonomy rather than independence has produced no fruit. There are those, notably in the Tibetan Youth Congress, who accuse him of being too patient, and the bombs which exploded outside Communist Party Headquarters and a government information building in Lhasa on March 18th and December 25th 1996 were signals from those who feel there is no other way to win, and nothing left to lose. As winner of the 1989 Nobel Peace Prize for his path of *ahimsa* (non-violence), the Dalai Lama pleads that violence can at best produce only short-term gains. But the Tibetan question is entering a new phase; there are plenty more twists and turns to come before a Dalai Lama once again looks down on his people from the high windows of the Potala.

7

RETURNING FROM THE BARKHOR WE climbed the stairs, and I all but collapsed onto the bed. I was having to make a determined effort to breathe deeply, and realised at once the problem.

'Altitude,' I said to Maria.

'But you'd think you'd have acclimatised, coming here by road,' she replied.

But I had not. The sheer shock of the new had kept me going all day. Now, walking up stairs exhausted me.

'A German athlete died of altitude sickness here last year,' said Hal, sticking his head around the door.

'Thanks, very reassuring,' I replied from my bed.

'No, he'd flown in from Kathmandu. He hadn't acclimatised at all. It would have been the best thing to have got straight back on and flown out again, but there wasn't another flight for a few days. They took him in at the Lhasa hospital but they gave him no treatment, only a bed. You'd think they'd have a pressure cabin in Lhasa, wouldn't you? But they did nothing for him. His friends had to run around saying, 'Where's the oxygen?' and feeding him and things. I was here at the time. I remember them coming back each day and telling it all to me. Then he died. They wouldn't allow the body to leave until his parents came and paid the bill. Horrible story.'

Hal invited himself in and sat on the end of my bed. It seemed part of his condition of being unable to relate to people that he failed to notice if their eyes glazed over or that conversation was not two-way;

or, if he did notice, he talked all the more in an effort to win back his audience. However, I reasoned that his present verbosity was probably a way of smoothing over our argument. We had still not forgiven him for that either and, short of an apology, could not. Neither could we bear the relentless intensity of the fellow, the inability to sit back and chat about nothing and make jokes like normal people did. But he was in the room next door, and we had to get on.

'There was a demonstration this morning,' he suddenly volunteered.

'Already?' said Maria. 'We've only been here a day. Did you see it?'

'No, it was in the Norbulingka, but I've got reliable reports. Four monks, two nuns. Two monks got away, the other three were arrested. They were beaten up during their arrest, taken away and beaten up some more. They were seen, covered in blood and bruises, being taken out of the police station and put on a truck to take them to jail.'

'That's terrible,' Maria empathised.

'Stupid, really. They were young, they had all their lives in front of them. Now, if they survive, they could be irreparably damaged by torture and excommunicated from the *sangha*. They'll have nothing left and what will they have achieved? If the news reaches the outside world it'll be a footnote on an inside page. They're too damned romantic, the Tibetans. They seem to think the outside world will come galloping in on white horses to save them, but at the end of the day both our governments care more about money and the Chinese market than human rights and dignity. It's tragic.'

Hal was evidently cut up, and so were we. For all his faults, I thought to myself, his heart was in the right place. I looked at him, sitting on the end of my bed, his hands in his pockets, his ankles crossed, his Bolivian-style hat pointing downwards as he stared at the floor. For a while, no-one spoke.

'What you need is some good food,' Hal said eventually. 'I'm going to the Lhasa Hotel for lunch tomorrow. Want to join me?'

'The Lhasa Hotel?' He was trying to make up, I thought.

'The Tibetans still call it that, and so do I. It's now known as the Holiday Inn, after they bought it out in 1986.'

'I see. Well, you obviously know all the details.'

'I have to.'

'So the food's good, is it?'

'The food's as good as it can be, but the staff, the Western staff, are really pro-Chinese. Any trouble means fewer guests. As far as the Holiday

Inn are concerned, everything would be OK if the Tibetans just shut up and stopped whining. Demonstrations for human rights and against illegal occupation are just bad for business.'

'So why go there?'

'It's a good place to keep my ear to the ground.'

At lunchtime the next day we followed Hal in a rickshaw. The hotel, four kilometres away out by the bus station, was so far from town that no tourist could really feel part of Lhasa at all, let alone mix with any Tibetans. From the Chinese point of view, this was convenient. Tourists could be herded from tour to tour with little chance of them straying from official eyes.

Hal led us through the maze of long corridors to the dining hall. Although a large quantity of food was set out, it was early and the huge room was almost deserted. We paid the Chinese cashier, and inspected the buffet. There was no vegetarian option, so we piled rice and boiled vegetables onto our plates. When we discovered that all the Tibetan restaurants in town were beset by beggars – mostly children but also adults who would come right in and stare at the food as one consumed it, all the bulging eyes, extended stomachs and rickets of Bangladesh in the middle of Lhasa – we would never quite feel comfortable eating in the Holiday Inn again.

We sat down. The waitresses, Maria observed to Hal, were all Tibetan, whereas the desk staff had all been Chinese.

'Deliberate,' he replied. 'They can't trust the Tibetans, and having them as waitresses gives the tourists a more "authentic experience", so at least they can go home saying they've seen one. Mind you, they used to dress Chinese women in Tibetan clothes and pin Tibetan names on their chests, but since people weren't so stupid as to be unable to tell a bronze face from a yellow one, they stopped it. Not only that, but some of the desk staff are really PSB. A few of the rooms are bugged, you see, so when a foreign journalist comes, the police make sure they get the right rooms.'

We finished our vegetables and returned with two trays piled high with fruit, chocolate cake and coffee. Maria, taking milk, was unable to find a teaspoon.

'There aren't any,' said Hal.

'What? Can't they get them?'

'Oh, they can get them. I told you, they can get anything. Only there's no point in bothering. The staff "liberate" them, you see. After the first batch had all gone they decided not to replace them any more. This must be the only hotel of its class in the world without teaspoons. Ironic, really, when you consider they wanted a hotel run by staff who hadn't learnt all the bad habits, like screaming at the guests, that get on your nerves in Chinese hotels.'

Hal, happy in his role as educator, was at his least intense. It was even pleasant to be with him when he was like this. All bulged out on chocolate cake, we went to town on the coffee, and I felt my strength returning.

'This is better than our last meal together, Hal.'

He glanced at me sourly, ungrateful for my bringing it up. It was my instinct to talk about things to smooth them over, but I had forgotten, in his present expansive mood, that he had little humour and even less insight.

'Yeah. Well.'

I spoke quickly. 'I suppose this place is more interesting later on.'

'Yup. At the moment the packages are out. But you'll speak to some people here who'll make you squirm, who are here because it's hip and obscure and gives them something to brag about with their home movies, and they don't care shit about the Tibetans.'

'Those people are pretty interesting,' said Maria, pointing.

I turned around. Behind me a gang of a dozen youths in leather jackets and jeans were strutting to a table in the corner, their plates piled high with the fruits of their privilege, swanking and swaggering even with each other. One or two were Chinese, most were Tibetan. I thought I recognised one of them.

'Isn't that the one who followed us at the river?'

Maria agreed. A mountain of food on his tray, he had not yet taken out his gum.

'This joint reminds me of Rick's bar in *Casablanca* sometimes,' said Hal. 'They're police alright. Such a give-away isn't it – the clothes, the behaviour? Only yesterday I was having coffee in the rooftop café and one of them was leaning towards me, trying to overhear what I was saying. Eating here is one of their perks.'

'A canteen for the police? I wonder how the Holiday Inn can justify it?' Maria mused.

Hal flinched a little, paused, placed both hands on the white tablecloth and glared patronisingly at her. 'The hotel is part-owned, you see,' he replied slowly. 'It's a joint venture between the British company Bass Plc, which owns Holiday Inn, and the Chinese government. OK? Now, when profits are at stake who cares about human rights, meals for the secret police or prisons full of tortured Tibetans? Why invest here at all? It's not the most ethical of companies, in my opinion.'

The meal over, Hal lit one of his bigger cigars. I looked at it, wondering how on earth he had room in his rucksack for clothes. He sat back, sighed and coughed a little, and toyed with the crumbs on his plate. A Tibetan waitress came over and refilled our cups.

'You wait until we get closer to the 27th,' Hal began, playing the wise man again. 'One year, I tell you, we had curfews, were confined to the hotel, the lot. They put guards on the gates at six in the morning. I used to go out at five-thirty to avoid them, and stay on the streets all day. Then one day – and they caught me in – they just trundled a bus to the front door, gave everyone half an hour to get on it, and drove us all straight back to Golmud. The city authorities may have different attitudes to the TAR, but when the pressure is on them, they have to act.' Another plume of smoke rose towards the chandeliers. 'Have you seen the Potala yet?'

'We're going now.'

'I wouldn't waste any more time or you might just leave without seeing it. I'm telling you, they can make things very difficult for us if they want to. You just wait.'

We headed towards the Potala, unsure whether Hal's counsel to see it without delay was more wisdom than hysteria. In front of the rugged outcrop of rock on which it was built, a queue of Tibetans and Chinese waited eagerly to enter a museum. They were kept in line by regular Chinese police with batons, who even climbed on the wall above them to lash out here and there. One young policeman, no more than twenty, grabbed an elderly Tibetan peasant by the scruff of his animal skin overcoat, and shook him about, smiling. The man looked terrified. When the youth saw us looking, he stopped. The people were queuing, we had been told, to see the ill-gotten gains of the daughter of the mayor of Lhasa, who had abused her position to embezzle millions of *yuan* from CAAC. Her house, apparently, had resembled a palace, but now she was in jail – her father's influence still useful in not having her shot – and her house had been transferred to the museum so that everyone could see her spoils. It was a popular exhibition, unfortunately closed to foreigners, and the police ushered us gently away.

Around the corner, on the lower slopes on which the palace of the Dalai Lamas stood, the ancient Tibetan village of Shol was in the process of demolition, what houses remained being converted into souvenir shops for tourists or turned over to Chinese artists to use as studios. The destruction of Shol was a keenly felt tragedy for the citizens of Lhasa, in whose hearts it had held a special place. In earlier times, those who lived there had counted themselves blessed to live under the gaze of the Dalai Lama, the nearest thing to a living Buddha, who could see, and presumably in doing so bless, their houses from his window above.

In anticipatory mood, we arrived at the large metal cage that let people in from two sides. A crowd of Tibetans stood miserably around it, their faces conveying their feelings, and they waved their hands angrily at us. We could go no further. The Potala was closed.

Mystified, we wondered what to do. Reasoning that the Potala could not be closed to the package tourists who had paid serious money for at best a few days in the city, we walked around the Lingkhor, the 'outer wheel' path for circumambulating the Potala. At the rear we found the road the Chinese had built to drive buses up Red Hill to the Potala's back door, and attached ourselves to a group of middle-aged Austrians. Having smuggled ourselves into Lhasa, it now seemed we would have to smuggle ourselves into the Potala, too.

A retired couple welcomed us, doubting their guides would even notice our addition. 'Two are absolute liars and spend their time trying to avoid us,' said the man as we began to climb up the hill. 'The third speaks no English and is completely useless.'

The woman complained bitterly in her rich, gravelly accent. 'We've seen the police in the Barkhor,' she said. 'All those shields and helmets and rifles. It makes me so *sad*, it is like the Second World War, the Tibetans in their own land are like the Jews in Europe. Don't they think they've done *enough* to the Tibetan people?' And then she added, in words that deserved to be writ large all over the Temple of Heavenly Peace in Tienanmen: '*If they'd only been nice to them for the last forty years, the Tibetans wouldn't be objecting so much to Chinese rule now.*'

It was funny how complicated problems could be reduced to piercingly simple truths.

'I feel so *sorry* for the Tibetans,' said the man again. 'I hope they *do* demonstrate on the 27th and the 1st and the world actually *does* something.'

We arrived at the top, and began to shuffle around in a room of near darkness. As our eyes adjusted to the light it became evident that the Potala, which is not only a palace but also the Namgyal monastery, was more interesting from the outside, for what was missing was more striking than what was on show. There were no Tibetans, no monks except for a few checking camera permits, no antiquities except for a few *chortens*, and of course no Dalai Lama. It certainly did not warrant a second visit, and with only ten rooms open, an hour was comfortably enough, unless one wanted to examine the minute detail of every mural, or to enjoy futile exchanges with programmed android tour guides.

'Why's a photograph so expensive?' the Austrian man asked one of the three guides, pointing at the *Fifty Yuan* sign for photos taken without a permit.

'Money goes to restoration,' she replied.

'Chinese did the damage. Why should foreigners pay?'

Good for you, I thought. The guide looked only about twenty, and was probably a high-flier to land this job. She exuded the air of thinking the same thing herself.

'Damage was done a long time ago. In Cultural Revolution.'

This was actually a lie; as the Dalai Lama himself complains: 'It is never said that the majority of the destruction was carried out long before the Cultural Revolution.' But this was our friend's argument, and I let him continue.

'Yes, by Chinese people,' he persisted.

'Cultural Revolution wasn't our fault. It was accident.'

'*Accident!* The Cultural Revolution was a bloody accident!' He exploded, reddening, the words coming from his lips like a gale. I realised she meant 'mistake', which is the official term for it. Probably her English was too poor to distinguish the nuance of difference.

'It was fault of Gang of Four,' came the stock, programmed response.

'Four people destroyed six thousand temples? They must have been very busy!' He looked at me. 'Don't you think?'

'Very busy,' I chimed in on his side. 'Four people, all those temples . . .'

The guide shut up. I wondered if she was wondering how she had been drawn into an argument with a foreigner against her training, or whether these arguments happened all the time with the intelligent tourists, and were taken as part of the job.

'I wonder what her parents did,' he said to me.

'Ask her,' his wife suggested, feeling no sympathy for the android whatsoever.

'Excuse me. What did your parents do during the Cultural Revolution?'

There was an intake of breath, and she moved away to the front of the group.

'Good for you,' his wife punched him on the arm. 'These people have no *conscience*. They just don't see that what they did was wrong, or that what they *are* doing is wrong. They are *brainwashed*. Brainwashed, brainwashed, brainwashed.'

Our tour group may have been astute, but this was by no means a feature of all the package tourists in Lhasa. Detaching ourselves from the friendly Austrians, we trooped independently but dejectedly from one ransacked room to another. Entering one room to find an elderly couple alone with their guide, a lama having just left by another door, we began to consider that some tourists and their guides almost deserved each other.

'He's a *most learned* lama,' the guide was saying. 'He spent a year in Beijing.'

'Yeah,' drawled the man. He was wearing checked trousers and a tweed jacket, and carried a huge video camera with a bulbous microphone. They cast cursory glances over the murals.

'Is this the monastery that was bombed?' he asked the guide.

'Who'd wanna bomb a monashtery?' replied the wife. She was frail but boisterous, and heavily made-up. I wondered why her plaster failed to crack when she talked.

'The Chinese of course.'

'*Why* would they wanna bomb a monashtery?' She exasperated him.

'Because they're commies, honey, and commies don't like religion.' 'Oh.'

Well, that was good enough. She could understand that. We hurried into the next room to get away from them, but they caught us up.

'Is the Dah-lai Lama a Yellow Hat or a Red Hat?' the man asked.

The guide looked perplexed. 'He wore a gold hat.'

'So what'sh with the hat? What differensh did the colour make?' rejoined the wife.

'Because you can tell what school he belonged to.'

'Like Yale or Harvard?'

'I mean what branch of the *Church*. They either wore red hats or yellow hats – but our friend here wouldn't know about it.'

'I haven't sheen any hatsh,' said the wife.

'That's because they only get them out for ceremoanies, honey,' the man explained, emphasising the third syllable. 'And the Chinese won't let them have any ceremoanies.'

'Oh,' said the wife.

'That throne is pure gold,' the guide proclaimed, pointing and trying to deflect the subject. It was clearly nothing of the sort.

'Gold? What gold? I don't shee any gold,' said the woman sarcastically, in the loudest of voices.

'If they're brought up in China, honey,' the husband explained peaceably, 'they probably don't know what gold looks like.'

'Oh.'

This man has a remarkable facility for satisfying his wife, I thought to myself.

'It probably was gold once,' I offered, butting in. 'I expect they've replaced it.'

'We've had enough of this,' said the man, shrugging the back of his left hand at their guide, as if he was not worth the effort of even pointing at properly. 'Everything that's yellow he says is gold. Next he'll be telling us the Dalai Lama's lavatory bowl is solid ivory.'

Halfway round we discovered the souvenir room and, sitting down for a break, found ourselves next to the gentle Pico Iyer. We had already met in the rooftop café overlooking the Jokhang square, when we had caught his wistful, Indian face gazing amusedly at two women picking nits from each other's hair below. Gentleness was his most radiant quality, and he moved about Lhasa with a quiet, sensitive affection. Humility was another aspect of his character, for despite a long conversation about the British education system, it was not until we later read his first book, *Video Night in Kathmandu*, that we discovered he was educated at Eton, Oxford and Harvard. Now, he was on a one-person tour with expenses paid by his publishers, who wanted him to write a book on the Potala for a series on ten great buildings of the world. We accompanied him as he examined this and that, peered here and there, but given the unrepaired destruction that was visible through the gaps in the many padlocked doors, he doubted he would be granted much access. Stepping into the sunlight on the Potala's famous switchback outer staircase, we commented that although the Potala was also a monastery, there had been a remarkable absence of monks.

'I know the answer to that,' said Pico, squeezing his guide's shoulder. 'It would seem I'm unique in Lhasa for having a pleasant and informative guide. Everyone at the Holiday Inn is complaining about theirs. Apparently there was a demonstration yesterday, and today all the monks are confined to quarters.'

I looked at the guide. 'Is that why the Potala is closed to Tibetans today?'

The girl, Chinese, smiled meekly but turned around, staring over the destruction of Shol far below us. A workteam had moved in, and the rhythmic thud of their sledgehammers rose upwards in the air.

'Yes,' said Pico quietly, as one confirming a secret. 'She told me that earlier. It's a punishment.'

A rare breath of wind blew, and her hair lifted a little off her collar as she half turned around. 'I like the Tibetan people,' she said. 'China hasn't always done good. I hope in the future there will be peace, and they will be happy.'

'Do other guides feel like you?' Maria enquired, touched.

Again she did not answer. A cloud of dust erupted below as another wall in Shol fell down. Pico spoke for her.

'She's being careful. I've found it takes a while to build up trust. But she's bright and good-natured, and it takes both those qualities in abundance to withstand the propaganda in their training. Perhaps that's why she's so rare.'

'*As rare as a star in daytime*,' I said. 'Old Tibetan simile.'

Back at the hotel there was good news and bad news. The good news was that people had begun arriving from Chengdu *with permits*, after a minor PSB station had begun issuing them at whim. Our numbers in the Yak had already doubled. Six had arrived that morning alone, having simply shown their permits to CAAC in Chengdu, bought tickets, got off the plane and taken a local bus into Lhasa. According to them there was some confusion at the airport on arrival, but the authorities had let them go.

The bad news was that the apparent liberalisation of policy in Chengdu coincided with a tightening of the screws in Lhasa. A Tibetan, too careless in expressing his views, had been overheard talking over lunch with two of the hotel guests. The police arrested the man as soon as he left, and the news filtered quickly back from other witnesses. The Western couple, two Canadians, were inconsolable, and blamed themselves for the arrest.

'Serves you right,' said Hal to their faces. 'You come here full of naivety and blunder about like a bull in a china shop, then wonder why things get broken. Ptah!' He snorted maliciously, turning to us as the woman burst into tears and her boyfriend led her away. 'Don't people realise before they come here that this is a totalitarian state with a fear of foreigners and that you can't just start talking to people without putting them in danger?'

Thus the joy that was felt at people beginning to get through from Chengdu was muted, and everyone became cautious. It seemed that Hal's prediction of accumulating awkwardness was already beginning to come true, and perhaps there was worse to come.

One morning, the police came to the hotel. A high-ranking policeman usually came in the evening to receive beer and a chat from the hotel manager, but this was the morning and this was different. They wanted a list of the names and nationalities of the guests. The sensitive anniversary dates were fast approaching. There had already been one demonstration, and also a number of fliers pasted on walls and dropped in the Barkhor calling for protest. It was important to the police, believing our presence was linked to the troubles, to keep tabs on who was here, and on our movements. We were followed that morning as we strolled around the Barkhor, by a Chinese man in a fawn jacket, and the armed patrols were noticeably increased.

Over the next few days, the expected numbers of new faces from Chengdu did not materialise. According to the six who had just arrived that way, this was mysterious. They had permits, and they had tickets. Plainly, that loophole had been somehow closed off. In Lhasa, the air remained tense. All the stalls which normally traded in front of the Jokhang had been cleared away since the last major demonstration. This was ominous. As the anniversary of the 1987 uprising grew closer, everyone without exception felt uneasy, as if something was about to burst the dam.

One evening, just as midnight was turning, we heard deep Chinese voices outside our door, followed by a loud and unsettling knock. We looked at each other. Maria threw some clothes on and went to answer it, while I stayed in bed and shivered as the cold night air blew in.

'Good evening. Can I see your passports?' The two high-ranking Chinese policemen were nothing if not polite, and the leader possessed the irony of a detectably upper-class accent. Maria handed them over, and they wrote down our details.

'When are you leaving?'

'One or two weeks,' Maria lied.

'You should leave in a few days.'

'Why?'

'I'm ordered to tell you to leave in a few days.'

'Why?'

'Those are my orders.'

'Can we go to Shigatse and come back?'

'Yes.' He smiled. 'What are you doing tomorrow?'

'Sightseeing. Why?'

'I'd like to invite you to some singing and dancing on Jaramalingka Island. There'll be free food and tea, and a bus to pick you up at nine. It will be a jolly good show.'

'I see.'

'Well, goodnight. We're sorry to disturb you.'

They disappeared, and we heard them knock next on Hal and Akio's door. Hal was, predictably, more obstreperous. We could hear them arguing – or at least Hal arguing, and the police keeping their cool.

'What d'you mean, *should* leave?'

'We're telling you you should leave.'

'You're not telling us we *must* leave?'

'No, I'm telling you you should leave.'

'And you can't give us a reason?'

'Those are my orders . . .'

The police made their way along the verandah and through the rest of the hotel. When they had gone, Hal, Akio, Gary and Jackie, a couple from Bristol recently arrived, and several others came into our room to compare notes and sat on the edges of our beds. Today was the 17th. We had been told to leave 'in a few days'. Hal, Akio and most others had been told to leave by the 22nd. Gary and Jackie had been given the 20th. This was a ridiculously woolly approach to such a high-level agenda as clearing individual foreigners out of Lhasa.

'A few years ago they just put us all on a bus and didn't let us out until we got to Golmud,' Hal reminded us for the umpteenth time. 'They're saying we should go, not that we must go, so this time they're being nice about it, trying to get us to go of our own free will, or at least reduce our numbers. To a Chinese that *would* be an order and they would do it, even though it was phrased as a polite request. They still don't appreciate that as a culture we have a different reaction to orders.'

'It's tomorrow that worries me,' said Gary. 'They're obviously planning something and want us out of the way.'

'You bet,' said Hal, fuming. 'When did the Chinese ever give anything away free? And you've seen how the stalls have gone from in front of the Jokhang? All those people have been told they can't work, and I don't suppose they'll be back until after October 1st. They're planning to go in and shoot people, making it real easy for themselves.'

'Why should they plan it for tomorrow?' I asked.

Hal looked at me superciliously, as to someone who really ought to know more. 'Tomorrow's the thirtieth day of the Tibetan month, a holy day, and the last holy day before the 27th. They must have strong grounds for expecting trouble or they wouldn't go to these lengths.'

'Well I'm not going to any song and dance show,' said Jackie.

'There's a special ceremony tomorrow in the Jokhang,' Hal continued. 'I think we should go to it *en masse* and show a bit of solidarity, and if anything does happen, we'll be there to get the news out.'

Everyone agreed, except Maria and I, too conscious of Hal's persuasive personality and too dubious of his amateur bravura.

'What about not getting involved?' I said, reminding him of some contrary pearls of wisdom he had uttered a few days before.

'Don't go then, if you're afraid,' he snapped nastily, sending his words out on seek-and-destroy missions as usual when he sensed opposition. 'Hell, look, if there're no witnesses, nothing's happened. We can't run the other way.'

'I agree with that,' I replied, 'but it seems stupid for us all to be together in one place. We'd be so easy to round up and we wouldn't be able to cover such a wide area. Wouldn't it be much better if everyone did their own thing, but bore it in mind to stay near the Jokhang?'

Hal bristled at the use of the word stupid to describe his idea. 'You do your own thing. I'll be real happy if you're not with us. It doesn't seem stupid to me that if we're all there in a block it will make a shooting less likely to happen.'

'It didn't before,' I reminded him, thinking of 1987 when Westerners had been present and a Dutch woman had been shot. 'I don't see why it should now. It could inflame the situation. If a demonstration starts they'll go in scattering people about anyway, and if it's a big one with flags they'll use guns whether we're there or not. We can hardly protect a demonstration, can we?'

'And what about the hotel staff?' said Maria. 'They'll be accountable if any of us is considered 'involved'. They may even be accountable if we don't go on this picnic.'

'Sure,' said Hal, controlling his anger and finding Maria easier than me to talk to. 'But balance the two things against each other. If we go on the picnic like good little children doing what we're told, there'll be no witnesses. What's more important? If the hotel staff spend a year in jail and news of another Tienanmen gets out, they'll think it the best year of their lives.'

It was Hal's way with words that made him so unlikeable, I thought, as he stalked out in a fit of pique, taking some of the more easily led ones with him. Gary and Jackie, who were already referring to Hal as '007', agreed with us, to stay close to the Barkhor but not as one large and provocative group, and went to bed. It was not easy to sleep, between stewing over our adverse reaction to Hal's personality and worrying about what tomorrow might bring for the citizens of Lhasa. In addition, we could still hear Hal in ranting mode through the walls.

'Some people don't listen to sense!' we could hear from the back of his room.

'Don't listen to reason!' came from the front as he paced up and down.

'I've been coming here for years, I *know* this situation. They just turn up first time and think they know everything!'

Silence.

'What can you do?'

Silence.

'Let them go their own way, I don't care!'

Silence.

'When I was here before, they brought a coach to the front and rounded us all up . . .'

Silence.

'D'you think Akio's in there?' I said to Maria.

'Hard to tell . . . It wouldn't surprise me if he was talking to the walls . . .'

We lay on our beds in the dark, eyes open, and waited for the storm to pass.

The Preciousness of Human Birth

IN THE BEGINNING WAS THE void. In the void there arose a wind, and the wind filled the void. The wind became full and swollen, and took the form of a double thunderbolt from which came clouds, and from the clouds came rain. Each raindrop contained enough water to fill a lake, and it rained for many years until a great ocean was formed. When the ocean was complete the wind moved again on its surface, whipping up the waves and stirring the tides. The ocean gave forth a cream-like foam which became thicker and thicker until it was solid, and in this way the earth was formed.

In the centre of the earth there arose a great mountain, Rirab Lhunpo, made of precious stones, of gold and silver, turquoise, coral and lapis lazuli. The top of the mountain is the best, the richest, the abode of the gods, but inhabiting the lower levels are the demi-gods, always fighting and squabbling to climb higher, for even on Rirab Lhunpo there is greed. The great mountain has four sides pointing North, South, East and West. Each side looks over seven great lakes and seven circles of smaller mountains to one of four lower lands, and the gods on the four sides at the top of the mountain are the rulers of the lands they face. Outside it all is Chi Gyatso, the outer ocean, about which little is known, for it is where only bad people go, when it is time to die.

The eastern world, Lo Phag, has the shape of a half-moon, and its people have moon-like faces. They live for five hundred years on the rice and vegetables they farm and, though they know not violence and do have some beliefs, they have no real religion. The western world, Balang Cho, has the shape of the sun and its people have sun-like faces. They live for five hundred years on the milk, butter and cheese that comes from their cattle. Though they are a strong people they too are disinclined to fight, but have no real religion. The northern world, Dra Minyen, is furthest from our own. The land is square and the people have square faces, and they live for a thousand years. In Dra Minyen no-one works, for food of all kinds miraculously appears, and the people who live there have all manner of riches. There is no violence and happiness is total – until it is time to die. In Dra Minyen, seven days before death a voice is heard, telling them they are going to die. The body begins to smell and no-one wants to know them, and the voices in the ears speak eagerly of the horrors that await the sloughing of the body. There is also no religion in Dra Minyen, and because there is no religion the people can do nothing to prepare themselves for what cannot be postponed.

And then there is our world, the southern world of Dzambu Lying. When our world was made there was a *prakcha* tree growing in a river, and when the fruit of the tree ripened and fell, it made a sound like 'dzambu!' The water spirits who ate the fruit shat pure gold, and although no-one knows any more the whereabouts of the tree, this explains why there is gold in our land.

At the beginning of things the beings who lived in Dzambu Lying were gods, who were reincarnated away from Rirab Lhunpo on account of their deeds. Being gods they did not need to work, and helped themselves to fruit from the trees between periods of meditation. But one day one of the gods noticed a kind of cream lying on the surface of the earth. Eating it, he found that it was good. He told the other gods about it, and soon all were eating the cream in preference to the other foods. They did not notice that the more they ate the more their powers and their lives reduced, and when all the cream had gone they were not gods any more, but human beings. That is how we came to be.

When we human beings appeared, at first we ate a plant called *myugu*. Each of us had our own *myugu* plant, and each day our own plant would produce one fruit, which was enough. Then one day, one person's plant produced two fruits, and he ate them both. The next day however, the plant did not produce at all, and being hungry he stole the fruit of his neighbour.

That person, finding no fruit on his plant, stole someone else's, and in this way stealing evolved, and the work of farming became necessary.

Worse was to come. While we still bore the male shape of the gods we once were, one man found his private parts were itching him, and tore them from his body. In this way women were made. Childbirth followed, which led to overpopulation. Instead of being kind, people looked to their own needs. Fighting came, and to save themselves from extermination the people elected a king, Mang Kur. He taught us to build houses and have our own land, so that each should know where his own property ended and his neighbour's began. We owe a big debt to Mang Kur, though old age, sickness, death, work and crime remain the lot of those who are born in our world.

Yet we must always remember our world is the best, because we have religion. In Dra Minyen, people may be perfectly happy for a thousand years less seven days, but will never become enlightened. First they are too happy to think about such things, then too terrified by what is suddenly upon them. Without suffering, there cannot be compassion. It would never need to arise. Without compassion there is no teaching of the Buddha, no drive to improve ourselves and help others. In our world, the balance of things allows us to think and reflect. That is why our world is the best.

Inside the southern world of Dzambu Lying, lies the land of Bod (Tibet). Of all Dzambu Lying's lands and kingdoms, Bod is the highest, and most blessed. We know it is the most blessed because the people of Bod are more religious than anywhere else, and there are so many religious teachers, even *bodhisattvas* living among us. Some people think this is because the people of Bod are descended from *bodhisattvas*.

A long, long time ago, when Dzambu Lying was still under water, the water level began to fall. The tips of mountains began to show through first, and this was our land. The land of Bod was first to be revealed to the air. It was, and is, a beautiful land, and everyone who lives there appreciates it. We have never taken the beauty of Bod for granted. When Bod appeared the mountains and the valleys grew rich with grass and wild flowers, and ran with clear silver water. In the morning warmth the dew would glisten and dazzle upon the colour-speckled carpets of the valleys, and in the evening cold the moon would rise and give light to the clouds and mountains. Such a land was home to many kinds of spirits, both good and bad, but as yet there were no people.

Chenrezig, the Lord of Compassion, chose the land of Bod as a most suitable place for meditation, though at the time he also chose to take the form of a monkey, with the name of Trehu. Trehu found a cave for himself on Mount Konpori, which today is above the town of Tsetang in the Yarlung Valley. He took a vow of celibacy, and passed day after day in silent contemplation. Nearby however, there lived a cannibal ogress, Tag Senmo, who was in reality the *bodhisattva* Droma. Tag Senmo was lonely, and began to disturb Trehu's meditation with plaintive songs and loud tears. Motivated by compassion, Trehu rushed to see whatever was the matter. Tag Senmo told him of her loneliness, and begged him to live with her and become her husband, but Trehu had taken a vow of celibacy, and vows are not to be broken. Driven again by compassion, Trehu went to the Potala where Chenrezig lived. Chenrezig gave him permission to end his retreat and cancel his vow, out of compassion for Tag Senmo. Thus it was that they were married, and the fruit of the union of the monkey and the ogress was six children, one from each of the six realms of the Buddhist Wheel of Existence − a god, a jealous god, an animal, a hell denizen, a hungry ghost and a human being. These children all multiplied, and their children multiplied and so on, and the descendants of the monkey and the ogress, who were really Chenrezig and Droma, are the people of Bod. Although they all look like human beings, they may in their troubled or peaceful minds be inhabiting any one of the six realms, but only if they are, mentally, in the human realm can they practise the *dharma* properly.

This story teaches us several things. The first is the preciousness of human birth. When one thinks of the countless millions of insects, animals and fish in the world, as well as of spirits and beings who live in the hell realms and other worlds, then one may begin to intimate how rare a thing it is to be born human. 'Imagine,' said the Buddha, 'a solitary, one-eyed turtle swimming beneath the ocean, while floating on the surface of the ocean is a single, wooden ox-yoke. What are the chances of that turtle, after a thousand years of swimming under water, suddenly deciding to surface and putting its head through the hole in the middle of the ox-yoke? Just so are the chances of precious human birth.' Even as a human we may not be born in a land where the *dharma* is known, so we should give even greater thanks for that. Another thing the story tells us is the essence of the Mahayana, that while being a monk is a wonderful thing, it is people who are not bound by vows and who live in the world who have the greatest opportunities for compassion. And compassion, well − that is what human birth is for.

8

WE NATURALLY HAD NO INTENTION of going along with police plans. When morning came we left the hotel and took a rickshaw to the Norbulingka or 'Jewel Park', the Summer Palace of the Dalai Lamas which had since been officially, if unimaginatively, renamed the 'People's Park'. It was a place of calm away from the city, but like many places in Lhasa, as a location of massacre following Tenzin Gyatso's escape, it bore the discomfort of its history.

Studded with modest buildings built over the centuries by successive Dalai Lamas, the Norbulingka held promise, but little was open and, peering through locked gates, all we could see was unrepaired destruction, though all was painted fresh on the outside, to look good to tourist eyes. We were allowed to see the palaces of the thirteenth and fourteenth Dalai Lamas and intrude into their (remarkably ordinary) bedrooms, but little more. As with the Potala much of value had long since been removed (including the gold, which had been visibly chipped off some statues), and the Chinese attempt to recreate the rooms was cold and killed any atmosphere. The gardens were infinitely more pleasant than the tampered remains inside.

In one brightly flowered garden we were fortunate to meet Henry Osmaston, a Geography Professor from Bristol University and a leading Ladakh specialist, on his fourth visit to Tibet. Henry was here on an agricultural and animal husbandry project, advising the Chinese government at their invitation. His opportunity of viewing the development of a Tibetan farmer's life at close quarters over many years had convinced him that things had substantially improved in the last decade, since farmers had been allowed to keep their above-quota produce. They were also, he was inclined to think, probably better off than prior to the Chinese invasion, although he agreed that was not to say they could not have been even better off without it, and the situation in the towns, of course, was something else.

Falling into an easy rapport, we chatted away keenly for some time. To meet someone as balanced as Pico or Henry was a relief compared with the bull-headed intensity of Hal, and the troubles a few miles away were temporarily forgotten. Tall, lean, bearded and carrying an air of complete unperturbability, Henry cut the figure of the archetypal Englishman in Asia with a battery of anecdotes up his sleeve, and we listened with fascination to his tales of life on the glaciers of India's disputed territory with Pakistan, the problems of spending winter in Zanskar, and how a few days before he had been mistaken for a corpse by a pack of dogs and magpies while sleeping out at Reting monastery.

'There was a sky burial site nearby, you see,' he said wistfully, 'where bodies are cut up and left for the vultures, and dogs and magpies scavenge for scraps too. It dawned on me that, seeing this inert body prostrate on the stone, they thought they'd found a bigger piece than usual and their luck was in. Luckily I woke up before they pecked my eyes out. It was my seventieth birthday as well. Now *there* was an intimation of mortality if ever I had one.'

Back at the Jokhang, things did not look good. Either the authorities had expected trouble, or had chosen today for troop exercises. A large, black riot control vehicle with mesh windows was positioned prominently in front of the shrine, and a number of riot police stood around it, their sleek black visors, shields and batons all glinting in the sun. Forty-six stormtroopers, three abreast, fifteen rows deep with one leading, stamped anti-clockwise around the temple with AK47s in their hands. In front of it all was Hal, smoking away in his Texan hat, surrounded by half a dozen other Westerners. Had anything happened?

'You're joking – with all this lot?' he sneered, pointing at the van and a further dozen armed police on the police station roof.

We walked off in the direction of the hotel. Passing the police station at exactly noon, a truckload of another forty armed police pulled up, disgorging its contents into the square. They leant against the police station wall or sprawled over the paving stones in the sunshine, rifles at their sides, laughing and joking as if on a picnic. Police now almost outnumbered Tibetans in the square. Perhaps the scene had been like this on September 27th 1987, I thought, when a group of monks entered the square behind their leader, who was bearing the Tibetan flag in his hands. A Chinese officer, who has still not been charged with murder, walked up to the Tibetan with the flag and put his pistol against the man's chest. Without even hesitating, he fired. The man fell, and another Tibetan, in one of those moments of bravery that make people into saints, picked up the flag, and the officer shot him, too. In moments the Jokhang square became a killing ground again, and for three days, Lhasa burned. For now, at least, we would not be witness to a slaughter.

The afternoon passed quietly. At seven we met Pico for dinner at the Holiday Inn. He chatted keenly about events from the perspective of the package tourists around him. The previous evening, when we had received nocturnal visits from the police, had not been smooth for them, either.

'There was an announcement,' said Pico, 'while all the guests were in the middle of their dinner. Some official just stood up and baldly declared that all visits to the Jokhang today were cancelled, and instead everyone was to be taken to see a song and dance show on Jaramalingka island. He didn't even say sorry.'

'How did that go down?'

'Terribly, as you can imagine. The two people at my table were on a tight package schedule, and today was their only opportunity to visit the Jokhang. When you think they paid two thousand dollars each to come here, and would now have to leave Lhasa without seeing its holiest shrine, they weren't exactly pleased, but people here didn't know what to seethe about most – the cancellation or the manner of it. Some told me they were planning to make their own way to town but we're a long way out, and not everyone has the confidence to do that.'

'Which is why they're on a package.'

'Quite. How's things at the Yak?'

We told him about the police visit, about the stalls being cleared from the Barkhor, the riot van and increased police numbers, the upsurge in Hal's egotism, the Chengdu PSB suddenly issuing permits and the strange and unfathomable case of the latest missing permit holders.

Pico laughed. 'I can give you the answer to that,' he said.

'What is it?'

'They're here.'

'Here?'

'Yes. They all arrived at the airport on the morning flight, and were prevented from leaving until they signed up for a very expensive tour committing them to a minimum of three nights in this place. They had to agree, as the alternative was a flight back to Chengdu or on to Kathmandu. Some, apparently, were quite stroppy and tried to walk straight out, the way one does in China, but the police pushed them back with electric cattle prods. They're not all here, as some are still trying to sweat it out at the airport.'

'The way one does in China.'

'Quite.'

'So that would explain how they're dealing with this sudden policy change by Chengdu. I wouldn't mind betting they've no control over Chengdu, and are having to route directives via Beijing to get them to stop. Could take weeks. By that time they'll have more stroppy Westerners out there than they can handle. Should be fun.'

'I'll tell you something else to cheer you up,' said Pico. 'Two middle-aged German package tourists missed everything today, since they were caught yesterday handing out Dalai Lama pictures in the Barkhor. They were taken to the police station and sentenced on the spot to spend all day in their room. The Holiday Inn staff even took them their meals.'

'Mind you,' said Maria, 'had they been independent tourists, they would have been shunted back to Golmud.'

'Yes, it could have been worse,' Pico agreed. 'They might not have been allowed their pudding.'

The confining of the Potala monks to quarters was evidence that, while the Chinese like to insist there is now freedom of religion in Tibet, the monasteries remain heavily controlled. Still uncertain as to when the axe would finally fall on us, and fully expecting it before the 27th, we set out to investigate Sera which, along with Drepung, was one of two great monasteries which lay within cycling distance of Lhasa.

There was a strange serenity about Sera that somehow spurned its past, like the calm that returns when a storm has wrung itself out, though most of it had yet to be returned to a state suitable for habitation or worship. In some rooms the religious murals had been roughly slapped over with black paint; in others, grease had been smeared on the walls. Many murals had been attacked with hammers and chisels or battered with holy statues, and now only bits of green elbow or blue knee remained here and there amid the gouged plaster. Still other shrine rooms were covered in giant graffiti, of red slogans or pictures of the marching PLA. The inner walls of one temple were glued ceiling to floor with faded Chinese newspapers. In several rooms, bullet holes showed where murals of the Buddhas and *bodhisattvas* had been used for target practice. But the most common method of attack was fire, and everywhere walls that were once a testa ment to antique spiritual landscapes of a breathtaking, intricate beauty, were now charred black with scorch. Amidst all this the odd group of Holiday Inn tourists were whisked in and out by their guides. They were taken only to the refurbished bits and away again, craftily shielded from any intimation of the scale of destruction which remained.

The most poignant example of Chinese vandalism lay in a shrine room which aroused our suspicions by being locked. From an upstairs balcony we found ourselves looking down on a huge mound of broken images, a hand sticking up here, a leg there, as if all the scattered remnants of the Red Guards' destructive energy had been gathered together and chucked into one big pile. There were, however, no heads, which would have been sold to the art markets of Hong Kong or Nepal. In another shrine room, a shining portrait of Mao had aura lines radiating from his beaming countenance while an incongruous battleship, symbol of the revolution, fired shells at the Potala. Mahakala, the black, wrathful protective deity, had his face gouged out and filled with red paint that dripped like blood. The people who did this were undoubtedly accomplished artists, but artists with a terrible art, exhibiting in a gallery in hell. The room was history, but little had changed. We wanted to throw up, and went outside into the air.

In the main shrine room, a major *puja* was under way. Most of Sera's four hundred and fifty monks and four lamas sat facing each other in rows, cross legged in red robes on red cushions. The chantmaster, an eighty three year old *Geshe*, was a master of 'overtone' chanting, the peculiarly Tibetan and Mongolian technique of producing three tones simultaneously from the vocal chords. At the end of a prayer the monks would go quiet, and only his voice could be heard in the stillness before they all joined in again. We sat against a wall at the back, absorbed in the timeless atmosphere of a multitude of flickering butter lamps, a crystal shaft of sunlight splicing the gloom of the great hall from the open, heavy wooden front doors. *Tsampa* and tea were brought round, and the monks mixed them both together into a paste, using the little wooden bowls it was now legal again to carry in their robes.

The womb-like cosiness was abruptly broken by the arrival of a Japanese film crew, who walked around the sides of the shrine room setting up spotlights and noisily clattering their equipment. Behind them a tall Westerner appeared, with no fewer than six heavy minders in tow. When the *puja* ended he introduced himself as Nick Kristoff, Beijing correspondent for the *New York Times*. Dressed stylishly in casual clothes, a soft woolly jumper beneath tousled, slightly curly hair and gently intelligent features, the warmth of the man was instantly communicated. This was his first visit to Tibet, he said; he had been trying to get in for years and been refused, then suddenly the permit had appeared and he was told, 'You're going on this date and coming back on that.' He had no doubt it was to do with China's eagerness to project an 'all's well' image abroad, and he was not likely to be taken in by cynical manipulation. As soon as we had begun to talk his minders moved in to interrupt us, using the polite method of forming a wall between us with their backs.

'Sorry about this,' he explained, smiling over their large and solid shoulders. 'I have to interview the Abbot and I guess they want me to get on with it.'

We moved to the back of the small crowd which formed while the party sat on the floor, and Kristoff took out his notebook.

'If *Geshe-la* says the wrong thing, he'll go to jail.'

We turned round to see a young monk, in his early twenties, standing behind us. It was brave of him to speak.

'He will have to be careful,' I agreed.

'Many of the monks here have been in jail. I, too, was in jail for six months.'

'Why?' I looked searchingly into his face. He had an intelligent look. He was eager to speak, but his eyes from experience kept flitting from left to right.

'I was arrested for demonstrating, in 1987. It was September, day-time, and I was wearing only light clothes. For six months I was allowed no visitors, and given no extra clothes. October, November, December,

January, February, March. The worst time. So cold. I thought I'd die from cold. Also I was handcuffed, all the time, for six months. It makes your shoulders very painful. And I was beaten often with sticks, and they put electric on my tongue and up here.'

He gestured towards his backside and went quiet. We did not know quite what to say.

'You're lucky they let you be a monk again,' I offered.

'Lucky, yes, lucky . . .' He chewed on the word so much I felt uncomfortable, that I had said the wrong thing. But he continued: 'I *was* lucky in jail. You know, so many people tortured badly – have to stand on ice, or special hot floors, very hot, sometimes two days. Many people, most people, they beat very badly, and use electricity more. Yes, I was lucky. Maybe I was young.'

In front of us, Kristoff, I felt, was having the wrong conversation.

'How is life now, as a monk?'

'We're very unhappy. We have police in the monastery. Some dress as monks. We have to be careful, who is near when we speak. And of course,' he added cynically, 'every time there's a demonstration we have to attend "political education" classes.'

Some of Kristoff's minders began to throw us glances.

'Don't say anything more. We're going over there. You stay here. We don't want to get you into trouble. It is best they don't see you talking to us.'

'OK.' He understood.

We went to sit on a wall in the monastery's main street, near the convoy of cars used to bring Kristoff and his six minders here. The interview over, Kristoff came up to us.

'I have fifteen minutes,' he said.

We told him about the shrine rooms we had seen. Would they make good pictures?

'Can you find them again?'

'I think so.'

'We must be quick.'

With a glance at his minders, who were observing us with more than a little suspicion, and with Maria staying put on the wall, we sprang off. From the corner of my eye I saw pandemonium break out around the cars. We dashed down a narrow lane. According to Maria afterwards, two attempted to follow us, a third went another way, all shouting into their portable radios. But the passages of Sera are narrow and many, and with a few turns it seemed we had lost them.

The pile of desecrated statues did not impress Kristoff. 'I'm interested in the present state of freedom of religion, not in the past,' he explained, correctly.

'But don't you think, in so far as all this is unrepaired, it remains the present? The monks have to live with all this.'

He took the point. The other shrine room, with the portrait of a deified Mao, did impress him. He took two or three photos and translated the slogans for me. '*Monks must study political economy from the victorious Red Guards.*' For a while we stood around, absorbed in the ironies of Red Guard art. 'It's every bit as much a religion,' Kristoff mused wistfully, shaking his head.

'What did the *Geshe* say?' I asked him.

'Well, naturally he was very guarded and phrased everything carefully, but I was impressed by the limits to which he was prepared to go. For example, he hoped the Dalai Lama could "use peaceful means to address the question of independence", and disagreed with the Chinese insistence that the reincarnation of the Panchen Lama *has* to be found in Tibet. No such criteria, he said, had ever been set. When I asked him how many of his monks had been arrested in the last three years, he replied, "more than ten", but of course I cannot rely on my translator, he may have said a hundred. And when I asked how many had been released, he replied, "only one".'

'You're not worried that your questions might get him into trouble?'

'Oh no. With the *Geshe*'s age, experience and position he would know that any act of self-sacrifice he might be tempted to make would be outweighed by the repercussions on the monastery as a whole.'

Kristoff's minders had not located us. Back at the cars we found they had been giving Maria a hard time, which perhaps we should have anticipated. She had, however, told them nothing. Now they had a go at me, slotting at once into interrogation mode, three of them together shoving their faces into mine, jabbing with their fingers, arrogance, hatred, toughness and power exuding at once from their leather jackets and dark suits. It was a rehearsed, practised method, and I realised what Maria had been through on her own.

'Why are you here?'

'Tourists.'

'No tourists. Tourists are on tours.'

'Well, we're here, aren't we?'

'You're independent travellers?'

'Why do you want to know?'

'Are you independent travellers? I'm asking you a question.'

'And I don't have to answer it if I don't want to.'

'What's your hotel?'

'Why do you want to know?'

'What is your hotel?!' They were working themselves up incredibly over the non-appearance of answers, an experience they would in no way have been used to.

'You give me a reason why you want to know.'

'What is your nationality?'

'Why are you asking all these questions?'

'What's your nationality?'

'Russian.'

'Show me your passport.'

'No.'

'Show me your passport!'

'You show me your papers!'

And so, for a while, it went on, with Kristoff watching it all in the car, until one man tapped his watch and said something, and they abruptly retreated, scowling angrily, and drove off down the hill. It only occurred to us later that, were it not for Kristoff's presence as a witness, we would almost certainly have been arrested.

In the Barkhor that afternoon, as the lowering sun sharpened the distinctions of light and shade, a monk approached us from a side alley. He looked more than his middle-age and carried the obvious bruises of a recent beating, doubtless a leaving present from his guards when he came out of jail. It was a strange encounter, for he fixed his eyes on mine a long way off, in such a way as to telegraph an attempt to communicate. As he drew near, my fears that he would endanger himself by speaking were unfounded, as he failed to reduce his speed but brushed past me very carefully, his hand fumbling against my own. I opened my fingers to receive the gift as he sped past. We continued for a minute or two, watching him disappear ahead of us, safely and without being apprehended, then stopped and looked around. Were we being followed? I held something hard within my palm, and resisted the urge to glance at it before we had encircled the Barkhor completely, and returned to the hotel.

In the safety of our room, we opened the little package. It was a piece of rice paper, wrapped around a larger piece of writing paper, meticulously folded. The rice paper had been block-printed in English with an appeal to the United Nations to open an office in Tibet 'in the name of human dignity'. The letter itself was in Tibetan, in *kuyk*, the fast form of *u-mei*, Tibetan handwriting.

Making sure we were not followed, we left the hotel again.

'We have a problem,' we said to a Tibetan friend. 'Can you translate something?'

He looked at us. He was young, a handsome man, with excellent English considering he had learnt it in the process of buying and selling. We knew him to be trustworthy, though such was his caution he had never, even to us, criticised the Chinese.

He nodded, and looked around the street. 'Follow slowly,' he said. 'From afar.'

We had done this before, and knew what to expect. Then as now, on the pretext of buying something we had followed him from a distance of twenty yards, occasionally and not ostentatiously looking behind ourselves, until we saw his tousled head appear smiling and beckoning from a doorway. Before we had gone for conversation, because he had invited us, and because he enjoyed dispensing hospitality in exchange for a little English practice. Now we were a little more worried. If anyone came in, I told myself, I would eat the piece of paper.

Inside, the house was poor by any standards. The walls were smoothly plastered and had been painted once, but were flaking and grimy now with cooking smoke. In the main room two ancient armchairs and a sofa were covered by small Tibetan carpets designed for sitting on, brown, with mythical white snow lions. The most dominant feature was the exquisitely carved and gaudily painted shrine, which occupied an entire wall. On it, statues stood in their delicate nooks, family photos were balanced alongside those of the Dalai and other lamas, and a row of butter lamps burned.

Our friend's wife entered with a thermos of butter tea, setting three small handleless bowls on a low coffee table in front of the old sofa. Having rapidly acquired a taste for Tibetan tea which Maria would never do in a hundred years, I prepared for Maria to slide her cup towards me when our host became distracted, a practice she pursued with such callous disregard for my cholesterol levels that I had already put away gallons of it, and was thus interpreting every incidence of indigestion with studied alarm. The woman poured it for us, overlaying her shy nervousness with a warm smile.

'*Awaa yerpay?*' Turning her palm downwards beside her rainbow apron, she enquired whether we had any children. In Tibet as much as in the rest of Asia, it was always the first question.

'*Notsoo may,*' we half apologised, predicting the look of sympathy that would follow.

'*Awaa yerpay?*' We returned the question.

'*Notsoo pugu too yer,*' she replied smiling, with visible pride, holding up six fingers. The one-child policy was not yet applied to Tibetans, unless they worked for the state.

We continued making pleasantries, and when she went into the kitchen I pulled out the letter and unwrapped it. No sooner had our friend taken it than his mood changed and he jumped up to draw the curtains, plunging us into near darkness.

'Tibetan houses have spies,' he explained.

'But your neighbours may see you bring us here,' Maria countered, disconcerted.

'In that case I say you look to buy something. This serious matter.' He drew his finger across his throat, and for good measure pointed a gun at his head.

'Can you translate it?'

He read it through to himself, quietly. Before he had finished a friend came by to say hello, and he stuffed it into his pocket. For a while they made polite conversation and then his friend, realising from the darkness and the drawn curtains that something was going on, made his excuses and left.

'No problem,' he said and, smoothing it out again, began to translate the document, which we would have to smuggle out and pass to the London-based Tibet Information Network. He peered closely at it to make out the words.

> In many parts of Tibet the Chinese have built huge prisons, torture centres, places for causing suffering ... In Kongpo at a place called Tramo there is an extensive prison holding several hundred thousand Tibetans. Likewise, in the small prisons there are no less than thirty Tibetans all the time, and in the major prisons, no less than a hundred Tibetans at all times. In the Lhasa city prison, no less than three

thousand Tibetans are held at all times. Moreover, in the prison called Gutsa there are no less than seven hundred Tibetans. In the Sangyip prison, there are no less than eight hundred Tibetans ...

As for food, in the morning they give out wooden bowls with a portion of light rice porridge and wheat about the size of a walnut. As for bedding, there is a grass mattress and a badly torn cotton sheet infested with lice.

Before the daily announcements, which are made three times a day, the prisoners' hands are hand-cuffed and their feet are manacled. As soon as they reach the place where the announcement is given the prisoners are slapped several times and are punched below the stomach. Then the announcements are made. While making the announcements, some Chinese say: 'You splittists – you're the ones who conspired in secret to divide the motherland. Your type has put up the different types of posters, posted up the Tibetan national flag.'

When they punish you they hit you with electric batons, they beat you while hanging you upside down, and when you're near death they splash you with a basinful of water and lower your rope down. When it is almost impossible to rise because of the pain, they drag you by the handcuffs into the prison cell. Then just before leaving the cell they each kick you once and warn you, 'You must all think well.' Saying this they close the door.

When it is about time for lunch, they push through a hole two steamed momos as tiny as walnuts and a ladleful of steamed vegetables. Then, after lunch, again we are taken to the place for announcements. Again, they continue punishment that is unbearable. Electric current is passed through the finger tips and it is impossible to tell whether it is your body or not. Then they disconnect the electric wiring and come up with another idea. They heat up an iron peg on the heater and poke you with it continuously. At the same time they hit you with batons and belts. Finally they handcuff you again and put you back in the prison cell. When you come round, your whole body is racked with pain, burning sensations, and throbbing with numbness. Even when you're dying of thirst, they only give you one wooden bowlful of water.

When parents or relatives of prisoners or other Tibetan people come to the prison doors with food, not only are they not allowed to take the food in to the prisoners, but they are scolded and abused. The Chinese draw a white line and warn, 'If you cross the white line, we'll

kill you. We've the authority to do so. We have the authority to put
you in prison. You might get beatings along with the others.' Then
they warn: 'From today onward, you are not allowed to come here ...'

It was dated, and signed with his name. We had sat, listening in silence.
I reflected on the bravery required to sign such a document, for if it was
found upon us ...

'Why did you hide it?' Maria suddenly asked, interrupting my
thoughts. 'The man who came in is your friend.'

He sighed, folded the letter and gave it back. He pointed at the door
by which his friend had left and at the kitchen, where his wife was busying
herself quietly. 'Everyone in Tibet has a relative in prison,' he explained.
'Including me, him, and her. They make people outside talk with threats
against people inside. I hid the paper because I don't want to give him
knowledge to talk about. That is also why he didn't ask.'

That evening, Kristoff came to the Yak. He had given his minders the slip
by arranging a tour of the Barkhor area at night, then hopping over to us in a
rickshaw instead. Again he wore a hairy woollen sweater and light-coloured
flannels, and in the relaxed atmosphere of our room he came over as careful
and academic, yet also humorous and warm, without superiority. He noted
with precision Hal's store of information, then sat back against the wall
on Maria's bed, his right foot on his left knee, and cradled his tea in both
hands for warmth. His task of providing the details over, Hal went quiet
and seemed to lose interest. Prompted by remembering he had won the
Pulitzer Prize for his coverage of Tienanmen, I asked Kristoff about the
unrest. Was there really a lot of social discontent in China?

'Yes. Lots.' He could not have sounded more definite.

'Because of the sudden availability of goods they can't afford?'
Maria guessed.

'Partly. But I don't think that's the main thing. The sudden availability
of information is far more important. Before, they had no knowledge of
the outside world and a limited, biased knowledge of their own. Now,
all of a sudden, the people of China have become more truly educated,
internationally aware. They know the nature of the world beyond their
borders and, more than that, they know the nature of their own regime.
Hong Kong, Taiwan and American TV have also made them aware of
lifestyles the goods in China's shops can't give them. Information is the

single most powerful factor in social discontent.' This was exactly what Wang and Li had said.

'Could an uprising happen again, then?' Maria wondered.

'Sure. Next week, or in ten years' time, and the system will fall. Anything could trigger it – death of leaders, probably – but it'll happen, as a result of the discord in towns and cities.'

'And China could break up?'

'It could. China's always been politically regionalised, and Beijing's already losing control over the provinces. China could easily go the same way as the Soviet Union, with Tibet the first piece to break off.'

'Could it happen?' Hal leant forward with a sudden renewal of interest.

'Entirely feasible,' Kristoff replied with conviction. 'And the Chinese know it. That's *why* they're so heavy on the Tibetans, and so quick to control the movements of foreigners. One senior *cadre* told me a few weeks ago that Tibet would close its doors to individual travellers for the next three years. Because, you see, they divine this link between individual travellers and instability. It's not justified of course, but the Chinese like to have control, and it's naturally harder to control individuals than groups. More than that, this is a "group culture" – the Chinese don't often act individually themselves, and they find it hard to understand why others do. Naturally they're suspicious, but it comes down to not understanding Western culture.'

'Being afraid of it, too,' volunteered Maria, 'after decades of propaganda.'

'Exactly.'

Kristoff's plane left at five the next morning. It was already midnight, and we had to let him go.

'I envy you,' he said jokingly as he left. 'Not least because you got here without using C.A.A.C. It always makes us wonder whether our latest report will be our last.'

For the next few days things were quieter, though the riot van stayed in its prominent position. Leaflets were dropped in the Barkhor calling for demonstrations, but none happened. Perhaps it was only a show of defiance, a baiting of authority in the face of the intimidation, but tour groups were again excluded from the Jokhang, just in case. The Potala remained closed to Tibetans, but the stalls returned, more people were on the streets, and we ambled around in the way we had become used to, not feeling we had to see things, but enjoying our presence in the jewel in the earth's crown before it was chipped off and melted down for good. There were new arrivals to chat to as well, as people from Chengdu completed their allotted time at the Holiday Inn and came over to the smaller hotels in the centre. However, in spite of the ease of getting through from Chengdu, only one Canadian had made it from Golmud for a week. According to him, monks and nuns were being refused bus tickets in Golmud until after the 1st, and things were difficult for them as they had not enough money to stay in even the cheapest hotels until that time.

With our numbers increasing dramatically by the day, it would be a very awkward operation for the authorities to clear everyone out by the 22nd deadline, now only a few days away. Indeed, according to the most recent arrivals, the PSB in Chengdu had been so rabidly issuing permits for Tibet that CAAC had stopped requiring them and begun selling tickets regardless. This was laughably beyond the TAR authority's control, and the best they could do was to hold people at the airport until they paid up for a minimum three-day tour at the Holiday Inn. Against this background we had to consider seeing places in Tibet other than Lhasa, and that meant the possibility of being picked up by the TAR police and taken to the airport. If we stayed however and the deadline was enforced, we might equally well be shunted back to Golmud. We decided to visit Samye, the birthplace of Buddhism in Tibet, a place of some importance and worth the risk. It was only later that we realised how far we had underestimated the risk we were taking.

The night before leaving we dined at our favourite Tibetan restaurant, and as usual emptied plates of food into bags for the malnourished beggars of all ages who trooped in to gaze importunately at the diners. In the morning we would leave for Samye, not even sure we would return. We slept restlessly, and in the deep of the night I had a dream which showed the extent to which the Tibetans had won our empathy.

We were in an East European city. There was a great excitement, but not a happy one. Crowds were pouring onto the streets, and rushing to the central square. It looked like Wenceslas Square in Prague, only bigger, and in the centre of the square was a stone tower. Tall, lean and pointing upwards into the night, the tower was evidently the focal

point of the demonstrations. Police and civilians mixed chaotically, but
no shots were being fired. Emotion had boiled over. Everywhere was a
kind of panic, but a singlemindedness of purpose. With no idea what
the purpose was we entered the tower, swept along in the throng, and
found a spiral staircase winding upwards. Following many people,
and with many people following us, we climbed. As we climbed we
passed numerous niches cut into the wall, and noticed that in each niche
there was a bird, a beautiful bird, a beautiful large bird all studded
with vermilion stones and wrapped in a bright but deep blue cloth.
There were so many of them, embedded in the high walls of the stone
tower, and we looked questioningly at each other, wondering what
they signified. The force of the bodies coming up from below jostled
us onwards and upwards, and when finally we reached the top of the
stairway, we understood. The most powerful form of protest was to
throw oneself from the tower. It was to this end that the thousands of
people were running to the tower, and the police were trying to stop
them. Things had come to such a pass, there was no point in the police
shooting people in order to prevent their suicides. Eyes streaming with
tears, men and women, old and young, flashed past and over the parapet
into the night, seeking in their own deaths the only way they could be
free. And when the people died, their bodies were embalmed within the
images of these exquisite, jewel-studded birds, were wrapped in the blue
cloth and placed in the niches in the tower. We stood by the ramparts,
looking over as people rushed past us and fell. Below, we saw the blue
cloaks being placed as if by angels on the bodies of the dead, the first
step in their magical transmutation into new birds, for new niches. We
felt the cold, raw wind on our faces, and wept violently.

Part 3

TRAVELS IN TSANG

Tsang, the largest of Tibet's provinces, is often referred to as the 'cradle' of Tibetan civilisation. When the nomads settled, it was here that the towns sprang up.

That happened late, but mythology has long memories.

Tibet's first king known with certainty was by tradition the thirty-third, Songsten Gampo, who ruled in the seventh century; a lord of military might, the rulers of China and Nepal gave him their daughters as dues.

By the time of the thirty-eighth king, Trisong Detsen, the Chinese capital Ch'ang An was in Tibetan hands, and Samarkand followed.

Trisong Detsen was no Ashoka.

Having sought to make Buddhism the jewel in the nation's crown, he was not about to let the empire dissolve like a sandcastle upon a beach.

Yet, being foreign, Buddhism had its enemies.

The forty-first king, Langdarma, wiped it from Tsang for three hundred years.

Almost.

Sometime in the eleventh century, Yeshe 'Od, a pious descendant of the royal line, was ransomed for his weight in gold.

Bringing the money, his nephew found they were short by the weight of his uncle's head.

'No matter,' said Yeshe 'Od. 'Let me be killed, and spend the money on inviting the good teacher Atisa from India.'

It was done, and Tibet has been Buddhist ever since.

Even Mao could not succeed where the evil Langdarma failed.

The meeting of two people is like the meeting of two chemicals — if there is a reaction, both are transformed.

C.G. JUNG

Dealing with Demons

ALTHOUGH KING SONGSTEN GAMPO'S WIVES, Wen Cheng and
Bhrikuti Trisun, are credited with introducing Buddhism to the Tibetan
people, it never really became established until the reign of Trisong Detsen
(755–97). Even then it had to contend with strong opposition from defenders
of the Bon faith, as well as with competition from China and India as to
what kind of Buddhism would eventually take root. The first monastery
in Tibet was at Samye, and the story of its construction, in the late
eighth century, reveals all of these tensions in Tibet's dawning religious
consciousness.

This was the time of Buddhism's finest flowering in China, heady
days of sublime philosophy and monastic expansion, especially for the Zen
school. As knowledge of Tibet's courting of Buddhism spread, so some
Chinese monks began to make the journey there in the hope of usurping
the role of the bride. Tibet's own eyes, however, were directed south. A
century and a half previously, the scholar-traveller Thonmi Sambhota had
been commissioned to devise a Tibetan alphabet by Songsten Gampo,
who had rejected written Chinese as unsuitable to the Tibetan language.
Thonmi Sambhota had gone to India, and returned with a product so
geared to the precise translation of Sanskrit that Tibetan texts today can be
reliably used to re-create lost Sanskrit works. Thus, Tibet's acquaintance
with Buddhism had until now been derived from Indian rather than Chinese
sources, and when Trisong Detsen conceived the idea of a monastic order
he naturally proposed to an Indian teacher, Shantarakshita, and not to a
Chinese master. The sudden arrival of the Chinese at Samye was like a

belated rush of the church door, while Indian Buddhism was being led up the aisle.

Shantarakshita (c.705–88) was a professor from Nalanda University in Bihar, and one of the greatest scholars in Buddhist history. He was an exponent of Yogachara-Madhyamaka, a rigorously logical school which taught that the world had the nature of Mind. He first visited Tibet in 763, but encountered such hostility from the native Bon religion that he was driven back to India. His parting advice to the king was to invite Padmasambhava, a scholar-saint with a reputation for subduing demons. Shantarakshita returned in 775, bringing Padmasambhava with him, and Padmasambhava is given virtually all the credit for the completion of Samye.

Padmasambhava was a member of the Indian *siddha* (powerful person) tradition, with paranormal powers. Such people were reputedly able to change shape, project their consciousness, even halt the sun in the sky. These abilities came from proficiency in Tantric Buddhism, or Vajrayana (the 'Thunderbolt Vehicle'), which had been the dominant form of Buddhism in northern India for over four hundred years, and it was through Padmasambhava that Vajrayana became the established religion of Tibet. With a root doctrine that the world is like a dream sustained by consciousness, and that real changes in both oneself and the world can be effected by meditation and ritual, it is hardly surprising that Tibetan Buddhism has such a reputation for 'magic and mystery'.

Of course, many of the stories about the *siddhas* are legends, and the life of Padmasambhava is studded with more legendary accretions than most. It is possibly true that he was born in Oddiyana (perhaps the Swat valley in Pakistan), but probably not true that he was found sprung from a lotus in the Milk-Ocean eight years after the Buddha's death, not least because this would make him over a thousand years old when he arrived in Tibet. Stories of kings attempting to burn him at the stake and the fire transforming into a lake, are typical of the *siddha genre*. The story of his being discovered and brought up by a king who would not let him leave the palace (a Buddha motif), like the story of his learning Tantra from the Buddha's disciple Ananda, are probably attempts by the Nyingma school, which looks to him as its founder, to relate him more closely to the Buddha himself. The rest of his biography is more plausible.

Given that Padmasambhava spent twelve years at Samye dealing with the matter, one can assume the subjugation of Tibet's demons was no pushover, even for him. During that time he assisted Shantarakshita in ordaining the first Tibetan monks, translated several important works and buried a number of supernaturally revealed 'treasure' texts (*termas*) in the hills because Tibet was 'not yet ready for them'. (The *Tibetan Book of the Dead* is an example.) It is commonly accepted that King Trisong Detsen gave him his wife, Yeshe Tsogyel, out of gratitude. This must have been something of a sacrifice, not only since the king had only been married to her for two years, but because his principal wife had lined up with the Bon opposition. The King's ministers were reportedly so scandalised that Padmasambhava was forced to return to India, leaving in typically legendary fashion by causing his horse to fly over the hills. Such a hasty retreat does suggest that the Bon demons were never finally quelled, even if Samye had been brought to completion. A final piece of intrigue continues in a prophecy he famously left behind him:

When the Iron Bird flies in the Sky,
The Faith will go to the Land of the Red Man.

There remained the issue of the Chinese, who had not departed but taken up residence, and were now shouting like jilted lovers when the priest asks: 'If any know a reason why this couple should not be joined together . . .' It was their last chance, and the reason they gave was that enlightenment arose suddenly, not gradually as the Indian Buddhists taught. In 792 King Trisong Detsen ordered a debate, and both sides sent for their ringers. From China, a monk named Mahayana argued the Zen corner. From India there was Kamalashila, whose works on meditation and philosophy remain seminal today. The winning side was to determine the form of Buddhism in Tibet, Indian or Chinese, and the losers were to be banished.

The debate was refereed by the King. As bridegroom also, and with China militarily encroaching further in the east, Trisong Detsen had to consider what kind of in-laws would come with the marriage. Though the debate was held in the Chinese monks' quarters, the dice, we can assume, were loaded. Kamalashila won. The Chinese in bad grace published the result as their victory, but were asked to leave. The way was now clear for peaceful development at Samye, and the Vajrayana was imported lock, stock and barrel from India. Kamalashila, unfortunately, having stayed on to write after the debate, was murdered three years later. It may have been a vengeful, lingering Chinese – or a sign that the Bon resistance was regirding its loins.

Exactly what constituted Bon in those days, which many people, including several of the King's ministers and his wife, struggled to defend, we do not know. No texts survive, because Tibet before Thonmi Sambhota was pre-literate. Today, Bon is virtually indistinguishable from Buddhism, since when it finally succumbed in the eleventh century it took the entire Buddhist cosmology and doctrine for its own – merely renaming everything, so that the Buddha for example was called Shenrab rather than Shakyamuni, but his life story was the same. Thus, Bon was influenced far more by Buddhism than the other way around. The popular notion that Tibetan Buddhism is a mixture of Indian Buddhism and native Tibetan beliefs is a great misconception. Tibet offered itself to India like a blank and open book, and Tibetan Buddhism is Indian Buddhism, in its Vajrayana form, transplanted to Tibet unchanged.

In spite of Trisong Detsen's fervent personal involvement in events at Samye, which was not even the capital, he continued in these later years of his forty-two-year reign to pursue the extension of the Tibetan empire. He was so successful that the Caliph of Baghdad, Haroun ar-Rashid, was forced to ally with the Chinese, who had lost their capital, Ch'ang-an, to counter the Tibetan threat to Muslim interests in Central Asia. It would seem therefore that problems of Bon opposition were due to the fact that Buddhism was foreign, rather than to any disgruntlement over neglect of state. When Trisong Detsen's son, Muni Tsenpo, acceded to the throne however, opposition to Buddhism did find economic dis-ease at home: Muni Tsenpo is recorded as attempting a complete redistribution of wealth on Buddhist grounds, so that every citizen possessed the same amount of money. He was dismayed to discover, say the records, that the rich still got richer and the poor still got poorer. The early Socialist did not last long, for he was poisoned by his own mother – Trisong Detsen's principal wife and champion of the Bon faith.

In 815 Tri Ralpachen came to power. Ralpachen was a strong king who halted Chinese advances on the weakening empire, but remained a champion of Buddhism. To boost the strength of the *sangha* he decided to request one monk from every seven families. The threat to Bon's national popularity that this represented was so great that the defenders of the old order decided to act, and Ralpachen was assassinated on the orders of his own brother, Langdarma. What followed has been the stuff of Tibetan folk songs and theatre ever since.

Langdarma's first act on seizing power was the ruthless repression of all forms of Buddhism, destroying temples, killing monks who refused to convert back to Bon and deporting Indian *pandits*. The repression was so fierce and total that scholars are able to refer to Buddhism in Tibet up to that time as the 'first diffusion'. It was to be another two centuries before a 'second diffusion' was possible, even though Langdarma did not last long. It was a Buddhist monk, Lhalungpa Pelgyi Dorje, who did the deed. Cunning and careful, he covered a white stallion with charcoal, donned a black cape with a white lining, and shot the king with an arrow during the performance of a play. Making his escape, he steered the horse across a river and reversed his cape, thus making a getaway as a white rider on a white horse while everyone was looking for a black rider on a black one. The tradition concludes with Lhalungpa escaping to a refugee Buddhist community in Kham, but spending the rest of his life in meditation in penance for his act.

Langdarma's murder signalled the end for the unified Tibet created by Songsten Gampo, and the kingdom degenerated into its own era of warring states, curiously contemporary with the break-up of China into the Five Dynasties period. Both nations being at their weakest, neither had the strength to bother the other, and there were no Sino-Tibetan contacts for another three centuries. Tibetan history virtually took a breather until the next glimmer of Buddhist activity in 1012, the 'second diffusion' when Tibet again prostrated itself towards India. This time, with the arrival of the gentle Atisa, patronised by various wealthy families and regional kings such as Yeshe 'Od, Buddhism would be allowed to grow unimpeded in Tibet for almost another millennium.

9

HAVING BOOKED OUR TICKETS ON a Tibetan rather than a Chinese bus, we found ourselves with the front two seats – the seats of honour. A large picture of the Dalai Lama hung above the windscreen, which was also strewn with prayer flags. All the passengers were Tibetan, and at once welcomed us warmly with a mixture of shy toothy smiles and energetic nods.

Stopping short of the checkpoint for leaving Lhasa, we were told to get out along with several Tibetans whose papers were perhaps not quite in order, and the bus continued to the post while we walked across a field. It was autumn now, and the field, turned to straw, was full of haystacks. We did not give the checkpost a wide berth; in fact we were close enough to see the faces of the police manning it, and they, no doubt, saw us. A lot, in that moment, became clear. In China, if something is not your job, then it is not your responsibility, and everyone wants to get away with the minimum responsibility necessary. It was the duty of the police to check the bus. If they found no-one without papers on the bus, then they had done their job. The fact that a group of people including two Westerners was walking over a field before their very eyes was neither here nor there.

Nevertheless, not to tempt providence, we walked a good hundred yards up the road the other side before sitting down to wait. The check took a long time. That they should follow the letter of their job so thoroughly and the spirit not at all was laughable. Yet our rucksacks were on the bus – if they went through the luggage, then what? We sat, waiting, gazing at the haystacks in the hot sun. An hour passed before the bus was released.

Everyone was all smiles as we got back on, greeting us like old friends though we had only met an hour ago. We sat down humbly, undeserving of their warmth. This was the touching quality of the Tibetans, their readiness to reach out to Westerners as if our continued presence was a magic wand that would eventually save them. It was because we were not so convinced ourselves, that our own smiles were rather awkward in return.

We drove across the Brahmaputra, the sacred river that spills its Himalayan waters into Assam and Bengal. Strong and fast flowing, its holiness here was spanned by a great bridge, guarded at both ends by armed sentries. They observed us, expressionless, as we crossed. We continued past the airport at an average speed of 40 kilometres per hour, keeping the great river on our left for much of the way. After a short time, most of the Tibetans got out at a miserable looking white-walled commune and the rest carried on to the town of Tsetang. We were dropped before then, in the middle of a vast nowhere, and pointed in the direction of another whitewashed shell, small and isolated on the shore of the river.

We walked towards the edifice, thirsty in the dry heat. The cloud of dust left by the bus drifted, and then settled. The space was immense. Beyond the northern banks great mountains rose, piercing the sky with god-like authority. East and west the river and the road came from nowhere and went, eventually, into hazy oblivion. The building was an empty shop. We walked behind it onto the pebbled sand and saw the ferry, a twelve-foot punt tethered to poles driven into the riverbed, festooned with prayer flags hanging limp in the breezeless air. It too was empty, but in the shade of a smaller derelict building ten yards away three rough men, an old and a young woman and three small children leant against the wall. They were all country people, in animal skin coats. They stared at us. I pointed at the boat; they nodded and we sat down, though they had taken the only shade that was left.

Apart from the people, the Brahmaputra, flowing firmly but more gently now on its way to India, was the only movement. There was not a breath, not a sigh, not the merest suggestion of wind. All was peace. That peculiarly Tibetan quality of light that comes with altitude enhanced everything. The mountains, though large and dominant, did nothing to diminish the sense of space. Arid though they were, there was an almost self-conscious assertiveness about them that brought to mind the Buddha's earth-touching pose. When the demon Mara had questioned his right to exist, he had simply and quietly touched the earth. It was a favoured Buddhist symbol, and the Buddha is often shown in that gesture. It was a statement of identity, like Yahweh's ultimate *I am that I am*. In the end we are all chthonic, earth-sprung. At least, I thought, contemplating the strength of the mountains, the Chinese have not been able to raze *them*. Here, in the great Tibetan landscape, is something they could not touch.

'A romantic thought, unfortunately, and hopelessly wrong.' Maria corrected me, taking a scoop of sand and sifting it idly between her fingers. 'The Chinese move the Tibetan landscape in many ways, from advanced deforestation to mining and nuclear testing, as well as for disposing of the West's nuclear waste on its behalf in exchange for a little hard currency.'

She was right, and in the end I corrected myself. Nothing was inviolable, neither human beings, nor the earth. Everything was subject to change. It was not a cheering thought.

Time passed. We played in the sand with the three ragged children, all girls. They were about six, seven and eight, yet had about them a strange air of maturity – a sense of humour yet devoid of the silliness which Western children learn. Instinctively inquisitive, they went into our bags and looked at the pictures in *Lonely Planet*, recognising without comment a statue of Mao Zedong. Two wagtails played tamely nearby; they gently lobbed stones at them, not to hit them but to enjoy the fun of keeping them on the move. They were beautiful, these children, exquisitely so, though their hair had not been combed since birth and probably would not be again until they wore plaits, and their snot, bright green on all of them, detracted not a jot from their preternatural looks. They played a game of pushing each other, standing feet apart, digging firmly into the sand and inviting a push on the chest, yet none could make the other fall. Their high cheekbones suggested strength of character. Like the mountains they were born and bred in, there was about them that which asserted itself without the effort of doing so. They knew who they were; and because they knew who they were they could not easily be knocked over – like the mountains.

The ferryman eventually came. A smooth but surly-looking brute, a young man in new jeans and T-shirt with a gold chain around his neck, he seemed distinctly out of keeping with the character of the place. When he saw us we noticed his eyes involuntarily gleam, and put ourselves on guard. The three girls took our lighter bags, the younger one our camera bag, and we watched nervously as they carried them in single file up the narrow plank into the boat. Then came the charade. The ferryman wanted a hundred *yuan* for the crossing. We queried it, thinking he could be meaning one *yuan*. He then wrote '50' on his hand. Still too high. He tried again. We refused. And he went home.

We made pillows of our rucksacks and lay down in the boat. A monk and a nun joined us, and everyone just sat. The rough countrymen, big and muscly in their animal skins with daggers poking from their waists, androgynous with their braided hair, got out their *malas* and began to hum mantras. The women, hair threaded through turquoise, stared across the river. The children sat on their hands, staring at us. An hour passed. An hour and a half, and the sun remained so hot I could almost feel the peeling process on my nose. The patience of everyone seemed as immense as the land they lived in. When we caught their eyes, the men smiled calmly. We tried to ascertain from one man how much he was paying. He wrote '50' on his hand. I jabbed at his chest, making clear I meant *him*, and he wrote '50' again. The girls joined in. The eldest wrote '5'. Possible, but it still seemed too much. Then the man prodded me. He wrote '30' on his arm, and raised his eyebrows. For the sake of the other passengers who for a matter of principle we could have trapped there until midnight, we agreed. He went off to play the go-between, borrowing a bike to go to the ferryman's house.

'Imagine dying with a *drachma* in your mouth and finding the fare over the river Styx had gone up,' said Maria, distractedly.

It was still another hour before he blessed us with his return, all smiles now which we returned with haughty stares. The journey, it is true, took a further hour — much longer than we expected as it was upstream and required negotiating sandbanks, but a small outboard motor did most of the work, and little punting was necessary. As we beached, the girls again took our bags, and two mini-tractor drivers, whose job it was to take us the final six kilometres to the monastery, pulled up. Looking sideways at us, the ferryman said something very obvious in their ears. This was the final straw. It was one thing to get what one could for oneself, quite another to encourage others to rip us off too. When the other passengers, furtively, guiltily turning their backs so we should not see, gave him not five *yuan* each but only one, it was our turn to imitate one of Hal's volcanic eruptions. Maria, PMT fuelled to boot, blew first. Umbrella shaking ridiculously in her angry fist, she ran towards him. The man cringed; the rest of the passengers stood on the sand, mouths open at the sight as she stood there swearing at him in words he did not need to understand. I ran to rescue her in case he retaliated, but my own anger took over. Dignity is inappropriately associated with aloofness and detachment, I thought; there are times when anger is just, and this was gross extortion, as well as leaving us all in the sun while he buggered off home. The fellow flinched, thinking I was going to hit him as I approached, index finger pointing like a gun. Yet an agreement is an agreement, and I was not going to renege. I counted out the sixty *yuan* and stuffed it into his chest, a few of the battered, over-used notes fluttering onto the sand. He picked them up and, snivelling even, held the money out to me. We turned our backs in disgust and threw our bags into a tractor trailer. The crowd, until now submerged in stunned silence, animatedly began to gossip. Yet we could not help but notice that the looks they gave us as we left were far from disapproving. Communities can be too much in the grip of a ferryman, and if he is a bad sort, he will not be much liked.

The incident receded a little as the strange landscape took over. On our left, hills with sand dunes blown up their sides were crested with snow, and small *chortens*, new ones, perched upon rounded rocks reflecting the sun. Painted buddhas and *bodhisattvas* were carved in relief from the stone and, together with many *aum mani padme hums*, decorated the lower slopes. Now and again the tractor stuck in the fine, dry sand, and we had to get out and push. Then, all of a sudden, like a golden button on a vast tray, the monastery of Samye came into view, so tiny from this distance against a horseshoe of hills. The only other passenger, a woman, got out shortly before the monastery, and paid one *yuan*. The driver deposited us at the gates, reduced his demand hastily from thirty to fifteen, and in the end settled for the ten we thrust at him unaware how lucky he was that we had nothing smaller.

We were glad to arrive. It had been twelve hours of not uncomplicated travelling and, after the peace and comfort of Lhasa, the day's later awkwardnesses were as rudely discomfiting as sitting suddenly upon a nail. We walked through the small gate in the outer wall that enclosed the monastery and the Tibetan half of town, and wondered which way to go. For no good reason we veered right. Underfoot, a mixture of sand and earth turned progressively to mud. The monastery gleamed in its new completion, but around it the town of Samye seemed as primitive and basic as its remoteness would have suggested several centuries ago. Mud-bricked buildings were scattered here and there, many still in ruins. Dusk was falling fast, and our hopes for the relative comforts of a hotel or guesthouse seemed futile. Nothing resembled a place to stay. A collection of peasant youths and monks hung around outside the only shop, which sold biscuits, sweets, jars of fruit and little else. They directed us to an unmarked three-storey building, inwardly sloping in Tibetan style and falling into dereliction at the back. We entered through the doorway; piles of wood and indeterminate farming machinery lay on the floor, and a set of steps, flimsy as could be, led up through the ceiling.

We took the steps; the house, half cave-like, was built into a little hillside, and the floor above was made of stone. We stuck our heads through the trap-door. A blackened kettle boiled on a wood-stove and, to the right, a door led off. There was no roof above us, and ahead, a ladder with rungs replaced by tree branches led to a square of cells on the top floor. The entire edifice seemed centuries old, and to have been neither cleaned nor touched beyond the odd sweeping since its creation. We hauled ourselves up and stared at the kettle. Its red embers were the only thing of colour, peculiarly inviting the eye with its suggestion of comforts, like hot water and caring humans. A figure appeared at the door on the right, hovering a while to take us in, then approaching quickly, smiling. It was a man, raggedly dressed, his hair in a pigtail wound round his head. He bowed repeatedly, his tongue stuck out as far as it would go and clamped between his teeth. This was the strongest form we had seen of this gesture – intended to show that nothing injurious is hidden in the mouth – which Lhasans have presumably come to consider rather unsophisticated. We followed him up the ladder, unsure if the rungs would take the weight of our backpacks, the wooden hand-rail swaying madly as we pulled upon it. In one of the upstairs cells two monks were stringing prayer flags together, and smiled happily. The man tried his bunch of keys on the other padlocked rooms. None fitted, or had ceased to work with disuse. He shrugged in apology. We were left with an unlocked room, a glassless window covered by an untouchable curtain letting on to the open landing. Pushing at the door, he looked at us as if we had no choice. The room inside was black, burnt out from ceiling to floor and covered with unremoved, chalked Chinese slogans. The worst of it was, it only had three and a half walls. Half the outer wall was so totally demolished that we could walk straight out onto the top of the hillock. Yet through this yawning gap we looked right over the monastery itself, its golden outlines beginning to fade under the gathering clouds and descending darkness.

'We'll take it,' I nodded, noticing warily from the corner of my eye that Maria was not, this time, appreciating the brighter side of life.

The light did not work. Given the absence of electricity elsewhere in the 'house', this should not have surprised us. The man came and went again, leaving us two lit candles which we used to look for our torch. Maria, pre-menstrual temperature rising again, swore, and used the torch to examine the tightly woven, antique straw mattresses for bed bugs. A wind blew; in the same moment the candles blew out and the torch broke, leaving us in pitch darkness as if by some spirit-led conspiracy. I felt on the table. There were no matches. I opened the door to feel my way downstairs; it had begun to rain, heavily so, and since the stairway had no roof I was progressively soaked while gingerly working my way down the makeshift ladder, the candle glow from the man's doorway and the red embers beneath the kettle the only guides for my eyes to follow. Then, slippery in the rain, one of the wooden branches turned beneath my foot and I slipped, swearing, my left leg disappearing through the ladder up to my groin, grazing my shins and simultaneously ricking, as I tried to hold on, the torn tendon in my left arm that had almost, after two years, begun to heal. It could have been worse; had I fallen off completely the ladder was so steep that I could have broken leg, hip or back on the stone floor below. At the noise, the man's daughter appeared with a torch, enabling me to extricate myself, and I followed her into their room.

They had a visitor. It was the go-between from the ferry whom I had taken for the girls' father, though they were now nowhere to be seen. He sat in his animal skin on the edge of the bed, smiling at me, probably telling his friend, who was also in good mood, the story of the fierce Westerners he had under his roof – in so far as he had a roof any more than he had walls. I looked up at the ceiling to check – yes, this room did have one.

'Matches?' I made a striking motion with my hands, and he went off to fetch a box.

Standing there, I examined the room. It was a fair size – probably his whole family lived in it. There was a shrine, the dim glow of its butter lamps the only provision of light. A row of cupboards stood against the far wall. In front of them was the bed. On a stool at the end of the bed the man's wife sat, looking at me blankly, a swaddled infant in her lap, copiously spitting onto her living-room floor and rubbing it in with her feet.

I nodded politely to defuse my approach, bent over and fingered the sheets on the bed next to her, raising my eyebrows questioningly. At first it seemed nothing registered, then suddenly she looked taken aback, giving me a look at once horrified, puzzled and condemning. When the man came back I repeated the gesture to him, and he nodded, gesturing that he would bring them up. I pointed at his thermos, and he filled one with hot water.

'*Thukjichay*,' I thanked him. He stuck his tongue out as far as it would go, and bit it. Armed thus with matches and hot water and expecting the imminent arrival of sheets, I made my way, carefully, back up the ladder.

Inside the room, I relit the candles, pronounced the torch dead, made some tea and stared through the missing wall at the rain outside.

'Well at least we're out of Lhasa,' I said, jovially.

Maria's PMT was in the red zone and, as I seemed unable to learn from experience, joviality was not the best tactic. In this instance she would have given anything to be back in Lhasa. On top of that we had had only one banana each for breakfast and nothing since, and had brought nothing with us because we had not seriously expected any humanly inhabited site the size of Samye to really be so deficient.

Half an hour later we were still sitting on the straw waiting for the sheets. I went down once more and repeated the previous gesture to the man's wife, with a vague hope that she would not clout me. This time she stood up, took me to a cupboard with sheets and bedding piled on the floor, and smilingly left me to it.

The cleanish linen I had selected was dampened by the tentative, careful journey back up the ladder in the dark and rain. My shins were gashed, my tendon pulled, and now my ribs were bruised. In different places I ached and smarted. My clothes were soaked, and I was both hungry and tired. I made Maria's bed with the drier sheets, my own with the damper ones, and then proceeded to get into it. But Maria did not move. Her eyes resembled the embers under the kettle on the wood-stove. Trouble, I thought.

'We haven't eaten.'

'I know, but when you're asleep you won't know that, and we can eat in the morning.'

'I can't sleep when I'm as hungry as this. Why didn't you read the book before we came?'

'Why didn't you?'

'Why should it always be me who makes all the preparations? I spend all my time looking after you and all you do is write. Now first of all go and pile up the rubble there to stop the rats getting in and then we'll go to the shop.'

Since I was already in bed this was not the kind of talk I wanted to hear.

'What rats? It's perfectly alright.'

'I can't sleep with that open hole there. Build a wall and we'll be safer.'

'I feel perfectly safe. The way that man stuck his tongue out I hardly think he'll come and rob us.'

'Look, I'm not going to sleep until it's done.'

I got up, dressed, went out into the rain, gathered a few bricks together and made a little wall, pissed with my back to the monastery, then knocked the wall down again attempting to get back in the dark. That accomplished, I prepared to get back into bed.

'What d'you think you're doing?'

'Going to sleep.'

'I'm hungry.'

'Maria, it's ten at night, it's pitch black, there're no lights anywhere, our torch doesn't work, we'll disturb them downstairs, and the shop'll be closed.'

'We can try.'

'Are you sure it's not your upbringing telling you you'll die if you go one day without food?'

'Don't bring my mother into this!'

'Look, it's suicide to go down that ladder, and come back again, in the rain without a torch. I told you what happened to me. Just go to sleep and we'll think about food in the morning.'

'I'll go myself then.'

'And what am I supposed to do with you if you break your leg? Take you to the casualty unit of the Samye Royal Infirmary?'

'Don't be so bloody sarcastic!'

'Why are you so bloody unreasonable?'

'It's not me who's unreasonable!'

'Look, sometimes, when the emotions are strong, the mind gets fixed on irrational courses. Please think about the dangers. It's not worth it.'

'Don't be so bloody sexist.'

We went. We knocked once again on their door and they readily gave us a torch. The shop unbelievably was open and we bought biscuits, stale rice puffs and *Jianlibao*, which we returned with and ate in a loud silence, before finally going to bed. I slept solidly for eleven hours and Maria was bitten by bed bugs.

Waking, I descended the ladder and returned with hot water from the permanently simmering kettle. Maria had not slept well but was in a better mood, and we made our apologies. We drank our tea and stared through the collapsed wall at the newly restored monastery in front of us. Everything was damp. The night had left snow on the crests of the hills where Padmasambhava's horse had flown, but heavy rain had fallen lower down. Now, shifting blocks of cloud interrupted a blue sky, and the wet rubble I had attempted to make into a wall stared back at me, a hopeless melange of dirt and insects. I walked over it onto the weed-ridden mound, and found the ground sliding, splashing and sucking underfoot, scotching any fanciful ambitions I may have had of searching in the hills for more buried texts.

With a game effort on Maria's part, we rose to investigate more thoroughly and began with a squelchy circumambulation. In the 1920s David-Neel had found Samye 'an abandoned place where can be found hardly more than twenty *trapas* (monks).' Given Samye's size and significance, this was incredible if true, for Samye had been historically the most important monastery in Tibet. Our room testified that not even the monks' quarters survived, and while the renovations were impressive, the only thing of age we saw at Samye was a crinkly, wizened walking stick, which a monk assured us had been Padmasambhava's personal staff. Bending us over like naughty children before the Head, he touched us gently with it on our backs.

There appeared to be only one 'restaurant' near the monastery, with a sign outside saying '*thukpa*' – meat and noodle soup. Ducking, we walked inside. The room was full of dirt and unswept dust; a great log fire burned away at quarter strength, and at one table sat the ferryman with the children from the boat. As we entered, he left. The three children, finding this hilarious, promptly amused the proprietor and his wife with the story of the crossing. The eldest indicated they were going back over the water that day and, prodding the air with her finger in the direction of the vanished ferryman, suggested with a frown that we might have our own problems. It was a wonder we had not thought of it. What if he refused to take us back?

Stomachs scarcely filled by a bowl of plain noodles, we left the tea-shop. Outside, a truck was preparing to leave. It contained a Chinese film crew. Since food and accommodation in Samye left so much to be desired and we had now seen the monastery, we decided to take a chance.

'Lhasa?' I enquired.

They were.

'Lift?' I stuck out my thumb.

'Two minutes,' he indicated on his watch.

We ran, collected our rucksacks and threw them into the back of the truck as it hooted and edged impatiently forward, and found the three children had materialised again, leaning against the back of the cab. We clung uncomfortably to the sharp metal sides as the truck bucked and bounced its way over the dunes. Looking back, the monastery reduced again to a little golden miniature in the distance. Perhaps, Maria wondered, the film crew would be official enough not only to get us over the ferry, but also past the checkpoints and back to Lhasa.

At the ferry, the occupants of the cab jumped out. One was the ferryman. He looked at us surprised, but continued to make the boat ready. The film crew consisted of two Tibetan men, a Chinese woman and a stuffed snow leopard, all of whom (including the leopard) worked for Lhasa TV. They smiled, but were self-absorbed and said little. To pass the time on the return journey the girls, still pretty and snotty at once but appearing now to be totally unescorted, sang 'Old Macdonald Had a Farm' for us in Tibetan, complete with an unchanged chorus of *ee-i-ee-i-o*. It was evidence, at least, of some schooling, though we wondered what animals other than yaks and chickens could possibly be included in the Tibetan version.

Safely transferred to the beach on the other side, we looked the ferryman coldly in the eye and negotiated a lift back to Lhasa from the film crew's driver, who had been waiting for them in his jeep. We were nervous of the airport, fearing we could be arrested and held there, yet it was at the airport restaurant – a shack by the road outside the gates – that they decided to have dinner. Throughout the meal we kept a permanent, nervous eye on the door for incoming policemen, but our attention was completely diverted by the sight of four foreigners on the road outside attempting to climb under the tarpaulin of a truck, parked and pointing in the direction of the city. We watched aghast as the driver came, and threw them off. Had they escaped from custody, and were now attempting to smuggle themselves into Lhasa?

The Pitfalls of Integrity

THE POST OF PANCHEN LAMA, tinged repeatedly with misfortune, has virtually since its inception played the part of the rope in the Sino-Tibetan tug-of-war. The office as created by the third Dalai Lama was achieved on merit; it was not until the 'Great Fifth' Dalai Lama, in tribute to the then Panchen Lama Chokyi Gyaltsen (1570–1662) who was his tutor ('Panchen' means 'Great Teacher'), predicted a reincarnation, that the office began to be transmitted in that fashion. At the same time, the Dalai Lama recognised the Panchen Lama as an 'emanation' of the Buddha Amitabha, thereby bestowing on the Panchen line an essentially spiritual function above and in contrast to the political role with which the Dalai Lamas sometimes sadly saw themselves saddled. Unfortunately history was not to allow the distinction to remain pure. Shigatse was far enough from Lhasa for its courts, encouraged by this new status, to jealously nourish autonomy; rivalry with Lhasa, once engendered, was allowed to fester and become a cancer in Tibet's political self-determination.

The trouble began with Chokyi Gyaltsen's reincarnation, properly speaking the second Panchen Lama, Lobsang Yeshe (1662–1737). In 1728, the seventh Dalai Lama was driven into exile by a punitive Chinese invasion intent on driving a wedge in the Tibetan-Mongol alliance. The Chinese emperor, seeking to divide the Geluk Church and weaken the role of the Dalai Lama, offered Lobsang Yeshe kingship of Tsang and Western Tibet. Weighing his duty to the exiled Dalai Lama against the military might of China, Lobsang Yeshe accepted part of the offer. He had intended it as a compromise, but it was a historic error of major proportion, for it acknowledged the emperor's right to 'give' bits of Tibet to whom he liked, and a corridor of influence was created for China to act in Tibetan affairs.

With the ninth, tenth, eleventh and twelfth Dalai Lamas all dying before their majorities, the consequent power vacuum in Lhasa allowed the office of the Panchen Lama to grow in importance. So soon after Lobsang Yeshe's blunder this was much to the dismay of the Lhasa Regents, and it was during this time that rivalry between the two courts reached its heights. When the 'Great Thirteenth' Dalai Lama attained his majority he hit Tashilhunpo with a large tax demand, ostensibly to support the army but also to assert Lhasa's authority, and perhaps, too, there was suspicion over the then Panchen Lama Chokyi Nyima's involvement in China's 1910 invasion of Tibet.

Chokyi Nyima showed his displeasure by seeking exile in China. This was something of a mistake for him personally since the Chinese refused to let him leave, eventually electing to return him with a military escort. His death in 1937 offset this scenario, but the Chinese had been reminded of the value of the Panchen Lama to their political machinations. In 1944 therefore, *they* 'discovered' the next Panchen Lama, also called Chokyi Gyaltsen (1938–89), on Chinese soil. Recognition of him was forced on the Tibetans in 1951 as part of the infamous Seventeen-Point Agreement.

Chokyi Gyaltsen had thus been born in China, selected at an early age by the Chinese, and brought up and schooled specifically as a mouthpiece for the occupying regime. For a while, it worked. Use was first made of him as early as 1949, when at eleven years of age he supposedly telegrammed Mao to request the 'liberation' of his country. In Lhasa he was seen as a puppet, the authenticity of his incarnation ridiculed. Even we encountered the myth in Lhasa that the 'true' Panchen Lama was in Scotland. In Shigatse however he was accepted, and because Shigatse was his seat, there was no uprising in 1959 and his monastery was left alone. However, by 1960 the PLA's own momentum of destruction carried itself to Tashilhunpo regardless. Some monks were executed, others committed suicide, and all but a handful from four thousand were sent to labour camps. The monastery was ransacked. This must have been pivotal in motivating Chokyi Gyaltsen's greater independent stance.

By 1961 the attempts of the Great Leap Forward to substitute wheat and rice for barley had brought Tibet to its knees. Avedon describes the situation graphically:

In Tibet, thousands were dying from starvation. Lhasa and Shigatse were dead cities, without stores, goods or commerce. Monasteries were gutted. Work gangs covered the countryside, prisoners and free alike toiling over dirt roads lined by dull green PLA convoys carting the harvest and religious wealth of Tibet to the People's Republic. With nothing left to lose, Lhasans abandoned their labour and converged on the Panchen Lama as he made his way out of Lhasa, petitioning him to plead with the Chinese for food and medical care. Their appeals galvanised him to act. Once in Peking he delivered a 70,000 character memorandum to Mao Zedong describing conditions in Tibet, included in which were demands for more grain for farmers, care for the aged and infirm, a genuine acceptance of religious freedom and a cessation of mass arrests. Mao assured the Panchen Lama that the proposals would be heeded.

He had made a stand, but promises made in Beijing were not brought to fruition in Tibet. So, in 1964 he became more bold. He agreed to denounce the Dalai Lama in public in Lhasa. A celebration of the forbidden *Monlam Chenmo*, the annual Great Prayer Festival established by Tsong Khapa, was specially licensed as the vehicle for the act. Then, with ten thousand citizens before him, he turned the vehicle around, praising the Dalai Lama and asserting Tibet's right to independence. After a particularly violent interrogation (*thamzing*), he was, at the age of twenty-seven, locked up in China's notorious Qin Cheng Number One jail. On release in 1978 he married, apologised for his 'crimes' and began again to fill a rubber-stamp role. In 1979 a poster on the Democracy Wall written by a former cell mate described his hunger strike and an attempt to commit suicide during torture. He was not officially rehabilitated until April 1988.

In 1989 however, Chokyi Gyaltsen died after a banquet in his honour in Shigatse, having made his strongest assertion of Tibetan integrity since that fateful day in 1964. As previously, it would seem he was motivated to speak by the conditions of his people. Before, it had been the destruction of his monastery, the imprisonment of his monks and an official *laissez-faire* attitude to mass starvation that had made him protest. This time, Tibet was still unsettled after yet more gratuitous loss of life in three years of uprising, from 1987 to 1989. At the beginning of March, 1988, in spite of cut telephone and telex links, the world's press was full of pictures and stories as Lhasa erupted during the Great Prayer Festival. Many died, and the Jokhang was stormed. On March 10th the Panchen Lama was required to speak. He did so, attacking the rioters, but also blaming the authorities. They had brought this upon themselves, he said publicly, by treating Tibetans badly in the past. In December there was more unrest, this time with foreign casualties. The following March the rioting was even more severe, and compounded by the Tibetan Youth Congress's public dissatisfaction with the Dalai Lama's policy of non-violence and the 'Five-Point Peace Plan', which sought compromise on the independence issue. At the worst point, on March 6th 1989, police opened fire on demonstrators causing a hundred casualties and thirty deaths. The Tibetans responded by taking control of the Barkhor, erecting burning barricades and storming a police station to release prisoners. That night, the police broke into homes, taking away young men, and in the morning martial law was declared. But the Panchen Lama did not live to witness that last orgy of death, for on January 25th 1989 he had made his last speech. In it, he stated that the detriment of China's rule over Tibet was greater than the benefit, that 'leftism' (old-style Communism) was a greater threat to Tibetan prosperity than 'rightism' (in Tibetan terms, the independence movement). On January 28th, he died. It is a universal Tibetan belief that in return for his words he was poisoned. In Lhasa he had again become, in life, a puppet. But in death he became a hero.

Given Tibetan belief in reincarnation of course, his death was not the end of it. In May 1995 the Dalai Lama announced the discovery of the new Panchen Lama in Tibet. The Chinese could not accept this without accepting the Dalai Lama's authority over the Panchen Lama's selection rather than their own. Out-manouevered, they spirited the nomad boy, Gedhun Chokyi Nyima, and his family away to Beijing, charged the Abbot of Tashilhunpo, Chadrel Rinpoche, with collaboration, and locked up seventy other lamas in a hotel until they 'agreed' an alternative choice – Gyaltsen Norbu, the son of medium-ranking party *cadres* in Nagchu. The irony of an avowedly atheist, nominally Communist government claiming the right to identify a true reincarnation as born to their own officials was not lost on the world's press, though exactly how those two *cadres* were persuaded to volunteer their own son is a story that did not surface. For now, whether the boy chosen by the Dalai Lama will ever fill his role remains to be seen. All that can be said is that, if he is alive, he is certainly the world's youngest political prisoner.

10

SAFELY BACK AT THE HOTEL, we caught up on the events of the last two days. People were talking about troop parades; two Danes had been in a group of five held at the airport for two days and prevented from leaving by police armed with electric cattle-prods. Eventually, they sneaked off on a passing bus and had no doubt that the four foreigners we had seen clambering over a truck had been part of their plane-load from Chengdu, still trying to get away.

The following day, escapes continued. Clearly no-one knew how to stop the Chengdu PSB issuing permits, and the police were too incompetent to hold so many people in the airport hotel. Numbers were building up there, and Lhasa had never seen so many individual tourists wandering around, making a mockery of their earlier ultimatum to us all to leave. At the same time people were disappearing, presumed arrested. A young Swiss had set off for Samye, intending like ourselves to spend one night there, and had not returned, nor had a New Zealander who had set off for Tsetang. Tibet was beginning to resemble a real-life game of Dungeons and Dragons – if you were in the wrong place at the wrong time, you got caught and removed from the board. If you had the right luck, bravery or magic spell, you survived. We had our own problem of an expiring visa, and had to consider the chances of having it extended anywhere in Tibet as virtually nil. As Hal said, the only extension anyone ever gets here is by the number of days it takes to get to Nepal.

This was one factor in deciding whether to go to Shigatse without waiting for the 27th. We had to balance the fact that if we stayed in Lhasa just for these crucial dates, we would have seen little else of Tibet. Another factor was that a Frenchman in that morning from Golmud, had been informed by our lady officer that all foreigners in Lhasa were to be rounded up and bussed or flown out on the 26th – in two days' time. Consoling ourselves that if any trouble blew up on that day there were now enough Westerners around for it to be well witnessed, we decided to go. We considered the decision understandable, but it earned us a stand-up row with Hal, who accused us of being deserters.

The Frenchman's tale seemed endorsed when we went to the bus station to buy tickets, only to be refused with the bizarre information that no independent foreigners were allowed to *leave* Lhasa for the next *three* weeks – not even to Golmud. We were, it seemed, under 'city arrest'. A certain amount of amused consternation spread through the Yak when we returned.

'First they tell us to go before the anniversary dates, then they tell us we have to stay for them,' said Hal, smiling wryly. 'It's obvious they plan to bus us all out in two days' time.'

The hotel staff meanwhile phoned the Lhasa City PSB for confirmation. That they knew nothing about it revealed the ruling to be the initiative of the TAR. The City PSB however, in a sign of the rivalry between the two authorities, promised to over-rule the directive. The staff then phoned the TAR, who admitted it was their policy because 'they wanted no disruption at this sensitive time'. The screws were definitely being turned, but not only on us. News arrived that the bus carrying pilgrims to Ganden had been withdrawn, and in the course of the afternoon several people with tours to Everest base camp found them cancelled, while taxi companies received orders not to rent to foreigners for the next three weeks.

The City PSB having promised to over-rule the TAR, we went ourselves to the police station in the morning and waited in the corridor of the dilapidated building while two Chinese police officers brought in a dejected Tibetan beggar and handcuffed him to the staircase. Half an hour later a woman police officer arrived and invited us in. We explained that we wanted to go to Shigatse, but the bus station was inexplicably refusing to sell us tickets. She hissed angrily into the air and went into the next room to telephone the bus station. While she was gone Maria hovered around her desk, her eyes lighting upon a curious volume entitled *Security English-Chinese Phrasebook*. Glancing at the door she beckoned me and flipped it open. Among various phrases in translation, one in the middle of the page stood out: '*I know I am wrong and I want to be punished.*'

Just that one phrase seemed to cast so much light on Chinese psychology, where so often magnanimity appears only to follow one's demeaning oneself. The most common punishment for foreigners in China is to write a confession, but I could hardly imagine anyone pointing sanely to such a phrase. We looked to see what else we might find – *please execute me* perhaps – when we heard a brief shout followed by the slamming down of a receiver and flipped it shut again.

Seconds later the policewoman returned, flustered and annoyed. 'Now you go. They give you ticket, no problem. If they say no—' she wrote her name and telephone number on a piece of paper, 'tell them to call me.'

Well, this is efficiency, I thought. 'Can you tell us why there's a problem for foreigners buying tickets?'

'No! I can't answer these questions. Go to the bus station!'

'Can you tell us what the prisoner outside has done?'

Her eyebrows almost left her face in anger at Maria's cheek. 'Go to the bus station!' she screamed again.

It seemed unwise to push the matter. The beggar, with whom we had been unable to communicate during our half-hour wait, was still standing handcuffed to the staircase when we left.

Facing the possibility that we might not get back into Lhasa, we spent all afternoon visiting our favourite haunts as if for the last time. We began with the rickety wooden bridge which stretched over the Kyichu to 'Thieves' Island'. In a city where even the telegraph poles were fair game for prayer flags, the structure of the old bridge stood no chance of remaining visible. Immeasurable layers of bright, tattered cotton, their printed prayers torn by the winds that blew their blessings over the land, had accumulated ceaselessly for centuries. At the beginning of the bridge a woman sat, threading more prayer flags for sale. We bought a string, in the traditional order of yellow, green, red, white and blue, and tied our own to the fluttering mass.

On the far side of the island the river separated into wide, fast-running fingers that scratched the land before the sheer southern mountains, in a great illusion of space just minutes from the city centre. The best views of the Potala could be had from here. Cut deep with the pain of impending loss, with the Potala as our backdrop, we hopped over the small rocks that jutted like stepping stones through the surface of the freshly melted water, dipping our fingers in its icy current, splashing ourselves like children, incongruously laughing against the thrust of deeper feelings. We looked at the river running clearly and noisily over the shallow stones and sand, and at the several picnicking Tibetan families on its banks. We recalled the parents who on our first morning in Lhasa had so keenly sent their little boy over with the simple message, *I like you*. It hurt like the thought of losing a new but dear friend to think that any time could be the last one saw Lhasa; it had grown on us, and it had grown inside us too. I was conscious that we were folding the city away in our hearts, like placing a beloved photograph in an inside pocket. No-one could take it away from us; only we could allow the memory to fade, and I could not conceive of that. In future moments of despair I thought, we would look back on our time in Lhasa as evidence that life itself had been worthwhile. We recrossed the Kyichu, circumambulated the Potala, and as darkness fell made two circumambulations of the Barkhor, deliberately leaving a further one to be performed another time.

In the morning we took a rickshaw to the bus station, a hundred yards south of the Holiday Inn on the road running past the Kyichu. It was efficiently organised, with eight numbered aisles leading to eight big glass doors. There were, however, no destination signs, in any language. At the front of the right-hand queue, passengers having their baggage weighed were being charged a weight-tax, and then their bags were loaded onto the roofs of two buses. A number of officials bustled them along like donkeys with loads. A Westerner we had not seen before was standing at the back of this queue and we asked him where he was going. He said he was going to Golmud. He was Israeli, and he wore only a T-shirt to keep out the cold.

'Do you have any other clothes?'

'Sure, they're going on the roof.'

'Don't you realise you're taking the highest civilian road in the world? At this time of year the snow will be feet deep by now, the bus'll be like a fridge, they may keep going at night and you've a high probability of breaking down?'

He gloated. 'I've been in the Israeli army. No problem.'

'What do they do for training – lock you in a deep-freeze? Come on, you can't tell me you're going to enjoy this.'

He shrugged, enjoying our disbelief. 'It won't be that bad.'

'Look, we came that way three weeks ago, and it was bloody

cold then in a heated truck. In a bus you'll be lucky if the windows close.'

'No problem, no problem!'

We talked a little further, but only until we could take no more and moved away. He had been in Lhasa for three days on a package tour – just so he could say he had been here, he said – but apart from the Potala he had not found anything 'to see'. This was a traveller of the proudest kind, for whom travel is essentially an endurance test, a means of self-validation in a hostile world, and the greater the hostility the stronger the sense of self. On reaching Golmud, we guessed correctly, he was going straight to Beijing, Hard Seat. He was also unfortunately typical of that most disliked breed of individual traveller, the ex-National Service Israeli. Like the legendary 'ugly American' anywhere or the reality of the British in Benidorm, young Israelis have an unfortunate reputation in Asia. Released from the army, these new incarnations of rampant racism and malevolent machismo cavalier their way around Bangkok and Saigon in muscle-revealing singlets with the basest colonial arrogance, intimidating trinket sellers, arguing over *sous*, picking fights, getting drunk, keeping everyone awake at night and seeing everyone else, particularly the locals, from an antagonistic viewpoint. Everybody hates them. Probably, they hate themselves too, which adds to their anger. The only thing different about this one was that he had wandered a little off his patch and was not in a group. We hoped he froze to death.

Our bus was a mixture of Chinese and Tibetans. It did not seem a coincidence that the only two monks and ourselves should be seated over the rear wheel arches. We had no reason to expect the road to be good, and would certainly not be nodding off.

At the checkpoint outside Lhasa a gun was unshouldered and aimed at the passengers by an adolescent soldier who stood in the front. His colleague only checked the papers of the Tibetans, not of the Chinese or ourselves. Yet the intimidation was soon forgotten. The old road was really a dirt track, treacherous, but subtly beautiful and grandly spectacular in turn, leading over two high passes, all hair-pin bends and sheer drops. As we began to climb the first pass, Kampa La (4794 metres), the undulating carpets of grass and vetch that rose and fell, first above and then below our window, were turned by billions of tiny alpines into a speckled riot of purple, pink, yellow and blue, stretching away like waves on an ocean of heaving earth. There were no trees, and soon our climbing left the grass level behind too, replacing it with the shades and intricate veins of desolate slate and rock. The air grew colder, and even more crisp. Mantras were murmured with increasing volume as we wound dangerously to the top of the pass and, at the exact spot marked by a cairn of stones and prayer flags, the Tibetans simultaneously rose, doffed their hats and showered reams of printed paper prayers out of the windows with a raucous, triumphant shout of 'Lha Gyal Lo!' (The Gods are Victorious!) before sinking, laughing, back into their seats. The Chinese, witnessing this display of undiminished devotion and undimmed spirit, shifted uncomfortably. Outside, the passing cairns were an other-worldly sight, erected by humans in the middle of a big nowhere of barren rock and still covered, under the tent of ripening blue, by a dazzling, unmelted morning frost.

Descending from Kampa La we could see the line where the grass began, and ahead a glint of water. The bus turned and tilted and slid its way down until, on our left, Lake Yamdrok suddenly appeared in all its fullness, another magical mirror reflecting in perfect tranquillity the totality of its surroundings. The wild beauty of everything was duplicated and enhanced in the water's clarity. What was outside was inside, and what was up was down – the blue sky, a few drifting clouds, the snowy mountain peaks, the green of the lower slopes and the russet hues of dry rock that separated the grass from the snow, all was as clear in the water below as it was in the air above. As we reached the level of the lake and drove next to it across the plain, an upturned rainbow appeared, hung like a horseshoe of light in the sky. We gazed at it. It *was* supernatural, this land, in the literal sense of the word. Indeed it would seem strange were it not inhabited by gods and ghosts and demons, but the demons here had the upper hand – a hydro-electric dam built on Lake Yamdrok with European aid had already drained it by thirty per cent, and in a few years' time there could be nothing left at all.

As twilight rose, we entered Shigatse. Shigatse was huge. We were dropped at the bus station and received directions to our hotel American-style, in blocks. 'Go three blocks down, go left two blocks . . .' The blocks too were massive, consisting of many buildings or single mega-buildings, all faceless monstrosities in the true tradition of Chinese functionalism. The streets were wide, soulless and empty, and it took a good forty minutes to hike through the concrete desert to what remains of the tiny Tibetan quarter.

We reached the Tenzin Hotel, a comfortable but basic affair with no running water, as darkness ate the last of the shadows. After eating and settling in we sat drinking on the balcony with Paul and Mark, an English pair from Bradford and Chester, who were busy working and travelling anywhere but home and had already proved good drinking companions in Lhasa.

Over beer and *Sports Report* on the World Service, they informed us the Shigatse PSB were happily issuing permits to anywhere except Everest Base Camp and the bus station was happily selling tickets to anywhere, including Lhasa. Best of all, Tashilhunpo monastery was beginning a three-day festival of 'lama-dancing' the next day; the only proviso was that some of the monks had thrown stones at a Scotsman the previous week, and Paul and Mark had themselves been rudely turned away.

With their beer flowing generously, we discussed the rather negative image that Tashilhunpo had managed to acquire. All of us, it seemed, had been warned by both monks and laypeople in Lhasa on no account to give the monks in Tashilhunpo Dalai Lama pictures, as they were in the habit of first asking for them, then reporting the foreigner to the police. Even *Lonely Planet* mentioned the stonethrowing, and I remembered Danziger, in *Danziger's Travels*, telling of how his companion was beaten up by the monks there. Whatever the combination of fact and rumour, the monastery was clearly a complicated issue, suffering as much as it gained through association with the Panchen Lama. We talked and drank and talked and drank until the last bottle was gone, and rose to totter off to bed.

'Oh, there's one thing we forgot to tell you,' said Paul as the courtyard below loomed in and out of focus. 'Every new arrival in the Tenzin Hotel gets a personal evening welcome from the PSB.'

We had unfortunately forgotten about that, indeed we had been in a drunken sleep for an hour when the loud knock came. Maria moaned. I swore, and got up. I had been naked under the sheets and warm carpet, and grabbed a hand-towel as I got blearily to my feet, shaking immediately with the cold. In my blurred and inebriated state I just did not consider the police, and thought it was probably the manager wanting to tell us something. As I awkwardly turned the handle I was surprised therefore when the door was thrust abruptly towards me, and a female police officer strode assertively into the room to demand our passports with two male underlings in her wake.

I was not, perhaps, as surprised as she was, for the towel I had chosen was not the largest of towels, and barely reached to each hip. This made the passports difficult to negotiate, as I really needed two hands to preserve appearances. Like some nightmarish party game I had to somehow retrieve the items from Maria and hand them over while keeping my hands by my waist without letting go of the towel, managing all the while not to turn my back on the officers as the towel was too small to stretch right around, all when it would have been hard enough in my condition to walk a straight line fully clothed. I gritted my teeth and attempted an obliging smile. My contortions on receiving the passports from Maria intensified the situation. The policewoman blushed. Indeed, she could hardly have been more embarrassed had I chosen a face flannel for the purpose. Her two male colleagues however were enjoying it, and she blushed again as they began teasing her. I guessed that 'Get out your gun and say hands up!' was probably the gist of their jokes. Passports in hand, I wobbled suggestively towards her, offering them on tip-toe from my right hip. 'Don't take the wrong thing!' her sidekicks might have said in their now barely concealed hysteria. The woman managed a 'thankyou' as she nervously took them, careful not to snatch in case I lost my grip, and smiled determinedly while her beetroot complexion deepened. The two men now ceased all attempts at containing themselves, doubtless relishing the thought of the weeks of ribbing that were to follow. For myself I stood there like a sot, shivering in the sobering cold, wondering how she was going to give them back. I watched as she checked them, trying to be cool, to keep her authority, refusing to be hurried. In the end she placed them sensibly on the bed, and with a very formal and proper nod, almost standing to attention, wished us a pleasant time in Shigatse. With that she turned and swept out, the jokes of her colleagues continuing behind her down the stairs and across the courtyard into the street below.

In the morning I noticed that an excellent view of the low white houses couched in the green-tinged but arid hills conjured up, curiously, a more Middle-Eastern than Asian feel. Out of sight behind the hills, leaning into them almost, was the great monastery best known as the seat of the Panchen Lama. With some hot bread inside us, we set out to test its more modern reputation for xenophobia.

We found Tashilhunpo an impressive sight, layers of gold-topped, ochre-red buildings rising from the base of a small mountain. The dance, on a specially constructed giant stage in front of the monastery, had already begun when we arrived. Traditionally, these performances were opportunities for the clergy to pay the laity back in entertainment for supporting them through the year (as well as fulfilling real ritualistic needs, such as exorcism), and were usually times of great excitement and laughter. On stage the monks had masks and costumes; off it the large crowd had donned their best clothes, fine *chubas* with silk blouses being much in evidence among the higher classes, the peasants managing as best they could. Everyone sat in large family groups, the women keeping their men's wooden bowls topped up with *chang*, everyone's cheeks bulging out with Tibetan cheese. Photographs were forbidden, and it did nothing to help their reputation that a number of monk-policemen made sure of that, one of them by hitting Maria's camera.

Maria wandered around nonetheless, avoiding the monk-police as best she could and discreetly taking pictures of the crowd. While I stood and watched, a young Chinese man came and stood by my side.

'Hello,' he said simply. He had a pleasant face, bespectacled, with unusually thick lips for a Chinese.

'Hello,' I replied, wondering what was coming next.

'You're enjoying it?'

'Yes, the costumes are excellent,' I answered politely. 'Are you a student?'

'No. I'm a judge.'

'A judge?' He looked about twenty. 'How old are you?'

'Twenty-two. I finished being a student last year. Now I come here.'

'Where were you a student?'

'In Guangdong province.'

'I see – so you studied law, and then the government sent you here?' It was the usual scenario for students in China to be given a posting by the government after graduating, and it could be anywhere. I imagined the same had happened to him. I was wrong.

'No – I studied social sciences, and I wanted to come here.'

'You *wanted* to come here?' No-one *wanted* to come to Tibet. Tibet was the short straw, which was why the wages were so high. 'Why?'

He laughed, acknowledging the strangeness of his desire. 'You see, I'm a Christian, an evangelical Christian. I know Tibetans are heathens and I want to convert them, so I requested Tibet, and they, of course, were happy to give me it.'

Maria, returning at this point, butted in. 'But the Tibetans at least have a religion — most Chinese don't have a religion at all. Why don't you work amongst the Chinese?'

He thought a moment. 'It's a good question. But they're worshipping devils here. Worshipping devils is worse than not worshipping anything.'

'Have you had any success?' enquired Maria, predicting the answer in her tone.

'No, but I'm still in my first year. There're problems also with the Chinese I work with, so I can't speak about it at work.'

That hardly seemed surprising. Yet he had given himself such an impossible task it was difficult to be angry with him, and he was so enthusiastically friendly and open — it is said that southerners are warmer than northerners in China, the opposite to what they say in Britain — he virtually made himself likeable. I changed the subject to his job, realising that 'judge' in China no doubt meant something a little different from in the West.

'You're very young to be a judge.'

'No — people start after they graduate.'

'So what are your duties — what kind of cases do you get to deal with?'

'Divorces.'

'Only divorces?'

'Yes.'

'I see. Are there many divorces in Shigatse?'

'Oh yes — many. Tibetans are always divorcing. I have to stop them.'

'You have to stop them? How?'

'That's my job. When people want to divorce they come to me and talk about their marriage, and I try to help them make a reconciliation.'

Aha, I thought. He was a marriage-guidance counsellor.

'Are you married?'

He laughed. 'No, no, I'm too young!'

'Have you ever had a girlfriend?'

He laughed again, embarrassed. 'No, no, not yet, I've never had a girlfriend!'

'Not even a kiss?' It was a little naughty of me.

'No, not even a kiss, and I don't want one! I'm too young! I only think about my job, my friends, and Jesus.'

The absurdity of China came home strongly in meetings like this. A marriage-guidance counsellor who was twenty-two and had never kissed anyone, an evangelical Christian attempting to convert fervent Buddhists in a Communist heartland. His life had absurdity and pointlessness written all over it, but because of his natural enthusiasm he had not yet noticed it himself. When he was gone, his place at my side was taken by a Tibetan woman, about sixty perhaps and heavily lined, aristocratic looking in expensive traditional clothes, a large picture of Mao pinned prominently to her breast.

Shigatse certainly seemed very Sinified. Whereas Tibetans and Chinese were like separate species in Lhasa, in Shigatse they visibly intermingled more. Dissent was certainly not in evidence, neither from the people nor from the monks, although lack of dissent did not extend as far as sharing China's National Day celebrations on October 1st, when ten trucks of soldiers drove around the city letting off firecrackers. It may not be unconnected that among Tibetans in Shigatse there is a vast and striking gulf between social classes. The poor are very poor, and live either in the countryside or in the hovels on the hill behind the monastery. Their major concern in life could not be dissent – even were they politicised – but mere survival. The richer ones have perhaps seen their living standards rise under the Chinese, and allowed themselves to be bought out. Further, Tibetans in Shigatse have not had to put up with the continual provocation that Lhasans suffer, and nor, in this land of controlled information, did they have much idea of what went on in other parts of the country (let alone in the outside world). Not kicking against the system, they have become more efficient sponges, absorbing the world according to the Party without a separate source for scepticism. So the monks can ask for Dalai Lama pictures, then report the giver to the police. Since the furore over the Panchen Lama's latest reincarnation however, one wonders if the way of things in Shigatse may yet change.

With the festival over, the monastery reopened for business, and as the crisp cold of the morning was transformed, desert-like in seconds into the fierce heat of mid-day, we walked up the cobbled courtyard to where a maze of little alleys separated the ochre buildings. In gaps of blue between the high roofs, flashes of black, outspread wings suggested a nearby 'sky burial', the proximity of the site having prompted a notice in the Tenzin Hotel informing foreigners that visitors attempting to photograph it would be 'educated and criticised'. Intriguing as that sounded, we were happy to respect Tibetan sensitivities and let this be the closest we got.

Whether Shigatse was obsessed with photography, and exactly how true were the rumblings about its monks, did not take long to confirm. On a pillar at the top of the steps of the first temple was a notice giving the prices for photographs in each of the halls. They wanted a hundred FEC (£11.36) for one snapshot, five hundred FEC (£56.81) to use a camcorder. The prices were so outrageous, I instinctively pulled my pen and notebook from my pocket, and began to scribble them down.

As soon as I did so a livid, middle-aged monk rushed at us from the darkness, followed by a younger monk in equally furious rage. Arms flailing they grabbed at my notebook and pen, and failing to get hold of them lunged at our tickets which Maria still held in her hands. Failing to catch those as well, they resorted to grabbing us, shouting and trying to muscle us down the steps. At first the scenario was so bizarre we found it amusing, but as they became rougher and more intent on throwing us out we became indignantly furious at their distinctly unmonkish behaviour. And why were they annoyed? Were they ashamed of the fees? They were, after all, stuck up there for all to see. And why did they instinctively relate to us antagonistically, when monks everywhere else saw foreigners as friends, as 'on their side'? The elder now put both hands around Maria's arm – no prohibition on touching women there – and attempted to wrestle her away. Both were slightly built and Maria, when she dug in her heels, had little real difficulty in resisting the assault. Fearful of the fracas being seen at the top of the steps and insisting on our right to be there, I simply walked forward into the depths of the temple; this caused the elder monk to release Maria and assist his comrade in arresting me, but their puniness was such that I had no trouble, with a mad monk on each arm, in walking right up to the shrine. To their consternation, I began to prostrate. As I did so they backed off. Confused and panting, they spoke to each other and disappeared. Convinced that they had run for help, we left the shrine room and dissolved into a large package tour in the Maitreya Buddha Hall where a party of Italians were admiring, but not photographing, Tashilhunpo's prize asset – a golden statue of the future Buddha, seated, and several storeys high.

We wandered with the package tour and had no further problems. When we left them, we found ourselves in the room where the Panchen Lama's embalmed and gilded body awaited transplantation to its *chorten*. It was seated, cross-legged and smiling on a cushion in a tank of glass, and in front of it a dozen monks continued a perpetual *puja* for his safe reincarnation and discovery. We gazed at the corpse. It was, of course, his original body, painted gold, with the lips painted red. We should not have been surprised that it looked just like him; it *was* him. To show respect, we prostrated. Three young monks beckoned us, removed two blessing ribbons from the shrine and tied them smilingly around our necks. For a moment there was the spirit again of Lhasa, and not all was rotten in the state of Tashilhunpo.

A Productive Friendship

THE CHINESE CLAIM TO TIBET, spurious ideas about Princess Wen Cheng and unity apart, rests on the notion that Tibet was incorporated into China under the Mongolian Yuan Dynasty (1260–1368). This claim is made irrespective of the facts that the Mongolians at the time were considered foreign, that the Chinese considered themselves under alien occupation and the end of the Yuan Dynasty a liberation, that centuries earlier a wall had been built to keep the Mongolians out, and that Mongolia is today an independent state. In spite of all that, Kublai Khan is now with political convenience considered Chinese, and so are Tibetans. While the absurdity of this reasoning has been likened to suggesting that France should be governed from London since both were once under Roman rule, it is also questionable to what extent Tibet was 'ruled' by the Khans.

In 1207 it came to Tibetan attention that Genghis Khan, undoubtedly a ruler of the bloodthirsty rather than the sage variety, was swallowing up parts of China and stood already on Tibet's borders. Rumours that his barbarous imagination stretched to boiling alive the leaders of the lands he captured doubtless also arrived with the news, and with some lateral thinking a delegation was despatched to befriend the fiend. It worked. An annual tribute was arranged, and the Mongolians did not invade Tibet.

When Genghis Khan died in 1227, the Tibetans rather rashly ceased the tribute. In 1240 Godan Khan, Genghis's grandson, invaded Tibet with thirty thousand troops, sacking villages, burning monasteries and killing monks and civilians at whim, in traditional Mongolian fashion. Then, curiously, Godan Khan suddenly stopped short of Lhasa and sent his envoys to look for 'an outstanding Buddhist lama'. They returned with the news that the lama of Drikhung was the richest, the lama of Taklung was the most friendly, and the lama of Sakya was the most religious.

The Sakya lama, Kunga Gyaltsen, was indeed renowned for his piety in spite of being the grandson of Kunga Nyingpo, who had personally studied with Virupa, a man from the same *siddha* tradition as Padmasambhava and who was famous for halting the sun in the sky in order to continue drinking in a tavern. Kunga Gyaltsen was also known as Sakya Pandita – the 'Great Teacher from Sakya'. At the age of sixty-three, his scholarship having enhanced the reputation of his monastery and perhaps earned him a life of quiet routine, Sakya Pandita one day received an unusual letter in the post:

> *I, the most powerful and prosperous Prince Godan, wish to inform the Sakya Pandita, Kunga Gyaltsen, that we need a lama to advise my ignorant people on how to conduct themselves morally and spiritually ... after much consideration I have decided that you are the only person for the task ... [and] I will not accept any excuse on account of your age or the rigours of the journey ... It would, of course, be easy for me to send a large body of troops to bring you here; but in so doing, harm and unhappiness might be brought to many innocent living beings. In the interest of the Buddhist faith and the welfare of all living creatures, I suggest that you come to us immediately. As a favour to you, I shall be very kind to those monks who are now living on the west side of the sun.*

His words on receiving it are not recorded, but in 1244 Sakya Pandita duly headed for the Mongolian camp at Kokonor, sending on ahead his two nephews, Pakpa, ten, and Chakna, six. It is said that by the time Sakya Pandita finally arrived three years later, the two boys had already 'won the heart' of the Khan, who gladly accepted Buddhist teaching and ceased throwing Chinese people into rivers as a means of population control. Far from embarking on a journey of disaster, a 'priest-patron' relationship with Mongolia was established, Godan Khan in 1247 investing Sakya Pandita with rulership over Tibet's thirteen provinces in exchange for religious teaching. Tibet now had central authority for the first time since Langdarma's assassination in 842, the Sakya School now became the dominant school of Buddhism in the land, and the town of Sakya became the *de facto* capital.

Godan Khan was succeeded by Kublai Khan, and Sakya Pandita by Pakpa. From the time that Kublai Khan and Pakpa met in 1253, their relationship was compared to 'the sun and moon in the sky'. Kublai Khan even consented to prostrate himself before Pakpa when receiving teachings, and to consult him on any matter concerning Tibet. Although later Tibetan accounts state that what won Kublai Khan over was Pakpa's magical prowess in competition with Taoists and Nestorians – he is supposed to have cut off his own arms, legs and head and reassembled them, which would be a hard trick to beat – it seems that what really impressed Kublai Khan about Pakpa was the young man's intellect. Since Kumarajiva had asserted Buddhism's distinctiveness from Taoism, the two religions in China had been in constant rancour, the Taoists claiming Lao Tzu pre-dated the Buddha and forging texts to 'prove' it. In 1254 Kublai Khan organised a debate between the two, in which the Taoists fell to the incisive questioning of the nineteen-year-old Pakpa, and were forced by him to admit their forgeries. In addition to having all Taoist texts except the *Tao Te Ching* destroyed, Kublai Khan's punishment – that the losers would convert to the faith of the victors – also showed the extent to which the Mongolians had become 'civilised' since the days of Genghis, a feat largely due to the influence of Buddhism.

Following that famous debate, Kublai Khan granted Pakpa supreme authority over Tibet – not bad at the age of nineteen – in a letter:

As a true believer in the Lord Buddha ... I have always shown special favour to the monks and monasteries of your country ... After studying under you ... and in return for what I have learned ... I must make you a gift ... This letter, then, is my present ... It grants you authority over all Tibet, enabling you to protect the religious institutions and faith of your people and to propagate the Lord Buddha's teachings ...

To the monks, I should say they should realise and be grateful that they have not been taxed; nor has their way of life been altered. We Mongolians shall not respect you, if your monks do not conscientiously carry out the teachings of the Buddha. Do not think the Mongolians incapable of learning your religion. We learn it gradually. I have high esteem for your monks and should appreciate it if they do not embarrass me in public by any undignified behaviour.

As your patron ... by this letter I have taken upon myself the sponsorship of your religion.

In 1260 Pakpa's authority was enhanced by the title 'Ti Shri' – Imperial Viceroy. In 1268, his intellect was again put to good use when he designed a script for the Mongolian language, consisting of 41 letters and capable of rendering 1,200 syllables. Kublai Khan immediately adopted it as the official script, though it was time-consuming to write and fell into disuse after the emperor's death. In 1270 Kublai Khan moved his capital from Karakorum to the new one being built at Beijing (in itself a momentous decision, marking a shift in Mongolian custom from nomadry to town dwelling, and thereafter, it has been argued, to their downfall). Pakpa travelled there with him, recording in his memoirs that Kublai Khan was 'very friendly' with a 'stranger from a faraway land', undoubtedly Marco Polo, who also records meeting Pakpa. Distance could not divide the friendship of the two great men, which remained sincere to the end. When Pakpa returned to Tibet in 1274 the emperor, at considerable risk of neglect of his state, accompanied him for several months as far as Amdo, so unwilling was he to relinquish his company. In 1280 however Pakpa died at his monastery in Sakya, poisoned by a petty attendant seeking to incriminate his secretary.

Following Kublai Khan's death in 1295, both Mongolian power in China and Sakya power in Tibet went into decline. There was never any doubt that Tibetan autonomy and the Tibetan way of life during this period were overshadowed by Mongolian power, but by the skilful creation of goodwill such power became a useful patronage. By comparing the letters of Godan and Kublai Khan to Sakya Pandita and his nephew, one can see how threat diminished and genuine support arose. Tibet soon became fully independent of Mongolian rule under the nationalist movement of Changchub Gyaltsen (1302–64), and China followed suit in 1368 with the new Ming Dynasty, whose rulers found it hard to find Tibetan lamas willing to visit them. It has also to be noted that throughout relations with the Mongolians there was never a moment when the practical administration of Tibet was not in Tibetan hands, and indeed, before 1950, aside from a few short-lived invasions, there never was such a moment in Tibetan history.

11

IN ORDER TO BETTER UNDERSTAND Shigatse we reasoned we could do little better than visit two doctors, Kathryn Stangl and Jean Guillermin, who had lived there for two years under the aegis of the Swiss Red Cross. We found them in their garden, sitting reading on two camp beds which they rotated to stay in the sun, as the fiercely contrasting cold shade shifted and encroached like a rogue tide. We had come at a good time, and they received us warmly. While Kathryn made us some tea, Jean explained how they had fallen into their post.

The Swiss Red Cross centre had been established as the result of one of the Panchen Lama's many humanitarian requests for his Shigatse prefecture (which, Jean repeated several times as if it measured the uphill nature of their work, is four times the size of Switzerland). The Panchen Lama had asked for a hospital, but received the reply that the prefecture had eighteen hospitals already, which was quite enough. What he got instead was the Swiss Red Cross centre for the training of Tibetan village 'barefoot' doctors. Since no matter where another hospital were sited most sick Tibetans would die before reaching it, this was a more sound and fundamental need. Some villagers had been 'identified' to fill the role of *amchi* or 'village doctor' a long time before, and for many this was their first opportunity of any training whatsoever. For two years Jean and Kathryn had run courses for thirty of these doctors at a time. No more than farmers with a low level of literacy, each was responsible for the health of about nine hundred people. At best they had received five or six weeks' training ten to sixteen years ago, with few or no refresher courses since. In many cases, even recently, the refresher courses had been in Chinese which they could neither speak nor understand. Few had half-way decent facilities, none had an adequate supply of drugs, bandages were non-existent as they were too expensive, several shared stethoscopes between them and one was keeping his syringes functional with sticking plaster. In addition to providing these 'doctors' with real training and pushing for better resources, Jean and Kathryn had also set up — remarkable in so short a time — the Shigatse School for Tibetan Medicine which, unlike the Lhasa school, would also teach Tibetan Astrology. This had opened in January 1990, and would initially train forty students on a six-year course. Their tour of duty was now about to end, and Jean talked with the deserved air of someone looking back on a success.

They had arrived, Jean concluded the story by opening another one, within days of the Panchen Lama's mysterious death, and found themselves at once being housed in his 'palace', in a field of intense and highly charged intrigue.

'Was he murdered?' I asked.

'Well,' said Jean, 'he'd recently become more outspoken about Tibetan autonomy, and two days after a major speech which had made international news on the strength of his demands, a banquet was given in his honour at the palace. He died that evening, officially of a heart attack, but in most unstraightforward circumstances. His wife, a nurse, was told he was having a heart attack but she wasn't allowed into his room, and all other people were also denied access to him. A doctor was called from Chengdu, not even from Lhasa let alone Shigatse itself, and of course, without attention, he died.'

'So you don't think he was poisoned?'

'If you look at his age, his build, his probable diet, his stressful life, it's quite likely he had an infarction. But why deny access to his wife? Why call a doctor all the way from Chengdu? There are so many unanswered questions.'

'It sounds like the rumours surrounding Jean Paul I,' said Maria. 'They didn't exactly kill him, but being ill they denied him treatment.'

'Yes,' Jean agreed. 'So it's both really; he was ill himself but they chose not to help him, and that would be considered murder in the West, even if he wasn't poisoned. But the belief that he was poisoned is very, very prevalent among Tibetans.'

Kathryn returned with the tea, and we commented on the cosiness of the garden, the prettiness of the marigolds and their blue and pink anemones. They had planted the garden themselves, and it had proved a continual source of comfort. When I mentioned Maria's habit of periodically sending back seeds to her mother, Jean wandered off to make a collection for us. Many Tibetan plants would grow in Europe, said Kathryn, because the altitude made them hardy, and they were used to the cold. Unfortunately they did not have the famous blue poppy, which even in Tibet is rare. Sipping the hot, scented Chinese tea, we shifted to the social aspects of Tibetan life, telling Kathryn about the 'judge' we had met, and the high divorce rate he had reported.

She laughed. 'We've met him too, and he told us exactly the opposite, but he's only been in his job a month.'

'What's the truth?'

'The truth is that in two years we've never met a divorced Tibetan. It's nothing to do with family pressure, rather life philosophy, that you have your karma and you may as well be patient with it. Tibetans are very good at putting up with things, much better than we are, and you also don't know what your relationship was in your past life, and so on. But they complain about each other all the time. Get a group of men together and they complain about their wives; get a group of women together and they complain about their husbands. It's their way of dealing with it, and it keeps them healthy.' She paused, and continued. 'Tibetan women are the strongest I've known. So are the men of course, but the women's strength means there's a higher level of sexual equality among Tibetans than among Chinese, better probably than in most of Asia, though they're of course still Asian and don't have our ideas of sexism. They marry late too, at about twenty-five, which allows them to develop as individuals before entering a relationship. And they've a very healthy attitude towards sex – in fact both sexes are quite flirtatious. They aren't shy like the Chinese! So all those things help, but the real reason for the low divorce rate is their mental way of dealing with problems.'

Jean came back, a handful of seeds cupped carefully in his left palm, which he poured into a rolled cone of paper for us. Kathryn looked up at him, pushing her hair from her forehead and protecting her eyes from the sun. Clearly they had no difficulties, I reflected, dealing with any problems that dual isolation imposed on their own relationship. They also seemed ideally suited to their work and placement. Jean was a tall, dark, lean and intellectual-looking fellow with glasses and a narrow jaw, Kathryn was buoyant and extrovert, positive and humorous. Maria mentioned the many reports reaching the West of enforced sterilisation. Jean leaned forward, taking the issue seriously.

'We've heard rumours that this was a reason behind the riots in Xinjiang a while ago, that closed the border with Pakistan. In Tibet, most of the rumours seem to be coming from Amdo and Chamdo. Among Tibetans these stories circulate very freely, and of enforced abortion too, but for ourselves we've no evidence. But of course different regions have different policies, and what's the case in Shigatse may not be the case in other prefectures. Perhaps that's why most of the rumours keep coming from the same places. We did meet a nurse in Dharamsala who'd escaped. She reported injections of phenol into the uterus as a method of sterilisation – pretty irreversible. We also heard of a conference in North Africa where the Chinese were invited to speak on this method, so we can certainly assume it's used.'

'Is Shigatse as different from the rest of Tibet as it appears at first glance?' I asked.

They looked at each other, deciding who wanted the baton. Kathryn replied first.

'It's a good question, and people familiar with Lhasa do notice a difference. I'd say that Shigatse's more protected. There isn't the information or access to the outside world here, so there's little grasp of the wider situation. When Lhasa erupts, not many people in Shigatse know about it. It may be unfair to say the people here have sold their culture for material gain, because they're not really politically aware, but of course a higher standard of living's a strong factor behind the lack of political opposition. If Shigatse were to see demonstrations I don't doubt the Chinese would have problems, but most Tibetans in Shigatse don't think in terms of 'sides' any more.'

Jean continued. 'My impression is that the monks here are certainly very cold. We've heard of people being asked for Dalai Lama pictures and then reported, and there are police inside the monastery, dressed as monks. A personal friend of ours had stones thrown at him for trying to go somewhere they didn't want him to. I think on the one hand Tashilhunpo escaped a lot of damage and received a lot of benefits because it was the Panchen Lama's seat and the monks have had to play a double game to keep their privileges. On the other hand, the easing of restrictions on monastic life has come very late, and many of the older monks will have experienced torture. We heard of a nun being stripped naked in winter and manacled to the floor. Water was thrown into her cell, turning instantly to ice and freezing her to the ground. But many of the monks are extraordinarily nice. In my view the monastery may well be extremely factionalised.'

The events of 1995 and 1996 surrounding the dispute over the new Panchen Lama bore this out starkly, and though Tibetan citizens there did not take to the streets, monk dissatisfaction brought Shigatse firmly into the arena of protest, with repercussions yet to be seen. For now, shivering at the last image, we realised there was not a lot of sun left to sit in and our own temperatures were falling.

'We'll be glad to leave such stories behind,' said Kathryn.

'But there are good memories,' Jean nodded, smiling. 'No matter what happens to the Tibetans, they never lose their sense of humour. They seem able to bring it out of the bag in any kind of crisis. It is,' he added in the tones of an ultimate truth, 'the strongest survival mechanism of all.'

It had been our intention to hire a vehicle to travel as far as Milarepa's cave near the Nepali border, but jeep hiring, it transpired, was better done in Lhasa, for all those in Shigatse mysteriously appeared to be 'broken'. We spent hours chatting up package tourists going that way in the Xigaze Hotel (where each room had an illuminated, mistranslated sign outside pleading not *Do Not Disturb*, but *Beg No Rummage*), but while they may have been willing to take us, their guides were more resistant. We could have hitched across miles of empty terrain, but ran the risk, by incurring police wrath, of being shunted over the border into Nepal itself. Conceding defeat, we opted instead for the once-weekly pilgrim bus to Sakya.

The pilgrim bus is one of the greatest joys of travelling in Tibet. The older men, so proud-looking in their huge coats, worn fashionably with one arm out and tied at the waist with thick string, so androgynously strong in their plaited hair, turquoise ear-rings, leather hats and knee-high boots, were today particularly in abundance. Perpetually, during the eight-hour journey, the bus reverberated with the deep hum of mantras which fell from their lips in a cadence of tones until, out of breath, they breathed deeply and began again with renewed energy. Although the road was in terrible condition and at times indistinguishable from the dried river beds we staggered painfully across, the scenery was beautiful, and we rose and fell with the mantras from the wheat and barley being harvested on the plains, all a mass of hay carts, horses, donkeys and scruffy, excited children waving and shouting at the bus, to the high, barren, snowy mountain passes which transported our companions into a collective hysteria of hat-doffing, paper-throwing and excited shouts of *Lha Gyal Lo!* followed by the receding bubbles of communal laughter. Discomfort in good company is not noticed, and while by rights we should have ached and moaned we would, if we could, have prolonged the journey even more.

The final, fifteen-mile long valley leading up to the tiny town of Sakya brought more excitement on board. Outside, we looked at a fairy-tale picture of harvesting that belied the frenetic hard work of the farmers. Field after field of golden hay was being cut and sheaved and transported on donkeys with red-plumed head-dresses, slung with red carpets and hung with rainbow strappings and jangling bells. In the background, the long line of mountains delineating the valley behind the river Trom was snow-capped, and gleamed like the hay under the blue sky. The word *sakya* means 'grey earth'; indeed the soil of the mountains was particularly grey and so, when we had escaped the supreme ugliness of the Chinese estate on the periphery of town, were the Tibetan houses. Cuddled by the mountains and bisected by the fast clarity of the river, the Tibetan houses were not the usual white and black but uniformly grey, with white stripes like goalposts at the edges of the walls and below the flat roofs, with additional strips of pink down the sides. (According to Batchelor, the colourings indicated their falling within the monastic fief, and therefore their taxability.) Though there was a certain communal charm, in truth the whole resembled a carefully laid-out factory, and the monastery, when we saw it, in its own grey cubic plainness in the centre of town, was more like a central warehouse or storage depot than a beacon of spiritual light.

We dismounted at the bus station and installed ourselves in the adjacent run-down Chinese hostel. A woman took our money and disappeared. Perhaps it was just as well. There was no electricity and the sheets were the filthiest we had ever seen. The glass in the windows was broken. There was spit all over the floor. We then discovered there was no water, and no toilet either, the few other unfortunate 'guests' visibly using the ditch at the edge of the bus station yard. Chinese functionalism was faltering, I thought, but then again the hallmark of functionalism is usefulness, but no more than is necessary; with so few guests anyway, why bother? People only require four walls to sleep between, like cattle. And after all, there was the ditch. Maria would simply have to hold her bladder until dark. Wandering the cold corridors we found another worker, and asked for clean sheets. She nodded, disappeared and returned, and we could not tell the difference from the old ones.

Outside, in the narrow, dusty dirt-track streets, where clusters of houses rubbed eaves as if cringing before some mythical giant, we found easily our compensation. Herds of donkeys, festooned with bells and piled high with the season's hay, rang like the pealing of a hundred church bells as they came at us this way and that, six abreast and filling the streets, forcing us against the walls, two herds often trotting towards each other and having to be sorted out by their peasant drivers who controlled them with loud shouts. Long after dark we would hear their bells, and long before dawn they would wake us up. There seemed to be no discernible activity on earth other than hay-reaping.

We found the monastery closed on our late arrival, but arrived at its doors together with a young lady on pilgrimage with her father. He, she conveyed in the method of holding up her fingers, was seventy-six. She, she said, flashing all fingers three times, was thirty. We transmitted back our own ages and, in the fun of the communication, a bond was formed. Using the Asian gesture of beckoning, with the arm stretched downwards and flicking the palm of the hand towards her own body, she invited us to follow them. When we hesitated to do so she repeated the gesture firmly, adamance in her face, and we duly obeyed.

They led us over the crystal river to the pilgrim route which wound around the monastic buildings on the mountain side of town, where most of the temples were destroyed but a few, slowly, were being rebuilt. For the most part it was an awkward, crumbly, sometimes dangerous climb, and her father, though he did not look seventy-six, certainly moved like an old man, arthritically and with a stick but without a word of complaint, pulling his stocky frame up steps and round narrow ledges and drops with muscles that must, once, have been thrice as strong as my own. She, worn but still pretty despite the days of accumulated grime smudged across her high cheekbones, went on ahead as they led us around the high ruins, holding her plain black ground-length skirt with each hand at the thigh, lifting it as she climbed but tightening it also, so that her strong but feminine shape pressed itself through the fabric. Now and again she turned around to see that we were following, her deep, inky-black eyes all compassion and concern. Deprived of language, we were communicating by smiles and looks, directing feelings through the gaze. Even from a distance those eyes of hers swallowed me. As we passed ruin after ruin I reflected that she had been born when the worst began to happen, twenty-one when it ended. Her father, head shaven but for a single pigtail split and bound tightly under his stetson, had seen and suffered more. Yet he had kept his faith and his culture, and passed them on to his daughter. What did he say to her in secret when she was seven? What hopes for the future could he find to reassure her with when she was nine? What terrors of fact was he forced to explain by whispers in the ear at night, while I was being told all was right with the world if my toys were all tidied away? In China they said nothing. The parent-child transmission of culture was extinguished in a pool of total fear, and because they said nothing, they have nothing now. But the Tibetan identity proved a mirror in which they saw their own spirit. Walls were demolished but words continued and, in a sense, everything was saved.

I braced my feet against some bricks and, turning, pulled her father up the final steps past the third temple, totally destroyed but now being rebuilt and in premature use as a nunnery. They offered butter at the shrine, saving enough for the main temple in the morning, and we sat down together on the hillside overlooking both sides of town. Cow dung, patted into pancakes and covered with straw to dry out, covered every tiny roof top awaiting its use as winter fuel. From Sakya's forest of little chimneys a thousand narrow columns of smoke rose with surreal uniformity, directly upwards into the thin, still air. The sun was setting but still bright. By the river far below it cast its rays onto the fields of cut and uncut hay, still bustling with energy so long as there was light to see. They gave us bread. We gave them biscuits. Above us on a small cone of earth three nuns stared down in their dirty red robes, shielding their eyes against the sun's fierce glare, smiling but still unused to the sight of foreigners. I wished for pocketfuls of Dalai Lama pictures to give out. Two urchins also came, no more than four and six, and played pick-up-jacks in the dirt while Maria photographed them. Across the river again, two Chinese trucks noisily started up, throwing dust and black exhaust into the air, their disturbance of the peace a rude pollution of our quiet intimacy. They led us back down the mountain again, and in the candlelight of their Tibetan hotel room the old man urged his daughter to give us more and more butter tea; we responded with Dalai Lama pictures and Dalai Lama rice, which she folded away as carefully as a treasure inside her purple cardigan, her father nodding sagely, and the evening passed thus in the happy solidarity of silently exchanged goodwill.

'The meeting of two people is like the meeting of two chemicals: if there is a reaction, both are transformed.' So said Jung, wisely. I thought now of those words and realised how well they worked as a motif for travelling. Few words had been intelligibly exchanged that day, but we were far from untouched, and so were the lady and her father. The root motivation of the traveller is dissatisfaction with the self, with one's poverty of experience, one's ignorance, one's lack of planetary understanding, and one travels, in the end, to be transformed.

We returned to our own hotel, wrapped ourselves in our own blankets rather than those provided, and slept soundly through the barking of a thousand dogs until awakened, far too prematurely, by the jangling bells of fresh herds of donkeys. In the morning the monastery opened promptly at nine, and lived up to its promise as possessing some of the finest and best preserved artefacts in Tibet. The monks, a refreshing change from Tashilhunpo, were all smiles and greetings and warmth. We joined the lady and her father in a long queue during a ceremony where a lama, seated smiling on his throne with lines of monks chanting musically below him in the main shrine room, blew a conch shell before placing it on our heads in blessing. We took it as a ritual confirmation of a blessing already received by merely being there, and though our stay in Sakya was short, we stored it away as a small jewel in the casket of memory.

Back in Shigatse, we went straight to the PSB to ask for a visa extension. With a mere eight days left to run, we would be in great difficulties if they gave us anything less than a month. We knew other people in the hotel had only been granted a few days – long enough, as Hal said, to get to the Nepali border. We had already been to see the police about it twice, models of politeness and deference. The first time a young, trendy, leather-jacketed policeman with a cross round his neck had promised us a month's extension, but not until less time was left on our current visa. It had been a delaying tactic, hoping we would disappear.

The second time, we had seen the young policewoman whom I had embarrassed on our first night. She had asked us to go to Sakya first – another delaying tactic. Now we were back a third time, having been to Sakya, and reminding her of her promise. We sat on Tibetan carpets designed for chairs in the pleasant, spacious office, leaning against traditional long Tibetan cushions, making ritual small talk before broaching the subject of extensions. She had, she said, to ask her boss, and at that moment her boss walked in, an older man with a younger friend. He looked at our passports.

'This PSB isn't allowed to issue extensions until only two days are left on the visa.'

'Well . . . that means we have to stay here longer . . .'

His friend had a kitten, the fluffy kind that calendars are made of, which he was trying to force into his trouser pocket, expecting us to laugh. We avoided his eyes by gazing importunately at the boss.

'How long do you want?'

'Two months would be nice, but one month would be OK.'

'Ten days is all.'

His friend hit the objecting kitten hard in the face. We neglected to laugh.

'But we want to go to Beijing, Shanghai, Xian, Guangzhou . . . ten days isn't enough.' I was naming places anywhere except Tibet.

'Two weeks. That's all.'

We looked at each other with slightly melodramatised dissatisfaction, but were half preoccupied with the kitten which was now being pulled out of his friend's pocket by its ears. The boss muttered something and walked out. The policewoman smiled.

'One month − Sssh!'

The Winds of Karma

ONCE, IN A LAND WITHOUT wisdom or wise teachers, a wise man was born. Walking across a wasteland without any particular aim, he came upon a skull. Picking it up, he sat down and wondered. Where had it come from, the skull? Well, plainly, it had come from death. And death, he wondered next, where had death come from? Obviously, he reasoned, death had come from old age or sickness. Where had old age and sickness come from? Without doubt, they had come from birth. Birth evidently followed from sex, and sex followed from clinging, desire, feeling and touching, which were habits and were rooted in ignorance. In a land without wisdom or wise teachers, he had worked it all out for himself by reasoning backwards, the essence of Buddhist teaching that all life involves suffering and the root cause of suffering is ignorance. But what to do about it?

The links between ignorance and death are known as the 'twelve-fold chain of dependent origination', and are represented on the outer rim of the 'Wheel of Life', an instructive picture to be found near the entrance of most monasteries. At the centre of the wheel are depicted a pig, snake and cockerel chasing each other's tails, symbolising the three poisons of desire, hatred and ignorance which keep the wheel turning. Between the centre and the rim are six pictures, representing the six different worlds which we all, at various times, inhabit. These are not places in the world so much as states of mind, for Buddhism always was concerned with the inner environment rather than the outer, and the attribution of a particular emotion to each realm also marks the wheel as an early form of character typology. The whole wheel is held by Shinje, the deity of death, indicating just where our compulsive behaviour is leading us, and precisely why it is necessary, somehow, to get off the wheel entirely.

At the top are the god realms, where people possess unbelievable riches and experience the most immaculate pleasures, every need or whim being answered as soon as it arises. Millionaires with yachts on the riviera, leading lives of leisure and following the sun, would fit in here where the predominant emotion is *pride*. Just below them on the wheel are the jealous gods, people who have plenty but still want more, who seem permanently unsatisfied no matter how much they have. Certain media magnates spring to mind here, where the principal mood is *jealousy*. The next realm down is the animal world, where behaviour is governed by the thoughtless instinct for self-gratification; perhaps most human beings live here, where *ignorance* underpins all. At the foot of the wheel the hell realms are divided into two, hot and cold, where seemingly interminable suffering is meted out according to the crime – a hot hell for deeds committed 'in the heat of the moment', a cold hell for more calculated acts – and the dominant mood here is *hatred* of one's situation. Above the hell realms is the world of hungry ghosts, where beings are depicted as having massive bellies but tiny mouths, surrounded by as much food as they could possibly wish for, but cruelly unable to satisfy their hunger. People whose love is unrequited, or who are stricken by poverty in a world of materialism abide here, where the main emotion is *greed*. Finally, marked by *desire*, is the human realm. Although a Buddha is depicted in each realm to show that the *dharma* is always available, it is only in the human realm that beings really possess the ability to reflect upon their thoughts and actions, to practise religion, and thus to escape from the wheel. We may live for years in one of these realms, or pass through several in one day; the trick is to stay balanced and mindful, improve the quality of our thoughts and exercise compassion for all sentient beings.

The twelve spokes on the outer wheel reveal the world to be driven by cause and effect, which in Buddhist terms is called karma. Simply put, karma is the results of your deeds, returning to you like a boomerang to its thrower. Steal now, and later in this life or the next you will be stolen from. More subtly put, the mind and the world are connected, co-extensive, and karma is the place where they meet. What happens to you now is the product of your past character, intellect and deeds. You took the road you are on and you cannot pass off what happens to you as someone else's fault, even if a meteorite should land on you from out of the sky. You may have been *ignorant*, but you still put yourself there. As a Jungian analyst once said, you simply cannot have a car crash that is not your fault – it is a deeper definition of fault that is required. Explaining how such a calamity should befall their country, Tibetans say: 'It is our karma, for bad deeds in our militaristic past, when our kings were bloodthirsty and we visited violence on our neighbours.' If this is so, I would not like to consider what may befall China, in times yet to come.

When death comes, the fate of the flow of consciousness which has separated from the body is also determined by karma. Where will it go? To what quality of rebirth will the mind be driven by the winds of karma?

Curiously similar to modern reports of 'Near Death Experiences', the *Tibetan Book of the Dead* (*Bardo T'ödrö* – 'Liberation by Hearing in the Bardo') also illustrates events after death in terms of lights, which the departed consciousness has to negotiate on the way to its next incarnation. This is not, like the *Egyptian Book of the Dead*, a matter of mythology, but a handbook designed to be read aloud, into the ear of the dead person, by an appropriately trained lama.

Properly speaking there are six *bardos* ('intermediate states'), three of which, After Birth, Dream and Deep Meditation, actually apply to life. It is the other three with which the *Book of the Dead* is concerned, beginning with the Time of Death Bardo. If death is expected, the lama may be able to be present at the moment of death. This is thought especially auspicious as this moment is believed to contain the best opportunity for enlightenment, when the mind, fleetingly, is presented with a vision of the clear light of ultimate reality. If that is missed then the person may also 'miss' their own death; they may see grieving relatives and not understand why they are grieving, talk to them and not understand why they do not respond. After a few days, still under the delusion that they possess a body, they enter the second Reality Bardo, the most terrifying of all. In this *bardo* the dead person experiences the fruits of their own mind as projections, seeing all manner of peaceful and wrathful deities accompanied by blinding lights and piercing sounds. From the bedside the lama encourages the person to recognise these as products of their own mind and not being real, to enter the brighter lights rather than shy away from them, to turn away from the dull, seductively smoky lights rather than be attracted. If the lama fails, then after about fifteen days, finally aware that they have died, the person enters the Bardo of Becoming. Now, the disembodied consciousness will review their past life, and make resolutions for the next. They may stand before the 'Lord of Death' as he weighs their deeds as black and white pebbles, and holds up a 'mirror of karma'. The person may manage a final glimpse of their family and, unable to reach out to them, feel the discomfort of 'a fish thrashing about on red hot sand'. Being without a body but by desire wanting one, the winds of karma gather, driving the person towards their next womb. It is said that at this time one sees couples making love (and animals, if one is heading that way), and is attracted to the parents-in-waiting. Landscapes loom before them, indicating which of the six realms is being entered. Right to the end liberation is a present, but dwindling, possibility, as one is driven into rebirth by the sheer quality of consciousness one established for oneself the life before.

Like much of Mahayana Buddhism, the teachings of the Wheel of Life and the *Bardo T'ödrö* are symbolic. Perhaps life is symbolic. Of what, and how, is for us to work out, but the recurring *leitmotif* in Tibetan thought of the mind-world relationship is a clue, the thread with which the whole system is woven.

With pessimism one could compare Tibet to an after-death state, waiting for its bad karma to exhaust before seeking rebirth. Padmasambhava buried the *Book of the Dead* in the hills because Tibet was not then ready for its teachings, and it has been argued that we are now ready, that Tibet's loss is our gain, that Padmasambhava knew this when he predicted, 'When the iron bird flies in the sky, the *dharma* will go to the land of the red man.' But this is at once pessimistic and selfish. Tibet is a real country that continues to exist because the spirits of its people have refused to allow it to be extinguished, and the teachings have survived there so far. It is the duty of Western governments and human rights groups to fight for Tibet with every sinew of *our* spirit, so that when the opportunity for liberation flashes before Tibet's eyes, we are there to help seize the moment when it comes.

12

ON ARRIVAL IN LHASA AFTER a two-week absence we began to catch up on events we had missed. There had been no demonstrations on the 27th or the 1st, though Tibetan shops and stalls had closed in protest on the 27th, and opened in protest when they should have closed, on National Day. Police presence on the streets for the entire period had been nervously increased, and black helmets, black uniforms, shields and truncheons were *de rigueur* in the daily Barkhor stomps. Harrassment of Westerners appeared to have increased *after* the sensitive dates had passed. Paul and Mark had been intimidated by plain-clothes police in the bank who told them to 'leave at once'. Gary and Jackie had been hauled off a bus near some hot springs, held in a cell overnight and released with their passports literally flung at them in the morning. Hal, to his nervousness, had himself been approached by a plain-clothes policeman in front of the Jokhang and warned to leave for 'political involvement'. Later, the same policeman had followed Hal around the Barkhor and back to his hotel room, where he asked him pointedly, 'When are you leaving?'

At the same time, the escapes from airport custody had continued. The New Zealander who had gone missing in Tsetang had turned up after being arrested, transported to Gongar airport and handed over to the police. There, he found himself held, amongst others, with a party of eight Japanese who had for a whole week held out against buying tickets back to Chengdu or on to Kathmandu. With one of the Japanese, a young woman, he had apparently scaled the airport hotel wall overnight, slept rough in the freezing hills next to an army base, hitched to Gyantse the following day, but being unsure of Gyantse's safety had got out before they arrived and walked around the town, finally hitching in to Shigatse and arriving back in Lhasa on the bus. The girl, the story went, had no more than a pair of flip-flops for shoes and appeared to have come to Tibet dressed for the beach. Yet for every escape there was an arrest. A Dutch couple who had escaped reported meeting a Canadian and a German, who had been arrested at the very last checkpoint on the outskirts of Lhasa, within sight of the Potala. It was still difficult to get in from Golmud, though a Japanese and an American had made a home run dressed as Chinese, complete with surgical masks, hats and blue jackets, with their rucksacks stashed in mail bags.

And then there was Daniel Wagner, the young French Swiss who had gone to Samye after us. He had even quizzed us about it beforehand, and we had given him no cause to think it a particularly risky journey. Daniel, in the wrong place at the wrong time, had simply been swallowed, though like Jonah he proved hard to digest. The police having begun to watch the buses, he had been spotted as soon as he dismounted at the ferry. Samye, they told him, was a 'closed area' open only to groups with guides. Like the police chief who had earlier kidnapped the Danes, they escorted Daniel for two days around Samye before 'fining' him, transporting him to the airport and handing him over to the Gongar police. They, smarting from the constant escapes, had begun to confiscate passports, but Daniel was not a man to be deterred by such niceties. We found him, showered and recovering, drying out his camera lenses in the hotel yard, having *swum* over the Brahmaputra the previous night and cadged a lift into Lhasa in an official jeep with a red flag by pretending to be ill. Whisked at speed through all the checkpoints he reached the Holiday Inn, a convenient point to make a spontaneous recovery.

Two hours later we saw him again, having been unable to cash his travellers' cheques against the photocopy of his passport. This, he acknowledged, was something of a problem. On top of that, his embassy advised him to return at once to the airport. Having gone to such lengths to leave it, and with a justified nervousness of how the police would greet his return, Daniel began to plot his own way out. In the end it was we who offered the solution. On the principle that the right hand in China rarely knows what the left hand is doing, Maria suggested that the PSB in Shigatse would know nothing of his case. He could go there and claim that he had lost his wretched passport *en route*. If that were the extent of their knowledge, they would be more likely to issue him with temporary papers to get to the Nepali border than to send him, passport and money-less, all the way over to Beijing. Taking this remarkable fellow to the Holiday Inn one evening, fortune presented itself in the form of a three-person Swiss film crew, heading for Nepal in a hired jeep. At Christmas we received a postcard from Daniel in Hong Kong. The ruse had worked, and he had been given a new passport in Kathmandu.

Our days in Lhasa drew to a close as they had begun, with my being ill, this time with 'flu. We hauled ourselves around the streets with the wistfulness of unwanted departure, our pain on leaving heightened by grief at the plight of the people we were leaving behind, and a raging anger against the ignorance and connivance of the outside world. One evening, however, in brooding mood after eating at the Holiday Inn, we retrieved our bicycles from behind the hotel and began cycling slowly back towards the Potala in the dark, when someone pulled alongside, greeting us in English with a quiet 'Hello'. We recognised her as the woman who had spoken to us about the wooden bowls in the Barkhor, and reminded her of it. It seemed fitting that we should see her at the beginning, and at the end of our stay, and she was happy to speak longer this time, disguised by the night and a curious law forbidding the attachment of lights to bicycles.

'Not only food bowls, but clothes!' she said. 'From '66 to '79 we had to wear blue suits. You can't imagine!'

'And prayer wheels and *malas*?' I asked.

'Of course, they weren't allowed.'

'Couldn't people hide them in their homes, for private use?'

'Too dangerous! Too dangerous, even to have them in secret. You can't imagine!'

We knew, of course, but to be told it first-hand brought it home. And yet in a way she was right. We could not imagine Tibetans without prayer wheels and *malas*, it was like shepherds without crooks. And for thirteen years! They must have thought they would never awake from their nightmare. Maria asked her about the Barkhor.

'Nothing. They took all that away. It was empty.'

'Didn't people circumambulate?' enquired Maria.

'You can't imagine, you can't imagine! But we did, you know, but not obviously.'

When we had met her the first time she had played the role of purveyor of information, and now, under cover of the dark, she seemed to be taking a humorous pleasure in our education. Certainly, in spite of the topic, she was lifting our mood.

'What about language?' It was a question I had badly wanted to ask, to find out how far the repression had gone.

'They couldn't stop us speaking Tibetan at home, but they tried to stop us using honorifics. They stopped Tibetan in schools, made us learn Chinese, and removed all Tibetan from public view – road names, shop names and so on. You could walk around Lhasa and not see the Tibetan alphabet.'

'What's it like in schools now?' asked Maria.

'Now better, but the big problem is they're sending our brighter children to China, to Shanghai and other places far from Tibet, for high school. So parents of such children can't see them for years, and the children become like Chinese. Then they go to work in China and marry Chinese. Our population is reduced and we lose our best brains. This policy is a *big* human rights abuse. Why not give them a good education in Tibet?'

We had heard of this policy, and imagined (from the lack of adolescent Tibetans on the streets) that it applied not only to the brightest. In fact, four thousand Tibetan children of secondary school age are in China for education in any one year, making the policy a major platform in the progressive extinction of Tibetan culture.

'Do you have to let them go?' I asked.

The reply was obvious. 'What can we do? They're our children. We want what's best for them. Their happiness comes before our culture. We just hope they don't forget, and when they come back to visit, we remind them.'

I returned to the past. 'What happened to you in '59?'

'Well, I went to jail. All my family not killed in the uprising went to jail. My family was labelled reactionary because we were involved in the uprising, and that's what they did to us. We lost our house, everything.'

'You didn't get your house back later, with an apology?'

'None of those involved in the uprising did, though some others did get such things. I went to our old house when I came out of jail. It had "No Entry" written in Chinese on every wall with white paint. Now it's been given to a government worker. I try not to walk past, if I can help it.'

Another confiscated home, the Potala, was approaching on our left, and with it the lights of the town. We dismounted and walked a little to continue the conversation. I asked her about the old Tibet, before the Chinese came.

'It wasn't perfect, but no-one starved and we were happier. The Chinese like to call Tibet a "serfdom", and what they mean is a bad relationship between the peasants and the landlords, but you know, the truth is that Tibetan peasants were nomadic, and if one landlord was bad they'd simply pack up and move to another one. Tibet's a big country with much land; landlords always needed the peasants so generally they treated them well, unlike our new landlords who in 1959 imposed upon us a greater serfdom than we'd known before, making us work the land to provide their soldiers with food.'

'Haven't there been any improvements?'

'Yes, small ones, but it doesn't equal the loss of our freedom and culture, and who's to say that if His Holiness had stayed then the improvements and material progress would not have been greater? Now they're changing the face of our city without consulting us, without a care for our feelings. Well, that's the Chinese. Already I can't recognise Lhasa from when I was born. The Barkhor and a small quarter are all that's left, and some of the Barkhor's been flattened to make their police stations. I'm afraid Lhasa's becoming another Chinese city. Really, it already is, there're so many of them here. And you can't imagine how many spies there are, how careful we have to be. I can take you for a walk around Lhasa and say to you, "this man is a spy, that man is a spy," and to you they look normal, dressed in Tibetan clothes. But we know who they are. We're all asked in our communes to spy on each other, and in junior school children are interrogated about the parents. We have video cameras and listening equipment on the streets, soldiers on rooftops, and they say we are free. Ha!' She threw up her right hand and tossed her braided hair in disgust.

'Why haven't you escaped to India?' Maria wondered. 'There must have been times when you were tempted.'

'Tempted, yes, there were times, but now I'm old I don't care. Freedom's in here.' She thumped her chest. 'When I was younger I seriously considered it, but my conclusion was, what of the people left here? We need each other, even if we can't exchange our secrets. And what if we all went? We're already outnumbered three to one in Lhasa. If we all got out, Tibet would be no more. So I thought about these things, and I stayed.' She was silent for a moment, and then continued with a mischievous smile: 'Of course like everyone else I live for the day when His Holiness returns, and we see them off!' She spoke firmly, as if possessed of the belief that it would definitely happen. We had come to the beginning of the street lights, and ahead the empty road was bathed in a raw yellow glow.

'Please excuse me,' she said. 'We're very close to town now. I must go. Please tell the world about us. Sometimes, we think they forget.'

'What is your name?'

'Droma,' she replied.

Droma, I thought. The Tibetan name for the goddess Tara, born from a tear drop. For a moment before she turned to go she gazed at us, an exchange of soul in a freezing of time. Before coming to Tibet, I had no idea that human eyes could convey so much; now, it was like watching the universe unfold. The pain, the immense, tragic injury of the ripping and tearing of the spirit shone simultaneously with an enveloping sunburst of defiance.

'Take care,' said Maria.

'Don't let them forget,' she repeated, and was gone.

We walked along in the cool night air, pushing our bicycles towards the town. It was naivety in some westerners who criticised the 'Tibet Good China Bad' stance, reflected Maria. Some situations *are* simplistic. The invasion was wrong, the occupation illegal in international law. Racism is wrong, pure and simple, it is not 'alright in some ways'. The same for the Holocaust. Have the Chinese done any good for Tibet? Not before 1980, when the bulk of the 1.2 million deaths occurred, and the Tibetan way of life, from religion to language to clothes and food bowls was literally erased. What about since? Not in terms of employment, where priority is given to Chinese, nor in health – Tibet is the least developed 'part of China' in health resources and, since all medical care must be paid for, Tibetans are less healthy than Chinese. (In 1995 a hospital in Lhasa refused to admit a woman about to give birth without pre-payment. The husband left her to borrow money, and when he returned found both mother and baby dead, lying where the woman had given birth, on the steps of the hospital.) Certainly not in education, which is not in Tibetan after primary school, and with the universities of Lhasa and Shigatse being for Chinese only, Tibetans are sent away to 'the motherland' for their studies. Nor do they benefit economically, since the Chinese receive four times local wages to encourage them to stay there.

Culturally? Religiously? Politically? Just where is the benefit? Some things just *are* black and white, she concluded, like Tibet and the Holocaust.

The next morning, Hal left for Golmud. Our best wishes to him were sincerely meant for much as he annoyed us, we knew he was more valuable than gold. Most other Westerners had gone too, getting out before the onset of winter. There was the sense of a circle becoming complete. Our numbers were once more fewer than ten, as they had been when we arrived. One of them was Daniel, still reporting daily to the TAR for an argument over how to be reunited with his passport, though he knew full well he was leaving without it. The hotel seemed empty, like a ballroom after a party, the revellers departed. Life in the streets went on as before, perhaps with a little less tension until the next anniversary date, in March, of the Dalai Lama's flight and the 1959 uprising. We wondered how many individual Westerners would be here then, for the next chapter in Tibet's unfinished history. The Chengdu route seemed closed off at last, and no-one had got in from Golmud for a fortnight.

And then a party of fifteen arrived, having walked over from another, mid-level, hotel. We sat on the sunny verandah and chuckled at their tale of the pliability of truth and rules in China today. In Chengdu they had gone to CITS, who had offered them the usual expensive Holiday Inn package. Undaunted, they visited another travel agent, who told them Tibet was closed.

'But we've met people coming out,' they replied, which was true. They had met Paul and Mark.

'China's at war with India,' came the immediate, stunning excuse to fob off the foreigners.

When they pointed out that there had been nothing about this on either the Chinese news or the BBC or VOA, another unlikely excuse was on hand.

'There are bad forest fires – the hills around Lhasa are burning.'

'But there aren't any trees.'

'And Lhasa's under Martial Law.'

'Martial Law was lifted ages ago.'

'Well it's come back now.'

Only when one has been in China for some time do stories like this cease to stretch credibility. The Chinese do not usually question a ruling, and when they do the excuse is utilitarian, the truth immaterial. It is after all a land where truth is functional, a question of aim and motive rather than fact. Their persistence paid off, however, with the third travel agent, who sent them in as a two-day, fifteen-member scientific expedition. They became, therefore, international botanists, though several of the motley crew would have been more at home in Kathmandu than Kew, and one immediately asked where the 'hash' was. Their resourcefulness in skirting the rules was outdone only by the arrival, on our last evening, of perhaps the best home-run of all — an American who had cycled it from Golmud. It had taken him twenty-four days, hiding in the hills in daytime, cycling only at night when the checkpoints were closed, walking around those that were not. The higher ground outside the Lhasa valley, he reported, was already thick with snow and ice, and without his mountaineer's sleeping bag he would certainly have perished. We were pleased we were still there to see him — another living paean to the tradition of arriving in Lhasa by stealth.

Sadly but unavoidably, we had to face our own departure. Like Shakespeare's schoolboy crawling like a snail unwillingly to school, we sloped off to the bus station to buy our tickets. Ridiculously unable to arrive by bus, the authorities were happy enough now for us to leave that way. Our last evening was predictably gloomy. Had it not been for Maria or the situation, I brooded, I would have donned a monk's robes and stayed put. We contented ourselves with a last evening *puja* in the Jokhang, taking a *thangka* we had bought in an artists' co-operative to be blessed.

The monks, overjoyed, beckoned us towards the Jowo. For a full blessing, it was traditional to leave the scroll in his lap overnight; as we were leaving for Golmud in the morning, a shortened version would have to do. We stood back and watched as they reverently placed it in his lap and then, mantras murmuring, unfurled it before him, holding the *thangka* aloft before his gaze, arms high for several minutes, while others ritually bathed it in the rich smoke of Tibetan juniper incense. I felt my eyes trapped by the Jowo while they held it there, bewitched by the moment into believing the statue sentient, a feeling that, I confess, has never quite left me. The *thangka* was then carefully rolled, grains of blessed barley placed inside it, and a yellow silk *katha* taken from the Jowo's lap and tied around it. We made a donation, prostrated three times, and the monks wished us well and saw us out.

To ensure our return, once more we circumambulated the Jokhang twice, poignantly conscious that this time the third circuit would be longer in coming. Those last walks around the Barkhor, late at night with few people around and only the lighted butter lamps of household shrines to catch the eye, perpetuated to the end the contradictory pull of intense, contrasting emotions which the spirit of Tibet and the Tibetans automatically engendered. Lhasa had been, for us as for those who live there, both crucible and crucifix, rendering us irrevocably transformed and scarred. 'My religion is kindness,' said the Dalai Lama. We could only hope that human rights would be the global religion of tomorrow.

That night, in the midst of depression, I was cheered by a dream. I was standing in front of the Jowo, which seemed larger than ever and towered above me, inclining slightly, its golden visage radiantly smiling. I prostrated three times, finishing in the standing position again, but with my hands together at my heart and my head bowed. The Jowo leaned forward, put out its hand and, touching my head, blessed me. Inside, something irrupted. Waves burst over the rock of my brain and trickled down, tingling pleasantly inside my scalp, and I woke up, smiling like the image of the Jowo.

In the morning, in the freezing cold before dawn, an excommunicated monk drove us to the bus station in a borrowed rickshaw, and we overpaid him monstrously. We had been seated over the rear wheel arch again, but for some time scarcely noticed the discomfort. Early rays of light fell upon Drepung as we drove by, the martial music of the army compound at its feet blaringly summonsing the soldiers to morning exercises. The heavily manned checkpoints on the outskirts were no longer there as we turned north, entering the valley we had arrived through in early morning darkness. Now it stood revealed by the rising sun as green but autumnal, most of the harvest hay now gathered and cleared away, fields freshly furrowed to be left until spring. The earth would turn hard in the bitter winter cold, but there would be little snow except on the mountains that rose suddenly a hundred yards either side of the road, and they had been snow-capped for weeks. I stared at the mountains, a run of pointed ridges all in a line. Even Tibetan mountains can look like monks, I thought, heads peeking above folded rocky robes, lines of shadow, lines of light, row upon twisted row sitting solid and unshakeable in meditation in the morning sun. Below them, *chortens* stood in fields again, sacred stones were piled high and low for the spirits' and our noticing, and on a sunbeam an elf somersaulted, oblivious to the wounds of the world. Commune compounds and haystacks fluttered with prayer flags and Chinese standards alike, the one by instinct, the other by order, impaling us also with the relentlessly Kafkaesque truth of this land where internal freedom and external constraint co-exist like inharmonious *yin* and *yang*, fighting dragons in the vicious circle of Tibetan life. The latter at least has passed its zenith and failed to win; perhaps the other can only rise from its nadir. I looked at Maria, lost in her own reflections beyond the muddied, rattling window.

'We shouldn't be sad,' I said. 'At least, not for ourselves. We've crowned our lives by coming here.'

Maria was silent. And then it all poured out: 'I think I've learned how vital resistance is to the human condition. If you can't stand up, prepared to be knocked down, you're not fully human. If no-one could ever do that, we wouldn't, as a planet, be worth our own existence. Resistance is part of daily life for the Tibetans, and they're as human as humans come. It's so easy for people at home to turn to the football results and forget what drama of bravery and suffering they've just read about in a main article, but it's cruel. For evil to succeed it's only necessary that the good do nothing. We can't do nothing. If not enough people in the West agitate on Tibet's behalf, there soon won't be a Lhasa, or even a Tibet to come to. This country isn't a spiritual Disneyland of levitating lamas, it's human and painfully real.'

'I know . . .'

Romance and reality. My answer trailed off as I gazed through the glass. I saw no more elves on sunbeams, just a grim succession of milestones giving the distance to Beijing.

Update

AT THE TIME OF GOING to press, conditions for independent travellers have eased, a one-way ticket including a three-day tour of Lhasa being available in Golmud for around £100. Of course, there could be one policy in the morning, another in the afternoon and another in the evening – the important thing is to try.

Conditions for those who live in Tibet however continue to get worse, especially for monks and nuns who as of October 1996 were threatened with excommunication unless they signed denunciations of His Holiness the Dalai Lama. As excommunication virtually guarantees unemployment and restriction to one's home town, the pressure to conform is immense. The drive to eradicate pictures of His Holiness, which led to rioting, deaths and the closure of Ganden monastery in the summer of 1996 still continues, and for a while yet visitors may be seeing empty frames placed upon empty thrones. However, some upheaval in China itself following the death of Deng Xiaoping and the return of Hong Kong is imminent, and the ripples of change could reach Tibet. We must hope, and of course, act; if the mind and the world are not that distinct, then optimism may well be the father of fortune.

Now you have read this book, please join:

FREE TIBET CAMPAIGN
(formerly Tibet Support Group (UK))
9 Islington Green, London N1 2XH

Tel: 0171 359 7573

You *can* make a difference!

Additional Reference

The Buddha

Siddhartha Gautama, later to become the Buddha, was born around 563 BCE, contemporary with Confucius. He was born into the royal family of Kapilavastu, an ancient kingdom in modern-day Nepal. Predictions made at his birth that he would become either a great holy man or a great king worried his father, Suddhodana, for were the boy to embark upon a spiritual quest not only would he not see much of him, it would probably mean the loss of his son and heir. Suddhodana therefore forbade Siddhartha to leave the palace, lavished upon him everything he desired, and obscured from his sight any signs of old age, sickness, death or holiness, in the hope that the motivation for spiritual pursuits would not arise. Inevitably, Siddhartha's curiosity about the outside world got the better of him, and he did see all four of the forbidden sights, the last, a holy man in meditation, prompting him to leave his father, wife, child, kingdom and earthly inheritance in pursuit of the answer to suffering.

Studying first with renowned Hindu teachers, then with five diehard ascetics on a regime of little more than a few grains of rice a day, Siddhartha became, according to one source, so thin 'you could see his backbone through his stomach'. This was a great contrast to his previous life of wealth and luxury, but it was only after accepting a bowl of rice pudding from a passing milkmaid that he gained the strength to meditate properly, and realisation of the errors inherent in extremes later led him to characterise his teachings as 'The Middle Way'. Sitting under a pipal tree, in four watches of the night he recollected his previous lives, gained clairvoyance, understood the causes of suffering and the workings of karma, and finally attained full, complete and perfect enlightenment (*bodhi*), after which he was known as the Buddha – the enlightened one. In the forty-five years that followed he travelled, taught and established a body of monks and nuns before dying, at the age of eighty, possibly from eating poisoned food.

Buddhism

Later in his life, the Buddha reportedly held up a handful of leaves, pointed to the rest of the forest and said: 'Only so much have I shown you.' He did however take care to express what teachings he thought we could understand as simply as possible, beginning by codifying his essential insight, the 'Four Noble Truths', in the manner of a doctor's diagnosis: all life inevitably involves suffering (*duhkha*), the primary cause of suffering is desire (*tanha*), the cause of suffering has a cure or antidote, and the cure is to follow the 'Noble Eightfold Path', which consists of Right Understanding, Right Thought, Right Speech, Right Action, Right Livelihood, Right Effort, Right Mindfulness and Right Concentration, all of which may be broken down into varying levels of guidance. Release from suffering is marked by the attainment of *nirvana*, literally the 'blowing out' of the fires of desire, hatred and ignorance. These fires feed on our failure to perceive the crucial 'Three Marks of Existence', that all things will fail to deliver any ultimate satisfaction (*duhkha*), that all things are in a constant process of change and nothing lasts (*anitya*), and all things – including ourselves – are devoid of any ultimate self, is-ness or independent identity (*anatta*). Such are the basic building blocks on which the rest of the system is constructed.

Theravada Buddhism

Theravada ('Teaching of the Elders') Buddhism claims to be the original teaching of the Buddha, free from later interferences. Its central characteristic is the idea that there is only one Buddha for each world system, and for us that was Siddhartha Gautama. The best the rest of us can hope for is to become an *arhat* whereby, following perfection in the four meditative stages (*jhanas*) one becomes free from further rebirths and enters *pari* (complete or total) *nirvana* at death. In pursuit of this goal the things of the world are considered a distraction, and the life of a monk is the highest ideal.

Buddhism suffered greatly from the Muslim invasions of India, as a result of which very few Buddhists were left there after the twelfth century CE. Sri Lanka, Burma, Thailand, Laos and Cambodia are the principal strongholds of Theravada today.

Mahayana Buddhism

Around a hundred years after the Buddha's death a schism arose between two wings of his followers, the conservative Elders (*Sthaviras*) and the more progressive – and more numerous – 'Great Assemblyists' (*Mahasanghikas*). At the root of the schism was the concept of the *arhat* which, the *Mahasanghikas* contended, was a state in which ignorance and desire still abided. Over time, the *Mahasanghikas* developed into the Mahayana ('Great Path', as opposed to the pejorative Hinayana, or 'Narrow Path', by which they knew the Theravadins) and, assisted by the philosophical conclusion that *samsara* (this world) and *nirvana* were the same (a logical consequence, really, of *anatta*), the goal of enlightenment was asserted over that of *nirvana*. The ideal of the *arhat* was replaced by that of the *bodhisattva* ('enlightenment-being'), which signified anyone who had oriented their consciousness towards enlightenment. Anyone could enter the *bodhisattva* path, which led to complete control over one's rebirths and, eventually, to Buddhahood, and was pursued not for one's own sake but for the benefit of others. A *bodhisattva*, crucially, will spurn their final entry into *nirvana* as a selfish act, opting instead for continued enlightened existence for the sake of all sentient beings, and there are thus numerous god-like 'celestial *bodhisattvas*' who have transcended human birth completely, but choose to remain in our world system in order to respond, out of compassion, to human suffering. A *bodhisattva* may become a Buddha, and there may be any number of Buddhas around us. Moreover, living in the world is seen as superior to being a monk, because the opportunities for helping others are greater and because it would be selfish to remain cloistered once the necessary realisations have been achieved. The world is also a great teacher, as Mahayanists like to say.

Mahayana Buddhism became the dominant form of Buddhism in China, spreading from there to Korea, Japan and Vietnam. It entered Tibet however from India, in the form of Vajrayana (the 'Diamond' or

'Thunderbolt Path') or Tantra, a term which signifies the transformation of the individual through meditation, mantra (sacred sound) and ritual.

Confucius

In 551 BCE, when Western history was still waiting to begin, Confucius (K'ung Fu Tzu) was born into a society already of some maturity but with a prevailing sense of loss of direction. This was a disunified China of 770 squabbling states in which people were already looking back to a mythical 'Golden Age' and wondering how to return to it. Confucius saw himself as the man who could arrest the wrong turn of history, not by saying anything new, but by codifying the supposed old ways. 'I transmit but I do not innovate,' he said, 'and am devoted to antiquity'. His system was essentially a moral code, not at all a religious one. He spoke of loyalty (*chung shu*), good-ness (*jen*) and righteousness (*i*), of filial piety (*hsiao*), brotherliness (*t'i*) and propriety in conduct (*li*), and of the importance of breeding and education.

According to Mencius (Meng Tzu), Confucius himself started out as a lowly clerk in the state granaries. He progressed, some accounts say he became prime minister of Lu, but it is generally thought that he was frustrated in his civil service career by a hereditary hold on the top jobs. Thus, while he accepted the inheritance of nobility he was a convinced meritocrat, 'Promote the worthy and employ the capable' becoming a well-worn Confucian motto. Taking his frustration with him, Confucius became an itinerant politician, wandering from state to state in the fruitless search for a patron, eventually retiring back in Lu and contenting himself with a small band of disciples. These disciples did a better job than their master of spreading the word, and by 59 CE he had become so popular that Emperor Ming Ti made him a god (of learning), and ordered the people to make sacrifices to him. While he lived no-one listened, but since his death he – or at least the ethical system attributed to him – has affected the lives of more people than any other human being.

Confucianism

China's ancient insistence on keeping records and obeying rules undoubtedly betrayed a fear, even then, of disorder and chaos (*luan*). This fear is still used today to explain China's totalitarianism, and the age of the fear, like the history of an obsession or psychosis, reveals its grip on the Chinese mind. Confucius may have failed to sell his ideas himself, but a long line of emperors after him found them very useful for keeping the common people in their place. The replacement of the rule of Ch'in by the Han Dynasty was at first a liberation (and saw a great leap in living standards), but later Han rulers, too debauched to follow any rules themselves, still used Confucianism to enforce order in the land. The problem as to what was or was not Confucian, caused by Chi'in Shih Huang Ti having burnt all the books was used to their advantage by adding bits that suited them and by steamrolling their acceptance. (Only *The Analects* can truly be attributed to Confucius, and even that is not totally pure.) For example, the rather Bacchic spring festival custom of boys and girls going off into the woods together was replaced by another, totally made up, that males unmarried by thirty and women by twenty should be paired off for life on the spot by the village go-between.

It was in the field of family and male-female relations that Confucianism really made its mark on China, with women suffering most through segregation and footbinding. Most Chinese could surely only have approximated the more absurd rules of the canon, that man and wife should not bathe together, a wife should not hang her clothes on her husband's clothes-horse, a concubine should not approach the husband's bed without properly fastened house-shoes nor spend the whole night with him if the wife was at home, that a man should copulate with each of his concubines every five days until they reach the age of fifty or he the age of seventy, and so on. Many travellers, like Marco Polo, wrote of the civility and politeness they encountered in China, but this was at the expense of a system where everyone knew and accepted their place without the facility of complaint or revolt, and the family or workplace could function unchallenged as a unit of repression. This was tyranny without the appearance of tyranny, and the whole system existed to stifle dissent.

How then was Confucianism overthrown so readily? The last dynasty, the Ch'ing, was notoriously corrupt, powerless and hated. In a last ditch effort to save itself it tried to revitalise Confucianism, thus identifying it with the old order in people's minds. The Nationalist Revolution of 1911 did not deliver immediate strength, the government at the Versailles Peace Conference after the First World War meekly handing over Germany's share of China to Japan without a fight. A much-quoted banner at the consequent May 4th 1919 student-led protest read: 'Down with the old curiosity shop of Confucius!' The May 4th movement, inspired by the Russian Revolution two years earlier, demanded an end to beliefs in gods, spirits, religions and – holy of holies – filial piety. Politically Confucianism was identified with feudalism, with disparity between rich and poor, with oppression, particularly of women who were not only secluded from the world but denied education, forced into marriage and concubinage, and even footbound at the will of men. It perpetuated 'superstitions' inconsonant with the modern, atheistic, scientific knowledge of Communism. Two years after the May 4th demonstration Mao, then an assistant librarian at Beijing University, co-founded the Chinese Communist Party with the sentiment: 'I hated Confucius from the age of eight.'

Taoism

The origins of Taoism are traditionally ascribed to two sages, Lao Tzu and Chuang Tzu. Though it is unlikely that they ever lived, the works that bear their names probably stem from the 4th century BCE. These exceptionally sublime collections of mystical insights are based on the idea of the *Tao* (the 'Way') – a term suggestive at once of the origins and the process of the universe – as an ideal with which we should live in harmony. For Chuang Tzu this was expressed, with some humour, in the ideas of inaction (*wu wei*), of being natural (*tzu jan*) and of yielding or 'going with the flow'. Many of his aphorisms, suggestive of tough times, are about survival. A stiff branch covered in snow will snap, he points out, whereas the branch that gives will remain intact. There is also advice on yoga and breathing techniques, and wisdom on approaching death. The more famous *Tao Te Ching* (*The Book of the Way and its Virtue*) attributed to Lao Tzu is in similar vein, but oriented towards good government, such as advice on winning the people's hearts by ruling them without seeming to (through the exercise of *wu wei*). That this subtle mysticism and unprecedented emphasis on yoga is quite anomalous in the body of Chinese thought is for me suggestive of Indian origins, although, ironically, later Taoists spent centuries trying to argue that Lao Tzu had gone to India instead of dying, and called himself the Buddha.

Taoism started at its height, and thereafter was all decline as it became a religion. Taoists today will distinguish themselves as either *Tao Chia* – following the philosophy of Chuang Tzu and Lao Tzu – or *Tao Chiao* – religious Taoists. The latter accept the philosophy, but also some of the stranger accretions to Taoism which history produced. In Hong Kong today there are alchemists (*fang shih*) who believe, like Ch'in Shih Huang Ti, that immortality through diet, lifestyle and the ingestion of compounds is a plausible achievement. Similarly there are those who believe in the mushroom-shaped islands of P'eng L'ai where immortals ride the air and drink the dew. (Intriguingly, these true optical illusions were captured appearing off the east coast on a home-movie camera in 1996.) Again there are the 'hygienists', who pursue immortality through breathing techniques and yoga – especially of the sexual kind. The rationale for this is that each ejaculation will shorten one's life, but redirection of the *ch'i* (vital energy) at the moment of orgasm will lengthen it. Thus, by developing the muscular control needed to withold the semen a man could enjoy sex for longer and with many partners, at the same time lengthening his life span. The mythical Yellow Emperor was decreed to have become immortal after making love to a mere twelve hundred women in this manner and – importantly – it was supposed to work for women too. What Chuang Tzu and Lao Tzu would have made of this we cannot know, but it was the attempt to put down the mass orgies that began to conflagrate across the country on full moon days that led to the Revolt of the Yellow Turbans, and thereafter to the driving underground of Taoism.

It was this last aspect which led to the creation of the secret societies which have so characterised China since, and have on numerous occasions played crucial roles in historical events. At the end of the last century hundreds of Taoists in a castle in Shandong burned themselves to death rather than surrender to the Confucian authorities who were persecuting them for their sexual yogic practices. In 1950, a Communist newspaper reported on the 'cleaning up' of a secret society, *I Kuan Tao*, that 'the shamelessly lustful leaders of *I Kuan Tao* carried out beauty contests . . . and made members engage in promiscuous sexual intercourse, promising the participants immortality and freedom from disease'. As late as 1957, long after the victory of Mao, official newspapers were reporting the putting down of Taoist uprisings in 'half the provinces of China'.

Naturally, China's secret societies were not always religious, or political, but criminal, as may be seen in the notorious Triads which flourished in Hong Kong under the British occupation. Ominously, as

Hong Kong reverts, the Triads have moved onto the mainland. (We saw them operating openly in Beijing in 1992, with their leather jackets, gold chains, flash cars and 'minders', whereas they had not been noticeable in 1990.) In January 1993, the holiday resort of Ling Xiao Yan was largely destroyed by armed rioters who blew up thirty buildings including the police station and a power plant, and attacked and looted many others in an orgy of violence lasting three whole days – probably a response to a moral mayor who had refused to cut them in on the tourist business. He was a foolish man. Those expecting China's fearsome PLA and *Wu Jing* to tackle the evil Triads in the way they have tackled the gentle Tibetans are in for a disappointment. Tao Siju, China's Public Security Minister in 1993, stated publicly that: 'There are many overseas [i.e. Hong Kong] organisations who are mistaken for the Triads. Really, I think they are also very patriotic. I have contacts with them!'

Perhaps the most likely and best scenario for the future of China is a return to the period of 770 squabbling states, and history can begin again.

Bibliography and Recommended Reading

Travel

Bass, Catriona, *Inside the Treasure House*, Abacus 1990

Batchelor, Stephen, *The Tibet Guide*, Wisdom 1987

Danziger, Nick, *Danziger's Travels*, Paladin 1987

David-Neel, Alexandra, *My Journey to Lhasa*, Harper & Bros 1927

Heinrich, Harrer, *Seven Years in Tibet*, Rupert Hart-Davis 1953

Heinrich, Harrer, and Norbu, Thubten Jigme, *Return to Tibet*, Penguin 1985

Hopkirk, Peter, *Trespassers on the Roof of the World*, Oxford University Press 1983

Iyer, Pico, *Video Night in Kathmandu*, Black Swan 1988

Tucci, Guiseppe, *To Lhasa and Beyond*, Snow Lion 1983

Wignall, Sydney, *Spy on the Roof of the World*, Canongate 1996

Tibet General

Avedon, John, *In Exile from the Land of Snows*, Wisdom 1985

Barnett, Robert, and Akiner, Shirin (eds), *Resistance and Reform in Tibet*, Hurst 1994

Craig, Mary, *Tears of Blood*, HarperCollins 1993

Dhondup, K. (trans.), *Songs of the Sixth Dalai Lama*, Library of Tibetan Works and Archives 1981

His Holiness the Dalai Lama, *Freedom in Exile*, Abacus 1984

Hyde Chambers, Frederick and Audrey, *Tibetan Folk Tales*, Shambhala 1981

Norbu, Thubten Jigme, and Heinrich, Harrer, *Tibet is My Country*, Wisdom 1986

Norbu, Thubten Jigme, and Turnbull, Colin, *Tibet, its Land and People*, Penguin 1968

Shakabpa, W.D., *Tibet, A Political History*, Potala Publications 1984

China General

Buck, Pearl, *The Good Earth*, Methuen 1931

Butterfield, Fox, *Alive in a Bitter Sea*, Coronet 1982

Chang, Jung, *Wild Swans*, Flamingo 1991

Fathers, Michael, and Higgins, Andrew, *Tienanmen − the Rape of Peking*, The Independent/Doubleday 1989

Goullart, Peter, *Forgotten Kingdom*, John Murray 1957

Kristoff, Nick, and Wudun, Sheryl, *China Wakes*, Nicholas Brealey 1994

Li, Zhisui, *The Private Life of Chairman Mao*, Arrow 1996

Min, Anchee, *Red Azalea*, Victor Gollancz 1993

Saunders, Kate, *Eighteen Layers of Hell*, Cassell 1996

van Gulik, R., *Sexual Life in Ancient China*, E.H. Brill 1974

Xianliang, Zhang, *Half of Man is Woman*, Penguin 1983

Buddhism

Bechert, H. and Gombrich, E., *The World of Buddhism*, Thames & Hudson 1984

Bercholz, Samuel, and Kohn, Sherab Chodzin (eds), *Entering the Stream − An Introduction to the Buddha and his Teachings*, Rider 1994

Lauf, Detlef Ingo, *Tibetan Sacred Art*, Shambhala 1976

Powers, John, *Introduction to Tibetan Buddhism*, Snow Lion 1995

Rahula, Walpola, *What the Buddha Taught*, Grove 1959
Saddhatissa, H., *The Life of the Buddha*, Mandala 1976
Trungpa, C., and Fremantle, F., *The Tibetan Book of the Dead*, Shambhala 1975
Watts, Alan, *The Way of Zen*, Penguin 1957
Williams, Paul, *Mahayana Buddhism*, Routledge 1995

Chinese Philosophy

Ch'en, Kenneth, *Buddhism in China*, Princeton 1964
Lau, D.C. (trans.), *Confucius – The Analects*, Penguin 1979
Palmer, Martin, *The Elements of Taoism*, Element 1991
Smith, D. Howard, *Confucius*, Paladin 1974
Waley, Arthur, *The Way and its Power*, Unwin 1934
Watson, Burton, *Basic Writings of Mo Tzu, Hsun Tzu & Han Fei Tzu*, Columbia 1967
Watson, Burton, *Chuang Tzu, Basic Writings*, Columbia 1964

Other

Campbell, Joseph, *The Hero with a Thousand Faces*, Sphere 1975
French, Patrick, *Younghusband – The Last Great Imperial Adventurer*, Flamingo 1995
Zaehner, R.C., *Hindu Scriptures*, J.M. Dent & Sons 1938

Index